THE TAMING OF THE SHREW

Edited by
Beth Obermiller

Cover illustration by
Heather Cooper

PERFECTION LEARNING CORPORATION
Logan, Iowa

A NOTE FROM THE PUBLISHER

The purpose of the Parallel Text Series of Shakespeare's plays is to assist the reader in understanding and appreciating the work of the foremost poet and dramatist of the English language. That there are considerable difficulties in reading and understanding this language is apparent from a casual glance through the many modern editions of the plays, which are accompanied by copious notes on each page of the text. Even these heavily annotated editions often fail to go far enough in illuminating the richly poetic and elliptical language that in large part demonstrates Shakespeare's genius and primacy, and constitutes our frequent perplexity.

In providing a line-by-line, contemporary prose paraphrase of the play on facing pages we have, in a sense, merely carried the convention of using explanatory notes to its logical conclusion. No attempt has been made to translate Shakespeare into modern poetry — a presumptuous and virtually impossible task. Instead, we have tried to render the often unfamiliar and remote Elizabethan language into a neutral and comprehensible modern equivalent. By its very nature, this task sometimes neglects the richness and complexity of the text, which is, in part, created by Shakespeare's magnificent and original use of language. Thus, the paraphrase is offered as an aid to understanding, not as a substitute for reading the original. The reader will find that referring to the paraphrase will often clarify the surface of the text, but the rewards to be found in reading Shakespeare yield themselves only to the careful and dedicated student of the original.

The Past is Prologue

Shakespeare lives! So writes his most eminent
biographer, S. Schoenbaum, in the prologue to
Shakespeare: The Globe and the World (New
York: Oxford University Press, 1979). And the
evidence is all around us.

We find it in the language we use. When we la-
ment that "the course of true love never did run
smooth," whether we are conscious of it or not,
we are quoting from *A Midsummer Night's
Dream*. When we observe that a well-intended law
or regulation is "more honor'd in the breach than
the observance," we are applying — or perhaps
misapplying — a phrase from *Hamlet*. When we
inscribe "What's past is prologue" on the
National Archives building in our nation's
capital, we are dignifying a minor line from *The
Tempest*. Often without realizing it, we find
ourselves speaking, if only momentarily, in the
accents of a Portia or a Polonius, a Macbeth or a
Mercutio. And when we *do* realize it — when we
are conscious of the Shakespearean idiom
embedded in so much of our daily speech — we
take pleasure in those subtle turns of phrase that
continue to enrich our discourse. A veteran
gardener recently observed, for example, that
anyone who calls a rose by any other name has
probably been pruning.

Alongside the Greek classics and the King
James version of the Bible, Shakespeare's words
and works offer a cultural treasure chest from
which English-speaking peoples have been
drawing, in one way or another, for more than
three and a half centuries. Folks have been

following the advice given in *Kiss Me Kate* — brushing up on their Shakespeare — for quite some time.

But Shakespeare's presence is also reflected in a number of other ways. Consider, for example, the more than 800 operatic and symphonic compositions deriving from such plays as *The Merry Wives of Windsor*, *The Taming of the Shrew*, and *Othello*. Or Broadway musicals, such as *The Boys from Syracuse* (a take-off on *The Comedy of Errors*) and *West Side Story* (Leonard Bernstein's New York gang-war updating of *Romeo and Juliet*). Or literary works such as William Faulkner's *The Sound and the Fury*, a sustained allusion to Macbeth's "tomorrow and tomorrow and tomorrow" speech. Here in the United States, Shakespeare has been part of our lives since the earliest days of the republic — even on the frontier, where spinoffs and parodies of Shakespeare helped while away many an hour in the nineteenth century. We've all delighted in the fractured Shakespeare offered up by the Duke and the King in Mark Twain's *Huckleberry Finn*. Ah yes, numerous — but not always sweet — are the uses of Shakespeare.

Nor is there any reason to think that Shakespeare's influence will be any less vital in the future than in the past. In most of the countries of the world, Shakespeare continues to maintain his position as the most frequently performed playwright. Every summer in the United States, for example, Shakespeare festivals highlight the vacation map from Maine to Texas, from Alabama to Oregon.

Ben Jonson was right, then, when he prefaced the first collected edition of Shakespeare's plays with the words "he was not of an age, but for all time!"

The Stratford Years

But if Shakespeare was a man for all time, he was also very much a man of his own age. Christened at Holy Trinity Church in Stratford-upon-Avon in April, 1564, he grew up, the son of illiterate parents, in a small Warwickshire town more noted for its wool and leather goods than for its literary cultivation. His mother, Mary Arden, was the daughter of a well-to-do farmer. His father, John Shakespeare, was a successful glovemaker who held several important borough offices in Stratford before he suffered financial reverses during William's teen years. The birthplace house still stands.

It seems all but certain that young Shakespeare spent most of his weekdays at the nearby Stratford grammar school, where, having learned his ABCs and the Lord's Prayer from a hornbook, he would have gone on to study Latin

Holy Trinity Church, Stratford-on-Avon

Shakespeare's House, Stratford-on-Avon

under the supervision of a stern schoolmaster.
Sundays he would have attended religious
services, studying the catechism of the newly
re-established Church of England and worshiping
in accordance with *The Book of Common Prayer*.

It was a rigorous upbringing, and it equipped
Shakespeare with enough background to become
one of the most widely educated men who ever
lived — despite the fact that he never attended a
day at a college or university.

Judging from his plays and poems, we may
infer that Shakespeare was interested in virtually
every aspect of human life — in professions such
as law, medicine, religion, and teaching; in everyday occupations such as farming, sheepherding,
tailoring, and shopkeeping; in skills such as
fishing, gardening, and cooking. Much of what
Shakespeare knew about these and countless
other subjects he would have acquired from
books. He must have been a voracious reader.

But he would have learned a great deal, also, from simply being alert to all that went on around him. He would have observed the plant and animal life of the nearby woods that he would later immortalize, in *As You Like It*, as the Forest of Arden. While there, he may have hunted from time to time; one legend has it that he left Stratford because he had been caught poaching deer from the estate of a powerful squire four miles upstream. He probably learned to swim as a youth, skinny-dipping in the river Avon. He may have participated in the kinds of athletic competition that were popular in the Elizabethan equivalent of the Olympics, the Cotswold Games. Chances are, too, that he would have been familiar with indoor recreations such as hazard (a popular dice game), or chess, or any of a number of card games. His works make it clear that he was fully at home with a broad spectrum of pastimes characteristic of the daily life of Elizabethan England.

Once his schooldays ended, Shakespeare married, at the age of eighteen, a woman who was eight years his senior. Anne Hathaway was pregnant when the wedding vows were solemnized. That it was a forced marriage is unlikely. But we shall never know how close the couple were. What we do know is that a daughter, Susanna, was baptized in Holy Trinity in May of 1583, followed less than two years later by the christening of twins, Hamnet and Judith. Sometime thereafter, certainly by the late 1580s, the father was in London.

The London Years

London was approximately a hundred miles distant. Shakespeare may have traveled there by way of the spires of Oxford, as do most visitors returning from Stratford to London today. But why he went, or when, history does not tell us. It has been plausibly suggested that he joined an acting troupe that was one player short when it toured Stratford in 1587. All we know for certain is that by 1592 Shakespeare had established himself as an actor and had written at least three plays. One of these — the third part of *Henry VI* — was alluded to in that year in a testament by a dying poet and playwright. Robert Greene warned his fellow playwrights to beware of the "upstart crow" who, not content with being a mere player, was aspiring to a share of the livelihood that had previously been the exclusive province of professional writers such as "the University Wits."

If we look at what Shakespeare had written by the early 1590s, we see that he had already become thoroughly familiar with the daily round of what was rapidly developing into one of the great capitals of Europe. Shakespeare knew St. Paul's Cathedral, famous not only as a house of worship but also as the marketplace where books were bought and sold. He knew the Inns of Court, where aspiring young lawyers studied for the bar. He knew the river Thames,

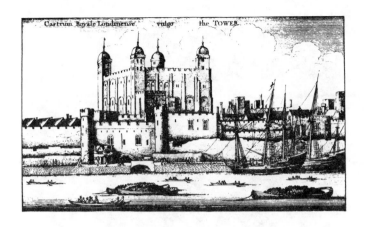

spanned by the ever-busy, ever-fascinating
London Bridge. He knew the Tower, where so
many of the characters he would depict in his
history plays had met their deaths, and where in
his own lifetime, such prominent noblemen as the
Earl of Essex and Sir Walter Raleigh would be
imprisoned prior to their executions. He knew
Westminster, where Parliament met when sum-
moned by the Queen, and where the Queen
herself kept her court at Whitehall Palace. He
knew the harbor, where English ships, having
won control of the seas by defeating the "invinci-
ble" Spanish Armada in 1588, had begun in
earnest to explore the New World.

In Shakespeare's day, London was a vigorous
city of approximately 160,000. If in its more
majestic aspects it was dominated by the court of
Queen Elizabeth — the sovereign most historians
regard as the greatest monarch in English
history — in its everyday affairs it was accented
by the hustle-bustle of getting and spending. Its
Royal Exchange was one of the forerunners of
today's stock exchanges. Its many marketplaces
offered a variety of goods for a variety of tastes.

Its crowded streets presented a colorful pageant of Elizabethan modes of transport and dress, ranging from countrywomen in homespun to elegant ladies in apparel as decorative as their husbands' wealth — and the Queen's edicts on clothing — would allow. Its inns and taverns afforded a robust diversity of vivid personalities—eating, drinking, talking, and enjoying games of all kinds.

London was, in short, a stimulating social and cultural environment for the poet whose works would later be praised as the very "mirror of life." And the young playwright took full advantage of the opportunity to observe humanity in all its facets. Without the broadening that London provided, it is doubtful that Shakespeare could ever have created such breathtakingly real characters as Falstaff, Prince Hal, and "all the good lads in Eastcheap."

Not that all was always well. Like any major city, London also had its unpleasant aspects. For one thing, it was riddled with conflict. Preachers were constantly denouncing the excessive use of cosmetics by women of the period. Even Hamlet speaks out against "your paintings," telling Ophelia "God has given you one face, and you make yourselves another."

In a similar vein, the city's Puritan authorities, regarding the theatres as dens of iniquity, closed them down on any available pretext, particularly during periods when the plague was rampant.

But even with the theatres closed, London was not free of vice and crime. In the Bankside district, prostitution abounded, as did gambling and drunkenness. Pickpockets, vagabonds, and other members of the fraternity of urban lowlife lay in wait for "conies" or unsuspecting victims. With so many "notorious villainies" for the "Belman of London" to bring to light, it is not surprising that some of the most interesting pamphlets of the period were muckraking tracts from reformers outraged by the sinfulness of the modern metropolis.

In such a setting did Shakespeare write and perform the greatest dramatic works the world has ever seen. And he did so in an area of the city that was accustomed to entertainments we would regard as the very antithesis of the sweet Swan of Avon's poetic sublimity. For if Bankside was to blossom into the finest theatrical center of that or any other age, it was also, for better or worse, the seedbed for such crude and cruel spectator sports as bear-baiting, bull-baiting, and cock-fighting. This may help account for the blood and violence one often sees on the Elizabethan stage, even in such Shakespearean works as *Titus Andronicus*, *Julius Caesar*, and *King Lear*.

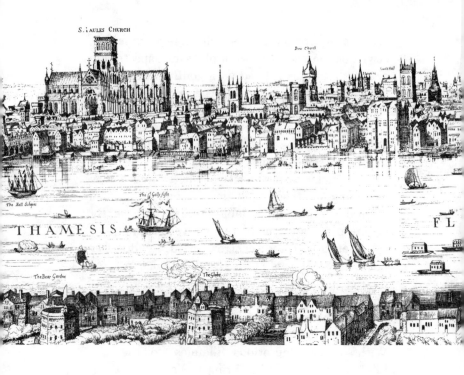

S. AULES CHURCH

Bow Church

Guild Hall

The Bell Sohpai

The Gelly fyfte

THAMESIS

FL

The Bear Gardne

The Globe

But of course there was more than murder and mayhem in the "wooden O" that served as amphitheatre for Shakespeare's works. On a stage largely devoid of scenery, the playwright and the actor made splendid use of language and gesture to establish locale, atmosphere, and meaning. And because the stage was surrounded on three sides by nearby spectators, the playwright and the actor benefited from a more intimate relationship with the audience than is customary in present-day theatres fitted with a curtain and a proscenium arch. For Shakespeare, this meant that he could allow a character to con-fide in the audience through asides, as does Iago in *Othello*, or to be overheard as he meditates in solitude, as does Hamlet in his celebrated "To be or not to be" soliloquy.

The limitations of the Globe and similar
Elizabethan theatres are obvious to us today. For
one thing, they were exposed to the sky and thus
could not operate comfortably in inclement
weather or in darkness. For another, lacking
spotlights and other modern paraphernalia, they
could not achieve some of the special effects we
have come to take for granted in the theatre of
our own day. What we sometimes forget,
however, is that these limitations could be
liberating for the playwright and the actor,
making possible a kind of dramatic invention and
flexibility difficult to duplicate in the more "ad-
vanced" theatre of the twentieth century.

The same was probably true in the Blackfriars
and other private indoor theatres of the period,
not to mention the halls at Court or the grea

palaces of the nobility. For it is well to remember that many of Shakespeare's plays were performed in theatrical settings other than the Globe, or its predecessor, the Theatre, or other amphitheatres of the period. Shakespeare's company was known as the Lord Chamberlain's Men from 1594 to 1603, when Queen Elizabeth died; after the accession of King James I, from 1603 on, it was known as the King's Men. Both designations implied a special relationship with the Court, and Shakespeare and his colleagues were invited to perform before the monarch more often than all the other acting troupes in the realm combined.

Shakespeare's real bread and butter, however, came from the immense cross section of the English populace who thronged to Bankside to see his plays performed. Despite the occasional caviling of such rival playwrights as Ben Jonson (whose admiration for Shakespeare was at times "this side idolatry"), we have reason to believe

Interior of Holy Trinity Church

that Shakespeare's dramatic works were immediately recognized for their artistic merits. By 1598, a critic named Francis Meres was comparing Shakespeare's genius to that of the greatest poets of antiquity — Ovid, Plautus, and Seneca — and finding the contemporary playwright superior to his classical predecessors. But unlike many great writers, Shakespeare was also a popular success in his own lifetime. He earned a generous amount of money, invested it wisely in real estate, both in London and in Stratford, and around 1613, eased into a gentleman's retirement — the owner of New Place, the second largest house in his native town.

There, three years later, he died. Fittingly, his death date, like the date tradition has agreed upon for his birth date, was April 23, the day England celebrated its patron saint. In the four centuries since the poet's birth, it seems no exaggeration to say that he has eclipsed even the heroic St. George in glory.

Epilogue

Shakespeare was laid to rest where fifty-two years earlier he had been christened. Shortly thereafter, a monument to his memory was erected above the tomb in Holy Trinity, and that monument is still in place for Shakespeare admirers to see today. But an even greater monument to his memory was produced several years later, when his theatrical colleagues assembled a large volume of his plays. The First Folio of 1623 was a labor of love, compiled as "an office to the dead, to procure his orphans' guardians" and "to keep the memory of so worthy a friend and fellow alive as was our Shakespeare." To that end, it was an unparalleled success, a publication that has aptly been summed up as "incomparably the most important work in the English language."

Among other things, the First Folio preserves what is generally considered the most reliable portrait of Shakespeare, the title-page engraving by Martin Droeshout. In dedicatory verses opposite the portrait, Ben Jonson attests to its authenticity. But quite properly, he then goes on to observe that though the engraver has "hit his face," he has been unable to draw "his wit." For that — for the mastery of language, of character, of poetic drama, of all that reminds us that, after all is said and done, "the play's the thing" — Jonson tells the reader, "look not on his picture but his book."

And so, for more than three and a half centuries, we have. We have read, and studied, and memorized, and performed — and yes, we have worshiped — the man Jonson praised as "Soul of the Age! The applause, delight, the wonder of our stage!"

Bardolatry — the word we use to refer to Shakespeare-worship — has had many manifestations over the intervening centuries. It has animated hundreds of Shakespeare festivals and celebrations, of which undoubtedly the most famous was the great Shakespeare Jubilee of 1769. On that occasion, thousands braved rainy Stratford weather to participate in ceremonies presided over by the principal actor of the eighteenth century, David Garrick. In a somewhat inverted form, Bardolatry has given rise to the notion that someone other than the son of ill-educated, small-town parents wrote the plays

we attribute to William Shakespeare. Hence
Francis Bacon, the Earl of Oxford, and other
members of the nobility have been proposed as
the "true" author of the works we still securely
hold to be Shakespeare's. And Bardolatry has
also occasioned an unceasing cavalcade of
Shakespearean curios and knickknacks:
everything from ceramic figurines and mulberry-
wood chests to Shakespeare-lovers' poker cloths
and Superbard T-shirts.

On the more serious side, appreciation of
Shakespeare has inspired notable works of art by
painters as diverse as Thomas Rowlandson,
George Romney, Henry Fuseli, Eugene Delacroix,
George Cruikshank, Arthur Rackham, Pablo
Picasso, Salvador Dali, and David Hockney. His
works have provided the basis of hundreds of
musical tributes, by composers ranging from
Beethoven to Mendelssohn, Tchaikovsky to
Verdi. And of course his plays continue to be
performed in theatres, in movie houses, and on
television screens.

The Bard is in our bones. Shakespeare lives.

John F. Andrews
Former Editor Shakespeare Quarterly
Folger Shakespeare Library

OOD FREND FOR IESVS SAKE FORBEARE,
O DIGG HE DVST ENCLOASED HEARE.
LESE BE Y MAN Y SPARES HES STONES
ND CVRST BE HE Y MOVES MY BONES

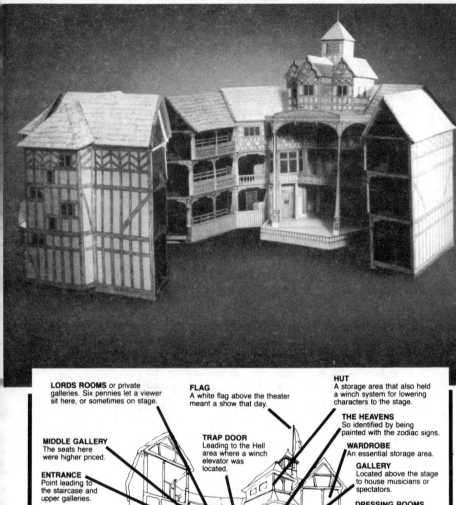

LORDS ROOMS or private galleries. Six pennies let a viewer sit here, or sometimes on stage.

FLAG
A white flag above the theater meant a show that day.

HUT
A storage area that also held a winch system for lowering characters to the stage.

MIDDLE GALLERY
The seats here were higher priced.

TRAP DOOR
Leading to the Hell area where a winch elevator was located.

THE HEAVENS
So identified by being painted with the zodiac signs.

WARDROBE
An essential storage area.

ENTRANCE
Point leading to the staircase and upper galleries.

GALLERY
Located above the stage to house musicians or spectators.

CORRIDOR
A passageway serving the middle gallery.

DRESSING ROOMS
Rooms where actors were 'attired' and awaited their cues.

MAIN ENTRANCE
Here the doorkeeper collected penny admission.

INNER STAGE
A recessed playing area often curtained off except as needed.

THE PIT
Sometimes referred to as 'The Yard' where the 'groundlings' watched.

TIRING-HOUSE DOOR
The rear entrance or 'stage door' for actors or privileged spectators.

STAGE
Major playing area jutting into the Pit, creating a sense of intimacy.

TIRING-HOUSE
Backstage area provided space for storage and business.

HELL
The area under the stage, used for ghostly comings and goings or for storage.

STAIRS
Theatergoers reached the galleries by staircases enclosed by stairwells.

STAGE DOORS
Doors opening into the Tiring-House.

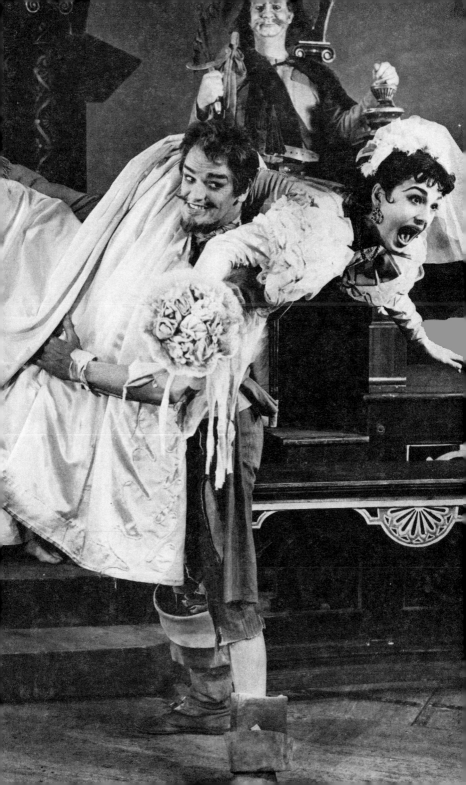

The Taming of the Shrew

DRAMATIS PERSONAE

A Lord.
CHRISTOPHER SLY, *a tinker.*
Hostess, Page, Players,   } *Persons in the Induct*
Huntsmen, and Servants.

BAPTISTA, *a rich gentleman of Padua.*
VINCENTIO, *an old gentleman of Pisa.*
LUCENTIO, *son to Vincentio, in love with Bianca.*
PETRUCHIO, *a gentleman of Verona, a suitor to Katherina.*
GREMIO,
HORTENSIO,   } *suitors to Bianca.*
TRANIO,
BIONDELLO } *servants to Lucentio.*
GRUMIO,
CURTIS,   } *servants to Petruchio.*
A Pedant.

KATHERINA, *the shrew,* } *daughters to Baptista.*
BIANCA,
Widow.

Tailor, Haberdasher, and Servants attending on Baptista
and Petruchio.

SCENE: *Padua, and Petruchio's country house.*

The Taming of the Shrew

CHARACTERS

A Lord.
CHRISTOPHER SLY, *a tinker.*
Hostess, Page, Players, } *Characters in the Induction.*
Huntsmen, and Servants.

BAPTISTA MINOLA, *a rich gentleman of Padua.*
VINCENTIO, *an old gentleman of Pisa.*
LUCENTIO, *Vincentio's son, in love with Bianca.*
PETRUCHIO, *a gentleman of Verona, Katherine's suitor.*
GREMIO, } *Bianca's suitors.*
HORTENSIO, }
TRANIO, } *Lucentio's servants.*
BIONDELLO, }
GRUMIO, } *Petruchio's servants.*
CURTIS, }
A Pedant.

KATHERINE, *the shrew,* } *Baptista's daughters.*
BIANCA, }
Widow.

Tailor, Haberdasher, and Servants attending on Baptista
and Petruchio.

SCENE: Padua, and Petruchio's country house.

The Taming of the Shrew

Induction

Scene i: [Before an alehouse on a heath.] Enter HOSTESS, *and beggar*, CHRISTOPHER SLY.

SLY
I'll pheese you, in faith.

HOSTESS
A pair of stocks, you rogue!

SLY
Y' are a baggage; the Slys are no rogues. Look in the chronicles; we came in with Richard Conqueror. Therefore *paucas pallabris*;
5   let the world slide; sessa!

HOSTESS
You will not pay for the glasses you have burst?

SLY
No, not a denier. Go by, Jeronimy! Go to thy cold bed, and warm thee.

HOSTESS
I know my remedy; I must go fetch the thirdborough.
            [*Exit.*]

SLY
10   Third, or fourth, or fifth borough, I'll answer him by law. I'll not budge an inch, boy; let him come, and kindly.
                [*Falls asleep.*]
            Wind horns. Enter a LORD *from hunting, with his train.*

---

4 *Richard* Sly means William the Conqueror who with his Norman army invaded and conquered England in 1066.   4 *paucas pallabris* or *pocas palabras,* is Spanish for "few words."

The Taming of the Shrew

Induction, Scene i: Outside a rural alehouse. Enter HOSTESS *and beggar* CHRISTOPHER SLY.

SLY

I'll get you, I will.

HOSTESS

I'll put you in the stocks, you rascal!

SLY

You wretch, the Slys aren't rascals. Look it up in the Chronicles: we came to England with Richard the Conqueror. So, in short,
5   let the world go by. Shut up!

HOSTESS
You won't pay for the glasses you broke?

SLY

No, not a penny. Go, by Saint Jeronimy. Go to your cold bed and warm yourself.

HOSTESS

I know what I have to do—I'd better get the constable.
        [*Exit.*]

SLY

10   Third, forth, or fifth constable, I'll give him a lawful response. I'll not budge an inch, wretch. Let him come, by all means.
        Falls asleep.
        Horns blow. Enter a LORD *, returning from the hunt, with his servants and fellow-hunters.*

LORD
Huntsman, I charge thee, tender well my hounds.
Brach Merriman, the poor cur, is emboss'd;
And couple Clowder with the deep-mouth'd brach.

15   Saw'st thou not, boy, how Silver made it good
At the hedge-corner, in the coldest fault?
I would not lose the dog for twenty pound.

1. HUNTER
Why, Belman is as good as he, my lord;
He cried upon it at the merest loss,

20   And twice to-day pick'd out the dullest scent.
Trust me, I take him for the better dog.

LORD
Thou art a fool; if Echo were as fleet,
I would esteem him worth a dozen such.
But sup them well and look unto them all;

25   To-morrow I intend to hunt again.

1. HUNTER
I will, my lord.

LORD
What's here? One dead, or drunk? See, doth he breathe?

2. HUNTER
He breathes, my lord. Were he not warm'd with ale,
This were a bed but cold to sleep so soundly.

LORD
30   O monstrous beast! how like a swine he lies!
Grim death, how foul and loathsome is thine image!
Sirs, I will practise on this drunken man.
What think you, if he were convey'd to bed,
Wrapp'd in sweet clothes, rings put upon his fingers,

35   A most delicious banquet by his bed,
And brave attendants near him when he wakes,
Would not the beggar then forget himself?

1. HUNTER
Believe me, lord, I think he cannot choose.

LORD
 Huntsman, I order you to look after my hounds.
 Bleed Merriman—the poor dog is foaming at the mouth—
 and mate Clowder with the deep-mouthed bitch.
15 Didn't you see, boy, how Silver proved his skill
 at the corner of the hedge where the trail was coldest?
 I wouldn't give up that dog for twenty pounds.

FIRST HUNTSMAN
 Why, Belman is just as good a dog as Silver, my lord.
 He barked even when the trail was completely cold,
20 and twice today he sniffed out the faintest scent.
 Believe me, I think he's the better dog.

LORD
 You're a fool. If Echo were as fast,
 I'd think he were worth a dozen like Silver.
 But feed them well and look after them all.
25 I'm planning on hunting again tomorrow.

FIRST HUNTSMAN
 I will, my lord.

LORD *(pointing to Sly)*
 Who is this here? Is he dead or drunk? Check and see—is he still
  breathing?

SECOND HUNTSMAN
 He's breathing, my lord. If he weren't warmed up with liquor,
 he'd find this was a cold bed on which to sleep so soundly.

LORD
30 What a monstrous animal—he lies there just like a pig!
 Grim death, your picture is foul and hateful!
 Gentlemen, I'll play a trick on this drunk.
 What would you think if we carried him to bed,
 dressed him in fine clothes, put rings on his fingers,
35 set a delicious feast beside his bed,
 and stationed well-dressed servants nearby when he awakened—
 wouldn't the beggar forget who he was?

FIRST HUNTSMAN
 Really, lord, I'd think he could hardly do anything else.

2. HUNTER
It would seem strange unto him when he wak'd.

LORD
40   Even as a flatt'ring dream or worthless fancy.
Then take him up and manage well the jest.
Carry him gently to my fairest chamber,
And hang it round with all my wanton pictures.
Balm his foul head in warm distilled waters,
45   And burn sweet wood to make the lodging sweet.
Procure me music ready when he wakes,
To make a dulcet and a heavenly sound;
And if he chance to speak, be ready straight
And with a low submissive reverence
50   Say, "What is it your honour will command?"
Let one attend him with a silver basin
Full of rose-water and bestrew'd with flowers;
Another bear the ewer, the third a diaper,
And say, "Will 't please your lordship cool your hands?"
55   Some one be ready with a costly suit
And ask him what apparel he will wear.
Another tell him of his hounds and horse,
And that his lady mourns at his disease.
Persuade him that he hath been lunatic;
60   And when he says he is, say that he dreams,
For he is nothing but a mighty lord.
This do and do it kindly, gentle sirs.
It will be pastime passing excellent,
If it be husbanded with modesty.

1. HUNTER
65   My lord, I warrant you we will play our part
As he shall think by our true diligence
He is no less than what we say he is.

LORD
Take him up gently and to bed with him;
And each one to his office when he wakes.
        [*Some bear out Sly.*] *Sound trumpets.*
70   Sirrah, go see what trumpet 'tis that sounds.

---

70 *sirrah* was a term used to address someone lower in status than the speaker. The word
was also used as a general snub.

SECOND HUNTSMAN
Things would seem strange to him when he woke up.

LORD
40 As strange as an illusory dream or unreal fantasy.
Then pick him up, and let's carry out the joke in style.
Carry him gently to my best bedroom
and hang my liveliest pictures on the wall.
Wash his dirty head in warm, scented water,
45 and burn sweet-smelling wood to perfume the room.
Get some musicians ready so when he awakens,
they can play a sweet and heavenly tune.
And if he should speak, be ready immediately
and with a humble, submissive, reverent tone
50 say, "What does your honor desire?"
Let someone present him with a silver bowl
full of rose water, sprinkled with flowers;
another carry the pitcher; a third one carry a towel
and say, "Does your lordship wish to cool your hands?"
55 Someone bring in an expensive suit
and ask him what clothes he wants to wear.
Someone else tell him about his dogs and horses
and that his wife is heartbroken about his disorder.
Convince him that he has been a lunatic,
60 and when he says he must be one now, tell him he's dreaming
because he's nothing else except a mighty lord.
Do all this, and make it convincing, gentlemen.
It will be wonderful entertainment
if carried out with a straight face.

FIRST HUNTSMAN
65 My lord, I guarantee you we'll play our parts
so he'll think, from our earnest attentions,
that he is nothing less than what we say he is.

LORD
Pick him up gently and carry him to bed,
and everyone take their places when he awakens.
        SLY *is carried out. Trumpets are blown.*
70 Servant, go and see who is blowing that trumpet.

        [Exit Servingman.]
Belike, some noble gentleman that means,
Traveling some journey, to repose him here.
        Re-enter SERVINGMAN.
How now! who is it?

SERVANT
        An't please your honour, players
75   That offer service to your lordship.
        Enter PLAYERS.

LORD
    Bid them come near. Now, fellows, you are welcome.

PLAYERS
    We thank your honour.

LORD
    Do you intend to stay with me tonight?

A PLAYER
    So please your lordship to accept our duty.

LORD
80   With all my heart. This fellow I remember
    Since once he play'd a farmer's eldest son.
    'Twas where you woo'd the gentlewoman so well.
    I have forgot your name; but, sure, that part
    Was aptly fitted and naturally perform'd.

A PLAYER
85   I think 'twas Soto that your honour means.

LORD
    'Tis very true; thou didst it excellent.
    Well, you are come to me in happy time,
    The rather for I have some sport in hand
    Wherein your coming can assist me much.
90   There is a lord will hear you play to-night;
    But I am doubtful of your modesties,
    Lest, over-eyeing of his odd behaviour,—
    For yet his honour never heard a play,—
    You break into some merry passion

---

85 *Soto* is a character who appears in John Fletcher's play *Women Pleased.*

Exit SERVANT.
It's probably a nobleman on a trip
who intends to rest here.
    Enter SERVANT.
Well, then, who is it?

SERVANT
If it please your honor, it is a troupe of actors
75   who offer to perform for you.
    PLAYERS *enter.*

LORD
Tell them to come here. Well, gentlemen, welcome.

PLAYERS
Thank you, your honor.

LORD
Do you intend to stay here tonight?

A PLAYER
If your lordship will accept our services.

LORD
80   Gladly. I remember this fellow
from the time he played a farmer's eldest son—
when you courted the lady so well.
I've forgotten your name, but really, that part
suited you well, and you performed it naturally.

SECOND PLAYER
85   I think it was the part of Soto your honor remembers.

LORD
That's right. You acted it very well.
Well, you've arrived at just the right moment,
especially because I have something amusing cooking,
in which your talents will really help me.
90   There is a lord who will watch your play tonight.
But I'm skeptical about your ability to keep a straight face
for fear that seeing his odd behavior—
because this lord has never seen a play before—
you might break into a fit of laughter

95   And so offend him; for I tell you, sirs,
        If you should smile he grows impatient.

A PLAYER
        Fear not, my lord; we can contain ourselves,
        Were he the veriest antic in the world.

LORD
        Go, sirrah, take them to the buttery,
100   And give them friendly welcome every one.
        Let them want nothing that my house affords.
                [*Exit one with the Players.*]
        Sirrah, go you to Barthol'mew my page,
        And see him dress'd in all suits like a lady.
        That done, conduct him to the drunkard's chamber;
105   And call him madam, do him obeisance.
        Tell him from me, as he will win my love,
        He bear himself with honourable action,
        Such as he hath observ'd in noble ladies
        Unto their lords, by them accomplished;
110   Such duty to the drunkard let him do
        With soft low tongue and lowly courtesy,
        And say, "What is 't your honour will command,
        Wherein your lady and your humble wife
        May show her duty and make known her love?"
115   And then with kind embracements, tempting kisses,
        And with declining head into his bosom,
        Bid him shed tears, as being overjoy'd
        To see her noble lord restor'd to health,
        Who for this seven years hath esteemed him
120   No better than a poor and loathsome beggar.
        And if the boy have not a woman's gift
        To rain a shower of commanded tears,
        An onion will do well for such a shift,
        Which in a napkin being close convey'd
125   Shall in despite enforce a watery eye.
        See this dispatch'd with all the haste thou canst;
        Anon I'll give thee more instructions.
                [*Exit a Servingman.*]

95   and then offend him. I tell you, gentlemen,
     if you should as much as smile, he will be irked.

A PLAYER
     Don't worry, my lord, we can control our laughter,
     even if he's the worst eccentric in the world.

LORD
     Go, servant, take them to the pantry,
100 and give them all a friendly welcome.
     Get them anything in the house they want.
          Exit SERVANT *and* PLAYERS.
     Servant, go to Bartholomew, my page,
     and see that he dresses just like a lady.
     When that's done, lead him to the drunk's bedroom,
105 and call him, "Madam" and give him respect.
     Tell him that I said—if he wants to win my love—
     that he should act honorably,
     just as he's seen noble ladies
     act toward their husbands.
110 Tell my page to greet the drunkard respectfully,
     with a soft, modest voice and humble courtsey,
     and say, "What do you command, your honor,
     that your lady and humble wife can do for you
     to show her duty and make known her love?"
115 And then, with kind embraces, tempting kisses,
     and with his head bowed to his breast,
     tell him to shed tears, as if "she" were overjoyed
     to see "her" noble lord well again
     after he had for seven years believed himself to be
120 no better than a poor, disgusting beggar.
     And if the boy doesn't have the woman's knack
     for crying up a storm whenever he wants,
     an onion will do the trick—
     which, if it's secretly carried in a handkerchief,
125 can't fail to bring tears to the eyes.
     See that these preparations are made as quickly as possible.
     I'll give you more instructions soon.
          Exit SERVANT.

I know the boy will well usurp the grace,
Voice, gait, and action of a gentlewoman.
130　I long to hear him call the drunkard husband;
And how my men will stay themselves from laughter
When they do homage to this simple peasant.
I'll in to counsel them; haply my presence
May well abate the over-merry spleen
135　Which otherwise would grow into extremes.
　　　　[*Exeunt.*]

Scene ii: [*A bedchamber in the Lord's house.*] *Enter aloft the drunkard* SLY, *richly dressed, with* ATTENDANTS: *some with apparel, basin and ewer, and other appurtenances; and* LORD, *like a servant.*

SLY
For God's sake, a pot of small ale.

1. SERVANT
Will 't please your lordship drink a cup of sack?

2. SERVANT
Will 't please your honour taste of these conserves?

3. SERVANT
What raiment will your honour wear to-day?

SLY
5　I am Christophero Sly; call not me honour nor lordship. I ne'er drank sack in my life; and if you give me any conserves, give me conserves of beef. Ne'er ask me what raiment I'll wear; for I have no more doublets than backs, no more stockings than legs, nor no more shoes than feet; nay, sometime more feet than shoes,
10　or such shoes as my toes look through the overleather.

LORD
Heaven cease this idle humour in your honour!
O, that a mighty man of such descent,
Of such possessions, and so high esteem,
Should be infused with so foul a spirit!

SLY
15　What, would you make me mad? Am not I Christopher Sly, old

I know the boy will skillfully mimic the grace,
voice, walk, and actions of a lady.
130 I can't wait to hear him call the drunk "husband."
How will my servants keep from laughing
when they pretend to serve this simple peasant?
I'll go and give them some advice. Maybe my presence
can stifle their overly merry spirit,
135 which otherwise might get out of hand.
     They exit.

*Induction, Scene ii: Bedroom in the lord's house. Enter on the balcony
at the back the drunkard* SLY, ATTENDANTS *(carrying clothing,
bowl, pitcher, and other items) and the* LORD, *dressed like a servant.*

SLY
     For God's sake, give me a pot of cheap ale!

FIRST SERVINGMAN
     Would your worship like a cup of sherry to drink?

SECOND SERVINGMAN
     Would your honor like a taste of this fruit conserve?

THIRD SERVINGMAN
     What clothes will your honor wear today?

SLY
5   I'm Christopher Sly. Don't call me your honor or your lordship. I never
     drank sherry in my life, and if you give me any conserves, make it
     salt beef. Never ask me what clothes I want to wear since I don't have
     any more doublets than I have backs, no more stockings than I have
        legs, and
     no more shoes than I have feet—no, sometimes more feet than shoes,
10   or such shoes as my toes can see through.

LORD
     Heaven cure your honor's mad fantasy!
     It's terrible that a mighty man of such noble ancestors,
     such belongings, and such good reputation
     should be possessed by such a foul spirit!

SLY
15   Are you trying to drive me crazy? Aren't I Christopher Sly, old

Sly's son of Burton heath, by birth a pedlar, by education a cardmaker, by transmutation a bear-herd, and now by present
profession a tinker? Ask Marian Hacket, the fat ale-wife of
Wincot, if she know me not. If she say I am not fourteen pence
20 on the score for sheer ale, score me up for the lying'st knave in
Christendom. What! I am not bestraught. Here's—

3. SERVANT
O, this it is that makes your lady mourn!

2. SERVANT
O, this is it that makes your servants droop!

LORD
Hence comes it that your kindred shuns your house,
25 As beaten hence by your strange lunacy.
O noble lord, bethink thee of thy birth,
Call home thy ancient thoughts from banishment
And banish hence these abject lowly dreams.
Look how thy servants do attend on thee,
30 Each in his office ready at thy beck.
Wilt thou have music? Hark! Apollo plays,
 [*Music.*]
And twenty caged nightingales do sing.
Or wilt thou sleep? We'll have thee to a couch
Softer and sweeter than the lustful bed
35 On purpose trimm'd up for Semiramis.
Say thou wilt walk; we will bestrew the ground.
Or wilt thou ride? Thy horses shall be trapp'd,
Their harness studded all with gold and pearl.
Dost thou love hawking? Thou hast hawks will soar
40 Above the morning lark. Or wilt thou hunt?
Thy hounds shall make the welkin answer them
And fetch shrill echoes from the hollow earth.

1. SERVANT
Say thou wilt course; thy greyhounds are as swift
As breathed stags, ay, fleeter than the roe.

2. SERVANT
45 Dost thou love pictures? We will fetch thee straight
Adonis painted by a running brook,

---

16 *cardmaker* Sly means cards used to separate wool before it was spun.   31 *Apollo* Greek
sun god and god of music.   35 *Semiramis* legendary queen of Assyria, renowned for her
lustful nature and great beauty.   46 *Adonis* one of Aphrodite's (or Cytherea's) lovers.
Aphrodite was the Greek goddess of love.

Sly's son from Barton-on-the-Heath? Born a peddler, trained to be a cardmaker, changed to a bear trainer, and now
working as a tinker? Ask Marian Hacket, the fat tavernkeeper at
Wincot, if she doesn't know me. If she says I don't have fourteen pence
20   on my tab for ale alone, chalk me up as the biggest liar in
the Christian world. Indeed, I'm not crazy! Here's—

THIRD SERVINGMAN
This is the kind of thing that breaks your wife's heart!

SECOND SERVINGMAN
This is the kind of thing that makes your servants despair!

LORD
This is the reason that your relatives avoid your house,
25   chased away from here by your strange madness.
O noble lord, think about your noble standing.
Call back your old, sane thoughts from exile,
and banish your pathetic, beggarly dreams.
Look at how your servants wait on you,
30   everyone in his place, ready to do as you command.
Do you want music? Listen, Apollo is playing,
    (Music plays)
and twenty caged nightingales are singing.
Or do you want to sleep? We'll take you to a bed
softer and nicer than the lustful bed
35   prepared for Semiramis.
If you say you want to walk, we'll scatter the ground with rushes
    and flowers.
Or do you want to ride? Your horses will be decorated,
their harness studded all over with gold and pearls.
Do you love hawking? You have hawks that will soar
40   above the morning lark. Or do you want to hunt?
Your hounds will make the sky answer their barks
and produce shrill echoes from the hollow earth.

FIRST SERVINGMAN
Say that you want to hunt hares, your greyhounds are as swift
as strong stags and faster than small deer.

SECOND SERVINGMAN
45   Do you love pictures? We'll bring you at once
Adonis, pictured by a running brook

And Cytherea all in sedges hid,
Which seem to move and wanton with her breath
Even as the waving sedges play with wind.

LORD
We'll show thee Io as she was a maid,
And how she was beguiled and surpris'd,
As lively painted as the deed was done.

3. SERVANT
Or Daphne roaming through a thorny wood,
Scratching her legs that one shall swear she bleeds,
And at that sight shall sad Apollo weep,
So workmanly the blood and tears are drawn.

LORD
Thou art a lord and nothing but a lord.
Thou hast a lady far more beautiful
Than any woman in this waning age.

1. SERVANT
And till the tears that she hath shed for thee
Like envious floods o'er-run her lovely face,
She was the fairest creature in the world;
And yet she is inferior to none.

SLY
Am I a lord? And have I such a lady?
Or do I dream? Or have I dream'd till now?
I do not sleep; I see, I hear, I speak,
I smell sweet savours, and I feel soft things.
Upon my life, I am a lord indeed
And not a tinker nor Christophero Sly.
Well, bring our lady hither to our sight;
And once again, a pot o' th' smallest ale.

2. SERVANT
Will 't please your mightiness to wash your hands?
O, how we joy to see your wit restor'd!
O, that once more you knew but what you are!
These fifteen years you have been in a dream;
Or when you wak'd, so wak'd as if you slept.

---

50 *Io* a Greek girl loved by Zeus, the king of the gods.   53 *Daphne* a nymph who was chased by the amorous Apollo. Her father saved her by changing her into a tree.

and Cytherea, hidden in the marsh grasses,
which seem to move and sway with her breath,
just like the waving marsh grasses dance in the wind.

LORD
50   We'll show you a picture of Io, showing her as a girl,
and how she was seduced and tricked.
It's so lifelike, it's like seeing it really happen.

THIRD SERVINGMAN
Or Daphne, wandering through a thorny wood,
scratching her legs so that the viewer would swear she bleeds.
55   And sad Apollo will weep at the sight,
the blood and tears are drawn so skillfully!

LORD
You are a lord, pure and simple,
and you have a wife far more beautiful
than any other woman in these declining days.

FIRST SERVINGMAN
60   And before the tears that she cried for you
overran her lovely face like envious floods,
she was the most beautiful woman in the world.
Even now, no one is more lovely than she is.

SLY
Am I a lord, and am I married to such a woman?
65   Or am I dreaming? Or have I been dreaming until now?
I'm not sleeping now—I see, hear, speak,
smell sweet smells, and feel soft things.
I declare, I really am a lord
and not a tinker or Christopher Sly.
70   Well, bring my wife here to me,
And I ask you once again, bring a pot of the weakest ale.

SECOND SERVINGMAN
Would you like to wash your hands, your honor?
O how happy we are to see you sane again!
How long we've wished that once again you would just know who
you were!
75   For the past fifteen years, you've been dreaming,
or when you were awake, it was like you were still asleep.

SLY
These fifteen years! by my fay, a goodly nap.
But did I never speak of all that time?

1. SERVANT
O, yes, my lord, but very idle words.
80   For though you lay here in this goodly chamber,
Yet would you say ye were beaten out of door,
And rail upon the hostess of the house,
And say you would present her at the leet
Because she brought stone jugs and no seal'd quarts.
85   Sometimes you would call out for Cicely Hacket.

SLY
Ay, the woman's maid of the house.

3. SERVANT
Why, sir, you know no house nor no such maid,
Nor no such men as you have reckon'd up,
As Stephen Sly, and old John Naps of Greece,
90   And Peter Turph, and Henry Pimpernell,
And twenty more such names and men as these
Which never were, nor no man every saw.

SLY
Now Lord be thanked for my good amends!

ALL
Amen.
          Enter the PAGE *as a lady, with attendants.*

SLY
95   I thank thee; thou shalt not lose by it.

PAGE
How fares my noble lord?

SLY
Marry, I fare well, for here is cheer enough.
Where is my wife?

PAGE
Here, noble lord; what is thy will with her?

---

89 *Stephen Sly, etc.* Stephen Sly was a real resident of Stratford, Shakespeare's birthplace. All the others named here may be real people. Greece may be a misprint for Green, a town near Stratford.

SLY
The past fifteen years! My word, that's a good nap!
But didn't I ever say anything during all that time?

FIRST SERVINGMAN
O yes, my lord, but they were meaningless words,
80   for even while you were lying here in this fine bedroom,
you'd say you'd been chased out the door.
And you'd complain about the hostess of the tavern
and say you'd accuse her at the court before the manor lord
because she served her liquor in stone jugs and not in clearly marked
    quart jars.
85   Sometimes you would call out for Cicely Hacket.

SLY
Yes, that was the lady's maid at the tavern.

THIRD SERVINGMAN
Why, sir, you don't know of any such tavern or maid.
Or any of the men you talked about such
as Stephen Sly, old John Naps of Greece,
90   Peter Turph, and Henry Pimpernell,
and twenty more names and men such as these
who never really existed and whom no one ever saw.

SLY
Well, thank God for my excellent recovery!

ALL
Amen.
    Enter the PAGE, *dressed as a woman, with* ATTENDANTS.

SLY
95   Thank you. You'll be rewarded for your good wishes.

PAGE
How are you, my noble lord?

SLY
Indeed, I'm doing quite well, for this is a pleasing situation.
Where is my wife?

PAGE
I am your wife, noble lord. What can I do for you?

SLY

100   Are you my wife and will not call me husband?
My men should call me "lord"; I am your goodman.

PAGE

My husband and my lord, my lord and husband,
I am your wife in all obedience.

SLY

I know it well. What must I call her?

LORD

105   Madam.

SLY

Al'ce madam, or Joan madam?

LORD

Madam, and nothing else: so lords call ladies.

SLY

Madam wife, they say that I have dream'd
And slept above some fifteen year or more.

PAGE

110   Ay, and the time seems thirty unto me,
Being all this time abandon'd from your bed.

SLY

'Tis much. Servants, leave me and her alone.
Madam, undress you and come now to bed.

PAGE

Thrice-noble lord, let me entreat of you
115   To pardon me yet for a night or two,
Or, if not so, until the sun be set;
For your physicians have expressly charg'd,
In peril to incur your former malady,
That I should yet absent me from your bed.
120   I hope this reason stands for my excuse.

SLY

Ay, it stands so that I may hardly tarry so long.

---

106 *Alice . . . Joan* Sly gives his "lady" humorously common names.

SLY

100   You're my wife, and yet you don't call me husband?
My servants should call me "lord." You should call me husband.

PAGE

You are my husband and my lord, my lord and my husband.
I am your obedient wife.

SLY

I'm certain of that. What should I call her?

LORD

105   Madam.

SLY

Alice, madam, or Joan, madam?

LORD

Just madam. That's what lords call their ladies.

SLY

Madam-wife, they say I've dreamed
and slept for fifteen years or more.

PAGE

110   Yes, and it seems like thirty years to me
since I've been a stranger to your bed all this time.

SLY

That is a long time. Servants, leave me and my wife alone.
    Exit SERVANTS.
Madam, undress and come to bed.

PAGE

My most noble lord, I beg you
115   to excuse me from coming to bed with you for a night or two.
Or if not for that long, at least until sunset.
Your doctors have strictly ordered
that, to avoid the risk of further madness,
I should not sleep with you, yet.
120   I hope this explanation will stand as my excuse.

SLY

Yes, it stands so that I can hardly wait another minute;

But I would be loath to fall into my dreams again.
I will therefore tarry in despite of the flesh and the blood.
Enter a MESSENGER.

MESSENGER
Your honour's players, hearing your amendment,
125   Are come to play a pleasant comedy;
For so your doctors hold it very meet,
Seeing too much sadness hath congeal'd your blood,
And melancholy is the nurse of frenzy.
Therefore they thought it good you hear a play
130   And frame your mind to mirth and merriment,
Which bars a thousand harms and lengthens life.

SLY
Marry, I will; let them play it. Is not a comonty a Christmas
gambold, or a tumbling-trick?

PAGE
No, my good lord; it is more pleasing stuff.

SLY
135   What, household stuff?

PAGE
It is a kind of history.

SLY
Well, we'll see 't. Come, madam wife, sit by my side and let the
world slip. We shall ne'er be younger.
[*They all sit.*] *Flourish.*

Act I, Scene i: [*Padua. A public place.*] *Enter* LUCENTIO *and
his man* TRANIO.

LUCENTIO
Tranio, since for the great desire I had
To see fair Padua, nursery of arts,
I am arriv'd for fruitful Lombardy,
The pleasant garden of great Italy;
5   And by my father's love and leave am arm'd
With his good will and thy good company,

---

127 *sadness* Elizabethans believed that sorrow affected the blood in this way.   132 *marry*
was originally from the oath "by the Virgin Mary." By Shakespeare's day, it had become
an intensifier like "really" or "indeed."   132 *comonty* Sly's pronounciation of
comedy.   s.d. *Flourish* trumpet fanfare.

but I would hate to fall back into my delusions.
Therefore, I'll wait, despite the urges of my flesh and blood.
        Enter a MESSENGER.

MESSENGER
    Your honor's acting troupe, hearing that you were better,
125   have come to perform a pleasant comedy.
    Your doctors think it would be very good for you,
    since your blood has been congealed by too much sadness,
    and melancholy is the germ of insanity.
    Therefore, they thought it would be a good idea if you watched a play
130   and switched to thinking about comedy and humor,
    which will prevent a thousand harmful things and lengthen your life.

SLY
    Indeed, I'll let them act their play. Isn't a comonty a Christmas
    game or an acrobatic trick?

PAGE
    No, my good lord. It's more amusing than that.

SLY
135   What! Is it household stuff, then?

PAGE
    It's a kind of story.

SLY
    Well, I'll watch it. Come, my wife, and sit by my side, and let the
    world pass by. We'll never be any younger.
        (They sit and watch.) Trumpet fanfare.

Act I, Scene i: Padua, a public place. Enter LUCENTIO *and
his servant* TRANIO.

LUCENTIO
    Tranio, since I really wanted
    to see beautiful Padua, known as a cultural center,
    I've come to rich Lombardy,
    great Italy's pleasant garden spot.
5   And since, with my father's love and his permission, I've been given
    his approval and your good company—

My trusty servant, well approv'd in all.
Here let us breathe and haply institute
A course of learning and ingenious studies.
10   Pisa, renowned for grave citizens,
Gave me my being and my father first,
A merchant of great traffic through the world,
Vincentio, come of the Bentivolii.
Vincentio's son, brought up in Florence,
15   It shall become to serve all hopes conceiv'd,
To deck his fortune with his virtuous deeds;
And therefore, Tranio, for the time I study,
Virtue and that part of philosophy
Will I apply that treats of happiness
20   By virtue specially to be achiev'd.
Tell me thy mind; for I have Pisa left
And am to Padua come, as he that leaves
A shallow plash to plunge him in the deep
And with satiety seeks to quench his thirst.

TRANIO
25   *Mi perdonato*, gentle master mine,
I am in all affected as yourself;
Glad that you thus continue your resolve
To suck the sweets of sweet philosophy.
Only, good master, while we do admire
30   This virtue and this moral discipline,
Let's be no Stoics nor no stocks, I pray,
Or so devote to Aristotle's checks
As Ovid be an outcast quite abjur'd.
Balk logic with acquaintance that you have,
35   And practise rhetoric in your common talk.
Music and poesy use to quicken you.
The mathematics and the metaphysics,
Fall to them as you find your stomach serves you;
No profit grows where is no pleasure ta'en.
40   In brief, sir, study what you most affect.

LUCENTIO
Gramercies, Tranio, well dost thou advise.

---

33 *Ovid* was a Roman poet who wrote an essay on love. He was banished by Emperor Augustus.

you, my trusty, reliable servant—
let's stay here awhile and perhaps begin
a course of learning and challenging studies.

10 Pisa, famous for dignified citizens
was my birthplace and before that, the birthplace of my father—
a merchant with a large trading market throughout the world—
Vincentio, a descendant of the Bentivolii.
Being Vincentio's son, raised in Florence,

15 it's fitting that I should do everything hoped of me
and make my fortune by good deeds.
Therefore, Tranio, I intend to study
virtue and similiar knowledge
that relates to the kind of happiness

20 that can be found especially through goodness.
Tell me what you're thinking, for I've left Pisa
and come to Padua like a man who leaves
a shallow pool to plunge into deep waters
and quench his thirst to the fullest.

TRANIO

25 Pardon me, my gentle master,
I feel as you do about everything.
I'm glad that you're sticking to your decision
to study the joys of sweet philosophy.
Only, good master, while we're admiring

30 this virtue and this moral discipline,
let's not be stoics or sticks, please,
or be so devoted to Aristotle's restrictions
that we completely reject the outcast Ovid.
Try out your logic with friends,

35 and practice rhetoric in your everyday conversation.
Use music and poetry to stimulate you.
Explore mathematics and metaphysics
as suits you.
There's no profit where there isn't some pleasure.

40 So, in short, sir, study what you like best.

LUCENTIO

Thanks very much, Tranio. You've advised me well.

If, Biondello, thou wert come ashore,
We could at once put us in readiness,
And take a lodging fit to entertain
45 Such friends as time in Padua shall beget.
But stay a while, what company is this?

TRANIO

Master, some show to welcome us to town.

Enter BAPTISTA, KATHERINA, BIANCA, GREMIO,
a pantaloon, and HORTENSIO. LUCENTIO *and*
TRANIO *stand by.*

BAPTISTA

Gentlemen, importune me no farther,
For how I firmly am resolv'd you know;
50 That is, not to bestow my youngest daughter
Before I have a husband for the elder.
If either of you both love Katherina,
Because I know you well and love you well,
Leave shall you have to court her at your pleasure.

GREMIO

55 To cart her rather; she's too rough for me.
There, there, Hortensio, will you any wife?

KATHERINA

I pray you, sir, is it your will
To make a stale of me amongst these mates?

HORTENSIO

Mates, maid! how mean you that? No mates for you,
60 Unless you were of gentler, milder mould.

KATHERINA

I' faith, sir, you shall never need to fear.
Iwis it is not half way to her heart;
But if it were, doubt not her care should be
To comb your noddle with a three-legg'd stool
65 And paint your face and use you like a fool.

HORTENSIO

From all such devils, good Lord deliver us!

---

s.d. *Katherina* throughout the paraphrase text, the spelling of Katherine's name has been
standardized to Katherine or Kate.   s.d. *pantaloon* is a comic old miser.   55 *cart her* both
prostitutes and shrewish women were sometimes punished by being exhibited to the public

If only Biondello had come ashore,
we could get ready at once
and find a place to stay that's fit to entertain
45   such friends as, in time, I'll make in Padua.
But wait a minute—who are these people?

TRANIO
    Some kind of show to welcome us to town, master.
        Enter BAPTISTA *with his two daughters* KATHERINE *and*
        BIANCA; GREMIO, *a pantaloon; and* HORTENSIO,
        Bianca's suitor. LUCENTIO *and* TRANIO *stand nearby.*

BAPTISTA
    Gentlemen, don't plead with me anymore.
    Just how determined I am, you know.
50   I won't give away my youngest daughter
    before my elder daughter has a husband.
    If either one of you loves Katherine,
    and since I know and love both of you well,
    I'll give you permission to court her whenever you want.

GREMIO
55   To bring her before the court, you mean—she's too rough for me.
    How about you, Hortensio—how would you like to marry her?

KATHERINE *(to Baptista)*
    I ask you, sir, do you want
    to make a fool of me among these brutish suitors?

HORTENSIO
    Suitors, girl! What do you mean by that? Not your suitors
60   unless you had a gentler, milder temperment.

KATHERINE
    Truly, sir, you have nothing to fear.
    Certainly I'm not even interested in marriage.
    But if I were interested, don't doubt that I'd
    comb your noodle with a stool
65   and bloody your face and treat you like a fool.

HORTENSIO
    From all devils like her, deliver us, good Lord!

---

on carts.   **58** *stale* means both "laughingstock" and "prostitute." Katherine is also playing
on the word "mate" ("stalemate"). **58** *mate* means "brutes," or "fellows" and
"husbands."

GREMIO
And me too, good Lord!

TRANIO
Hush, master! here's some good pastime toward.
That wench is stark mad or wonderful froward.

LUCENTIO
70   But in the other's silence do I see
Maid's mild behaviour and sobriety.
Peace, Tranio!

TRANIO
Well said, master; mum! and gaze your fill.

BAPTISTA
Gentlemen, that I may soon make good
75   What I have said, Bianca, get you in;
And let it not displease thee, good Bianca,
For I will love thee ne'er the less, my girl.

KATHERINA
A pretty peat! it is best
Put finger in the eye, and she knew why.

BIANCA
80   Sister, content you in my discontent.
Sir, to your pleasure humbly I subscribe.
My books and instruments shall be my company,
On them to look and practise by myself.

LUCENTIO
Hark, Tranio! thou may'st hear Minerva speak.

HORTENSIO
85   Signior Baptista, will you be so strange?
Sorry am I that our good will effects
Bianca's grief.

GREMIO
                    Why will you mew her up,
Signior Baptista, for this fiend of hell,
90   And make her bear the penance of her tongue?

---

84 *Minerva* Greek goddess of wisdom.

GREMIO

And me, too, good Lord!

TRANIO

Listen, master! Here's something entertaining brewing.
That woman is stark mad or amazingly willful.

LUCENTIO

70   But in the other girl's silence I see
ladylike gentle behavior and dignity.
Quiet, Tranio!

TRANIO

Well put, master. I'll be quiet and you look all you want.

BAPTISTA

Gentlemen, I'll immediately do as
75   I told you I would—Bianca, go inside.
And don't be unhappy, my good Bianca,
because I love you as always, my girl.

KATHERINE

A fine pet! She should
be crying if she had any sense.

BIANCA

80   Sister, be content with my unhappiness.
Sir, I'll humbly obey your wishes.
My books and instruments will be my company,
and I'll devote myself to them and practice.

LUCENTIO

Listen, Tranio—you can hear Minerva speaking.

HORTENSIO

85   Signior Baptista, will you be so unkind?
I'm sorry that our good will has been the cause of
Bianca's sorrow.

GREMIO

Will you cage her up,
Signior Baptista, on account of this devil,
90   and punish Bianca for her sister's shrewishness?

BAPTISTA
Gentlemen, content ye; I am resolv'd.
Go in, Bianca;
    [*Exit Bianca.*]
And for I know she taketh most delight
In music, instruments, and poetry,
95   Schoolmasters will I keep within my house,
Fit to instruct her youth. If you, Hortensio,
Or Signior Gremio, you, know any such,
Prefer them hither; for to cunning men
I will be very kind, and liberal
100   To mine own children in good bringing up;
And so farewell. Katherina, you may stay;
For I have more to commune with Bianca.
    [*Exit.*]
KATHERINA
Why, and I trust I may go too, may I not?
What, shall I be appointed hours, as though, belike,
105   I knew not what to take and what to leave? Ha!
    [*Exit.*]
GREMIO
You may go to the devil's dam; your gifts are so good, here's
none will hold you. Their love is not so great, Hortensio, but we
may blow our nails together, and fast it fairly out. Our cake's
dough on both sides. Farewell; yet, for the love I bear my sweet
110   Bianca, if I can by any means light on a fit man to teach her that
wherein she delights, I will wish him to her father.
HORTENSIO
So will I, Signior Gremio. But a word, I pray. Though the nature
of our quarrel yet never brook'd parle, know now, upon advice,
it toucheth us both, that we may yet again have access to our fair
115   mistress and be happy rivals in Bianca's love, to labour and effect
one thing specially.
GREMIO
What's that, I pray?
HORTENSIO
Marry, sir, to get a husband for her sister.

BAPTISTA

Gentlemen, be content. My decision is final.
Go inside, Bianca.
Exit BIANCA.
Since I know she is most delighted by
music, instruments, and poetry,
95   I'll board teachers in my house
who can properly instruct her. If you, Hortensio,
or you, Signior Gremio, know of any such teachers,
recommend them to come here. I'll be very kind
to clever men—and generous
100   to my own children in educating them.
And so, goodbye. Katherine, you must wait here
because I have something more to say to Bianca.
Exit BAPTISTA.

KATHERINE

Why, I trust I can leave, too, can't I?
Really, shall I be given a schedule as though
105   I didn't know when to stay and when to leave? Ha!
Exit KATHERINE.

GREMIO

You can go to the devil's mother. Your virtues are so great
that no one here will try to stop you. Their love is not so important,
   Hortensio, that we
may bide our time and endure this dry spell. Our
dough hasn't risen. Goodbye. Still, for the love I hold for my sweet
110   Bianca, if I can find somewhere a proper man to teach her
the subjects she loves, I'll recommend him to her father.

HORTENSIO

I'll do that, too, Signior Gremio. But I beg a word with you. Though
   due to the reason
for our quarrel, we've never yet consulted one another, you should realize,
   after careful consideration,
that it concerns both of us—so that we can again court our fair
115   lady and be happy rivals for Bianca's love—to try to get
one thing done above all.

GREMIO

What's that?

HORTENSIO

Indeed, sir, to get a husband for her sister.

GREMIO
    A husband! a devil.

HORTENSIO
120   I say, a husband.

GREMIO
    I say, a devil. Think'st thou, Hortensio, though her father be very
    rich, any man is so very a fool to be married to hell?

HORTENSIO
    Tush, Gremio, though it pass your patience and mine to endure
    her loud alarums, why, man, there be good fellows in the world,
125   an a man could light on them, would take her with all faults, and
    money enough.

GREMIO
    I cannot tell; but I had as lief take her dowry with this condition,
    to be whipp'd at the high cross every morning.

HORTENSIO
    Faith, as you say, there's small choice in rotten apples. But come;
130   since this bar in law makes us friends, it shall be so far forth
    friendly maintain'd till by helping Baptista's eldest daughter to
    a husband we set his youngest free for a husband, and then have
    to't afresh. Sweet Bianca! Happy man be his dole! He that runs
    fastest gets the ring. How say you, Signior Gremio?

GREMIO
135   I am agreed; and would I had given him the best horse in Padua
    to begin his wooing that would thoroughly woo her, wed her and
    bed her, and rid the house of her! Come on.
        [*Exeunt Gremio and Hortensio.*]

TRANIO
    I pray, sir, tell me, is it possible
    That love should of a sudden take such hold?

LUCENTIO
140   O Tranio, till I found it to be true,
    I never thought it possible or likely.
    But see, while idly I stood looking on,
    I found the effect of love in idleness;

---

143 *love in idleness* also is a name for the pansy, which was believed to spark love.

GREMIO
A husband! You mean a devil.

HORTENSIO
120   I say a husband.

GREMIO
And I say a devil. Think, Hortensio—though her father is very
rich, wouldn't a man have to be a complete idiot to agree to such a hellish
marriage?

HORTENSIO
Nonsense, Gremio! Though it's beyond your patience and mine to stand
her rudeness, there are many good fellows in the world,
125   if you could just find them, who would take her with all her faults and
big fortune.

GREMIO
I can't say. But I'd just as soon take her dowry with this condition—
to be whipped in the marketplace every morning.

HORTENSIO
Well, as you say, there's little to choose from among rotten apples.
But come;
130   since this restriction makes us friends, we'll remain friends
just until we can get Baptista's oldest daughter
a husband, thereby making the youngest free to marry, and then resume
our old rivalry. Sweet Bianca! May the winner be rewarded with
happiness! The fastest runner
gets the prize. What do you say, Signior Gremio?

GREMIO
135   I agree. And I'd give the man the best horse in Padua
who would begin courting her and who will really court her, marry her,
take her to bed, and get her out of this house. Come on.
    Exit GREMIO *and* HORTENSIO.

TRANIO
Sir, tell me, is it possible
that you should fall in love so suddenly?

LUCENTIO
140   O Tranio! Until I discovered it does happen,
I never believed it was possible or even likely.
But while I stood by, idly watching,
I discovered how strong love-in-idleness is.

And now in plainness do confess to thee,
145   That art to me as secret and as dear
As Anna to the Queen of Carthage was,
Tranio, I burn, I pine, I perish, Tranio,
If I achieve not this young modest girl.
Counsel me, Tranio, for I know thou canst;
150   Assist me, Tranio, for I know thou wilt.

TRANIO
Master, it is no time to chide you now;
Affection is not rated from the heart.
If love have touch'd you, naught remains but so,
"Redime te captum quam queas minimo."

LUCENTIO
155   Gramercies, lad, go forward; this contents.
The rest will comfort, for thy counsel's sound.

TRANIO
Master, you look'd so longly on the maid,
Perhaps you mark'd not what's the pith of all.

LUCENTIO
O yes, I saw sweet beauty in her face,
160   Such as the daughter of Agenor had,
That made great Jove to humble him to her hand,
When with his knees he kiss'd the Cretan strand.

TRANIO
Saw you no more? Mark'd you not how her sister
Began to scold and raise up such a storm
165   That mortal ears might hardly endure the din?

LUCENTIO
Tranio, I saw her coral lips to move
And with her breath she did perfume the air.
Sacred and sweet was all I saw in her.

TRANIO
Nay, then, 'tis time to stir him from his trance.
170   I pray, awake, sir. If you love the maid,
Bend thoughts and wits to achieve her. Thus it stands:
Her elder sister is so curst and shrewd

---

146 *Anna* sister and confidante to Dido, Queen of Carthage.   160 *daughter of Agenor*
Europa, beloved by Jove, chief Roman god.

And now I'll plainly confess to you—
145   you who are as much in my confidence and as much my friend
as Anna was to the Queen of Carthage—
Tranio, I'll burn, I'll waste away, I'll die, Tranio,
if I don't win the hand of this sweet young girl.
Advise me, Tranio; I know you can.
150   Help me, Tranio; I know you will.

TRANIO
Master, it isn't the time to scold you, now.
Affection can't be scolded away.
If you're in love, there's nothing left to do except this:
buy your way out of captivity as cheaply as you can.

LUCENTIO
155   Thanks very much, lad. Go on. This is soothing advice.
Your words will comfort me because your advice is good.

TRANIO
Master, you stared so longingly at the girl's face
that perhaps you didn't hear the jist of their conversation.

LUCENTIO
O yes, I saw the sweet beauty of her face.
160   She's just as beautiful as Agenor's daughter
who so humbled mighty Jove
that he knelt on the shore of Crete before her.

TRANIO
Didn't you see anything else? Didn't you notice how
   her sister
began to scold and kick up such a fuss
165   that a human ear could scarcely stand the noise?

LUCENTIO
Tranio, I saw her coral lips move
and noticed how her breath perfumed the air.
Everything I saw about her was sacred and sweet.

TRANIO
I see it's time to rouse him up from this daze.
170   Please, sir, wake up. If you love the girl,
put your mind and wits to winning her. The situation is this:
her older sister is so testy and shrewish

That till the father rid his hands of her,
Master, your love must live a maid at home;
175 And therefore has he closely mew'd her up,
Because she will not be annoy'd with suitors.

LUCENTIO
Ah, Tanio, what a cruel father's he!
But art thou not advis'd, he took some care
To get her cunning schoolmasters to instruct her?

TRANIO
180 Ay, marry, am I, sir; and now 'tis plotted.

LUCENTIO
I have it, Tranio.

TRANIO
                    Master, for my hand,
Both our inventions meet and jump in one.

LUCENTIO
Tell me thine first.

TRANIO
185   You will be schoolmaster
And undertake the teaching of the maid:
That's your device.

LUCENTIO
It is; may it be done?

TRANIO
Not possible; for who shall bear your part,
190 And be in Padua here Vincentio's son,
Keep house and ply his book, welcome his friends,
Visit his countrymen and banquet them?

LUCENTIO
Basta, content thee, for I have it full.
We have not yet been seen in any house,
195 Nor can we be distinguish'd by our faces
For man or master. Then it follows thus:
Thou shalt be master, Tranio, in my stead,
Keep house and port and servants, as I should.

that, until her father gets her off his hands,
your beloved must remain at home, unmarried.
175   Therefore, her father is carefully guarding her
so that she won't be pestered by suitors.

LUCENTIO
Ah, Tranio, what a cruel father he is!
But didn't you hear that he wanted
to get some knowledgeable teachers to teach her?

TRANIO
180   Yes, certainly I know that, sir—ah, now I've got a plan!

LUCENTIO
I have one, too, Tranio.

TRANIO
Master, I'll bet
that both our schemes are the same.

LUCENTIO
Tell me yours first.

TRANIO
185   You'll be a teacher
and accept the job of teaching the girl—
that's your plan.

LUCENTIO
That's it; do you think we can manage it?

TRANIO
It won't work. Who will act your part
190   and play Vincentio's son here in Padua,
entertain, study his books, greet friends,
visit his countrymen, and invite them to dinner?

LUCENTIO
Enough. Rest easy. I've got it all planned.
No one knows who we are yet,
195   and no one can tell from our faces
who is servant and who is master. So my plan is this:
Tranio, you will play the master in my place,
keeping house, my style of living, and my servants, just as I would.

I will some other be, some Florentine,
200   Some Neapolitan, or meaner man of Pisa.
'Tis hatch'd and shall be so. Tranio, at once
Uncase thee; take my colour'd hat and cloak.
When Biondello comes, he waits on thee;
But I will charm him first to keep his tongue.

TRANIO
205   So had you need.
In brief, sir, sith it your pleasure is,
And I am tied to be obedient,—
For so your father charg'd me at our parting,
"Be serviceable to my son," quoth he,
210   Although I think 'twas in another sense,—
I am content to be Lucentio,
Because so well I love Lucentio.

LUCENTIO
Tranio, be so, because Lucentio loves;
And let me be a slave, t' achieve that maid
215   Whose sudden sight hath thrall'd my wounded eye.
        Enter BIONDELLO.
Here comes the rogue. Sirrah where have you been?

BIONDELLO
Where have I been! Nay, how now! where are you? Master, has
my fellow Tranio stol'n your clothes? or you stol'n his? or both?
Pray, what's the news?

LUCENTIO
220   Sirrah, come hither; 'tis no time to jest,
And therefore frame your manners to the time.
Your fellow Tranio here, to save my life,
Puts my apparel and my count'nance on,
And I for my escape have put on his;
225   For in a quarrel since I came ashore
I kill'd a man and fear I was descried.
Wait you on him, I charge you, as becomes,
While I make way from hence to save my life.
You understand me?

---

202 *colour'd* servants dressed in dark blue clothes, while their masters wore more colorful clothing.   215 *wounded eye* pierced by Cupid's love arrow.

I'll become someone else—some Florentine,
200 or Neapolitan, or low-ranked man from Pisa.
     That's the plan and we'll carry it out. Tranio, take off your clothes
     immediately. Take my colorful hat and cloak.
         (They switch clothes.)
     When Biondello arrives, he must serve you.
     But first, I'll convince him to hold his tongue.

TRANIO
205 Yes, you'd better.
     In short, sir, since you want it this way,
     and I'm bound to obey you—
     for your father said to me when we left:
     "Serve my son well," he said,
210 although I think he meant something different from this—
     I'm willing to pretend I'm Lucentio
     because I love Lucentio so much.

LUCENTIO
     Do that, Tranio, because Lucentio is in love.
     Let me play the servant in order to win the girl
215 who, after just a short glimpse, has captured my wounded eye.
         Enter BIONDELLO.
     Here comes the rascal. Where have you been, servant?

BIONDELLO
     Where have I been! Wait, what's this? Where have you gone? Master, has
     my fellow servant Tranio stolen your clothes, or have you stolen his?
      Or both?
     Please, what's going on?

LUCENTIO
220 Servant, come here. This is no time for joking,
     so match your behavior to the circumstances.
     Your fellow servant Tranio, in order to save my life,
     has put on my clothes and adopted my style.
     And, so that I could escape, I put on his clothes.
225 I'm doing this because, in a quarrel that I had since coming ashore,
     I killed a man, and I'm afraid that I was recognized.
     So, I order you to serve Tranio as is proper,
     while I escape from here in order to save my life.
     Do you understand me?

BIONDELLO

230   I, sir! ne'er a whit.

LUCENTIO

And not a jot of Tranio in your mouth.
Tranio is chang'd into Lucentio.

BIONDELLO

The better for him; would I were so too!

TRANIO

So could I, faith, boy, to have the next wish after,

235   That Lucentio indeed had Baptista's youngest daughter.
But, sirrah, not for my sake, but your master's, I advise
You use your manners discreetly in all kind of companies.
When I am alone, why, then I am Tranio;
But in all places else your master Lucentio.

LUCENTIO

240   Tranio, let's go. One thing more rests, that thyself execute to make
one among these wooers. If thou ask me why, sufficeth my reasons
are both good and weighty.
            [*Exeunt.*]

            The presenters above speak.

1. SERVANT

My lord, you nod; you do not mind the play.

SLY

Yes, by Saint Anne, do I. A good matter, surely; comes there any

245   more of it?

PAGE

My lord, 'tis but begun.

SLY

'Tis a very excellent piece of work, madam lady; would 'twere
done!   [*They sit and mark.*]

BIONDELLO
230   Me, sir! Not a bit.

LUCENTIO
And not a syllable of Tranio's name from you.
Tranio has become Lucentio.

BIONDELLO
Lucky him; I wish the same thing had happened to me!

TRANIO
I could wish that, too, boy, if I could have the next wish after that:
235   that Lucentio really had Baptista's youngest daughter.
But, servant, not for my sake but your master's, I advise
you to be polite and discreet in everyone's company.
When we're alone, then address me as Tranio,
but everywhere else, I'm your master Lucentio.

LUCENTIO
240   Let's go, Tranio. One other thing remains for you to do—
you must join the perspective husbands. If you want to know why I ask
    this, be content with knowing
that I have good and important reasons.
     They exit.
     (The actors above speak.)

FIRST SERVANT
My lord, you're dozing. You're not paying attention to the play.

SLY
Yes I am, by Saint Anne. It's good stuff, really; is there any
245   more of it?

PAGE
My lord, it's just started.

SLY
It's a very excellent piece of work, my lady; I wish it were
over!
     (They sit and watch.)

Scene ii: [Padua. Before Hortensio's house.] Enter
PETRUCHIO *and his man* GRUMIO.

PETRUCHIO
    Verona, for a while I take my leave
    To see my friends in Padua, but of all
    My best beloved and approved friend,
    Hortensio; and I trow this is his house.
5   Here, sirrah Grumio; knock, I say.

GRUMIO
    Knock, sir! whom should I knock? Is there any man has rebus'd
    your worship?

PETRUCHIO
    Villain, I say, knock me here soundly.

GRUMIO
    Knock you here, sir! Why, sir, what am I, sir, that I should knock
10   you here, sir?

PETRUCHIO
    Villain, I say, knock me at this gate
    And rap me well, or I'll knock your knave's pate.

GRUMIO
    My master is grown quarrelsome. I should knock you first,
    And then I know after who comes by the worst.

PETRUCHIO
15   Will it not be?
    Faith, sirrah, an you'll not knock, I'll ring it.
    I'll try how you can *sol, fa,* and sing it.
        [He wrings him by the ears.]

GRUMIO
    Help, masters, help! my master is mad.

PETRUCHIO
    Now, knock when I bid you, sirrah villain!
        Enter HORTENSIO.

---

6 *rebused* Grumio really means "abused." He is using a malapropism—an unintentionally comic misuse of a word.   16 *ring it* Petruchio means he'll "wring" Grumio's neck.

Act I, Scene ii: Padua, before Hortensio's house. Enter
PETRUCHIO *and his servant* GRUMIO.

PETRUCHIO
    I've left Verona for a little while
    to see my friends in Padua, especially
    my best and proven friend,
    Hortensio. I believe this is his house.
5   Here, my servant Grumio. Knock, I tell you.

GRUMIO
    Knock, sir? Whom should I hit? Has someone rebused
    you, your worship?

PETRUCHIO
    Rascal, I told you, knock here firmly.

GRUMIO
    Knock here firmly? Why, sir, who am I, sir, that I should hit
10   you here, sir?

PETRUCHIO
    Rascal, I said knock (for) me here at this door
    and hit well, or I'll hit your foolish head.

GRUMIO
    My master has become angry. If I hit you first,
    I know who will be beaten for it afterwards.

PETRUCHIO
15   So you won't do it?
    I'll tell you then, servant, if you don't knock, I'll ring it.
    I'll see if you can sing your scales.
        (He wrings Grumio by the ears.)

GRUMIO
    Help, somebody, help! My master is mad.

PETRUCHIO
    Now knock when I tell you to, you rascally servant.
        Enter HORTENSIO.

HORTENSIO

20   How now! what's the matter? My old friend Grumio! and my
good friend Petruchio! How do you all at Verona?

PETRUCHIO

Signior Hortensio, come you to part the fray?
Con tutto il cuore, ben trovato, may I say.

HORTENSIO

*Alla nostra casa ben venuto, molto honorato signor
   mio Petruchio.*

25   Rise, Grumio, rise; we will compound this quarrel.

GRUMIO

Nay, 'tis no matter, sir, what he 'leges in Latin. If this be not
a lawful cause for me to leave his service, look you, sir. He bid
me knock him and rap him soundly, sir. Well, was it fit for a
servant to use his master so, being perhaps, for aught I see, two

30   and thirty, a pip out?
Whom would to God I had well knock'd at first,
Then had not Grumio come by the worst.

PETRUCHIO

A senseless villain! Good Hortensio,
I bade the rascal knock upon your gate

35   And could not get him for my heart to do it.

GRUMIO

Knock at the gate! O heavens! Spake you not these words plain,
"Sirrah, knock me here, rap me here, knock me well, and knock
me soundly"? And come you now with, "knocking at the gate"?

PETRUCHIO

Sirrah, be gone, or talk not, I advise you.

HORTENSIO

40   Petruchio, patience; I am Grumio's pledge.
Why, this's a heavy chance 'twixt him and you,
Your ancient, trusty, pleasant servant Grumio.
And tell me now, sweet friend, what happy gale
Blows you to Padua here from old Verona?

29-30 *two and thirty, a pip out* orginally was a term from a card game (pip being a marking
on a card). The phrase also came to mean "drunk." The thirty-two also may refer to
Petruchio's age and be Grumio's stab at his master's comparatively old age.

HORTENSIO

20   Why, what's the matter? My old friend Grumio! And my
good friend Petruchio. How is everyone in Verona?

PETRUCHIO

Signior Hortensio, did you come to settle the quarrel?
With all my heart, may I say that you are welcome.

HORTENSIO

Welcome to my house, my most honored Signior Petruchio.
25   Get up, Grumio, get up. I'll settle this quarrel.

GRUMIO

It doesn't matter, sir, what he claims in Latin. If this isn't
a legal reason to leave his service—Look, sir, he told
me to knock him and hit him firmly. Well, is it proper for a
servant to treat his master like that when, perhaps for all that I know,
30   he's out of his head?
I wish to God that I had hit him good.
Then I would not have suffered.

PETRUCHIO

What a stupid rascal! Good Hortensio,
I told the rascal to knock on your door
35   and couldn't get him to do it on my life!

GRUMIO

Knock at the door? O heavens! Didn't you say these words quite clearly,
"Servant, hit me here, rap here, knock well, and knock
me firmly?" And now you're saying "knocking at the door"?

PETRUCHIO

Servant, leave or shut up, I'm warning you.

HORTENSIO

40   Petruchio, please be patient. I'll swear by Grumio.
Why, this is an unhappy turn of events between you and him,
your long-time, trusted, pleasant servant Grumio.
So, tell me now, good friend, what fortunate wind
blows you here to Padua from old Verona?

PETRUCHIO

45   Such wind as scatters young men through the world.
To seek their fortunes farther than at home
Where small experience grows. But in a few,
Signior Hortensio, thus it stands with me:
Antonio, my father, is deceas'd;
50   And I have thrust myself into this maze,
Happily to wive and thrive as best I may.
Crowns in my purse I have and goods at home,
And so am come abroad to see the world.

HORTENSIO

Petruchio, shall I then come roundly to thee
55   And wish thee to a shrewd ill-favour'd wife?
Thou'dst thank me but a little for my counsel;
And yet I'll promise thee she shall be rich
And very rich. But thou'rt too much my friend,
And I'll not wish thee to her.

PETRUCHIO

60   Signior Hortensio, 'twixt such friends as we
Few words suffice; and therefore, if thou know
One rich enough to be Petruchio's wife,
As wealth is burden of my wooing dance,
Be she as foul as was Florentius' love,
65   As old as Sibyl, and as curst and shrewd
As Socrates' Xanthippe, or a worse,
She moves me not, or not removes, at least,
Affection's edge in me, were she as rough
As are the swelling Adriatic seas.
70   I come to wive it wealthily in Padua;
If wealthily, then happily in Padua.

GRUMIO

Nay, look you, sir, he tells you flatly what his mind is. Why, give
him gold enough, and marry him to a puppet or an aglet-baby,
or an old trot with ne'er a tooth in her head, though she have
75   as many diseases as two and fifty horses. Why, nothing comes
amiss, so money comes withal.

---

64 *Florentius' lover* Florentius is a fictional character who swore he would marry an ugly
woman if she answered a riddle that would save him from death.   65 *Sibyl* a seeress from
Greek and Roman myths who lived to a very ancient age.   66 *Socrates' Xanthippe* Socrate's
wife who was supposedly a shrew.   73 *aglet-baby* the figure of a woman on the tip of a lace.

PETRUCHIO

45   The kind of wind that scatters men throughout the world
to seek their fortunes away from home,
where little experience is gained. But, in short,
Signior Hortensio, this is my situation:
my father, Antonio, is dead,
50   and I've jumped onto this unknown path—
with any luck to marry and live as best as I can.
I have money in my purse and goods at home,
so I came abroad to see the world.

HORTENSIO

Petruchio, shall I be frank with you
55   and recommend you to a shrewish, unsuitable wife?
You'll thank me very little for my advice.
And yet, I'll guarantee you, she'll be rich,
very rich. But you're too good a friend,
and I won't recommend her to you.

PETRUCHIO

60   Signior Hortensio, friends like we two
understand each other without long explanations. So, if you know
someone rich enough to be my wife—
since wealth is the tune for my wedding dance—
if my bride is as ugly as Florentius' lover,
65   as old as Sibyl, as mean and shrewish
as Socrates' Xanthippe, or even worse,
I won't be bothered, and my
affections won't be dulled at all, even if she were as rough
as the stormy Adriatic sea.
70   I've come to Padua to marry a rich woman.
If I marry richly, then I'll live happily in Padua.

GRUMIO

You see, sir, he tells you plainly how he feels. Just give
him enough money, and then marry him to a doll or a lace-tip
or an old hag without a tooth in her head, even if she has
75   as many diseases as fifty-two horses. Well, everything's
fine if money goes with it.

HORTENSIO

    Petruchio, since we are stepp'd thus far in,
    I will continue that I broach'd in jest.
    I can, Petruchio, help thee to a wife
80   With wealth enough and young and beauteous,
    Brought up as best becomes a gentlewoman.
    Her only fault, and that is faults enough,
    Is that she is intolerable curst
    And shrewd and froward, so beyond all measure
85   That, were my state far worser than it is,
    I would not wed her for a mine of gold.

PETRUCHIO

    Hortensio, peace! thou know'st not gold's effect.
    Tell me her father's name and 'tis enough;
    For I will board her, though she chide as loud
90   As thunder when the clouds in autumn crack.

HORTENSIO

    Her father is Baptista Minola,
    An affable and courteous gentleman.
    Her name is Katherina Minola,
    Renown'd in Padua for her scolding tongue.

PETRUCHIO

95   I know her father, though I know not her;
    And he knew my deceased father well.
    I will not sleep, Hortensio, till I see her;
    And therefore let me be thus bold with you
    To give you over at this first encounter,
100   Unless you will accompany me thither.

GRUMIO

    I pray you, sir, let him go while the humour lasts. O' my word,
    an she knew him as well as I do, she would think scolding would
    do little good upon him. She may perhaps call him half a score
    knaves or so,—why, that's nothing. An he begin once, he'll rail
105   in his rope-tricks. I'll tell you what, sir, an she stand him but a
    little, he will throw a figure in her face and so disfigure her with
    it that she shall have no more eyes to see withal than a cat. You
    know him not, sir.

---

79 *help thee to* means both "find" and "become."   105 *rope-tricks* means both "rhetoric"
(and plays on the word "figure," as in figure of speech) and "roguish behavior."

HORTENSIO

> Petruchio, since we've gone this far,
> I'll tell you more of what I first said as a joke.
> I can show you, Petruchio, where to get a wife
80   who is rich, young, beautiful,
> and raised like a lady should be.
> Her only fault—and it's a big enough fault—
> is that she is intolerably mean
> and shrewish and stubborn—beyond all comparison—
85   so that even if my income were much less than it is,
> I wouldn't marry her for a gold mine!

PETRUCHIO

> Enough, Hortensio! You don't know the power of gold.
> Tell me what her father's name is—that will do.
> For I'll court her even if she scolds as loud
90   as when, in autumn, thunder makes the clouds ring.

HORTENSIO

> Her father is Baptista Minola.
> He's a friendly and courteous gentlemen.
> The woman's name is Katherine Minola,
> famous throughout Padua for her scolding tongue.

PETRUCHIO

95   I know her father, though I don't know her.
> And Baptista knew my dead father well.
> I won't sleep, Hortensio, until I've seen her,
> so let me be so bold as
> to leave you now, though it is our first meeting—
100   unless you want to go there with me.

GRUMIO

> I beg you, sir, let him go while he's still in the mood. Really,
> if she knew him as well as I do, she'd think scolding would
> have little effect on him. She might call him half a dozen
> rascals or something like that. It wouldn't bother him. Just start him
> off, and he'll rant
105   and rave. I'll tell you, sir, if she's just a
> little obstinate, he'll spit a figure of speech at her and hurt her
> so much that she'll be as blind as a cat. You
> don't know him, sir.

HORTENSIO

Tarry, Petruchio, I must go with thee,

110   For in Baptista's keep my treasure is.
He hath the jewel of my life in hold,
His youngest daughter, beautiful Bianca,
And her withholds from me and other more,
Suitors to her and rivals in my love,

115   Supposing it a thing impossible,
For those defects I have before rehears'd,
That ever Katherina will be woo'd.
Therefore this order hath Baptista ta'en,
That none shall have access unto Bianca

120   Till Katherine the curst have got a husband.

GRUMIO

Katherine the curst!
A title for a maid of all titles the worst.

HORTENSIO

Now shall my friend Petruchio do me grace,
And offer me disguis'd in sober robes

125   To old Baptista as a schoolmaster
Well seen in music, to instruct Bianca;
That so I may, by this device, at least
Have leave and leisure to make love to her
And unsuspected court her by herself.

Enter GREMIO, *and* LUCENTIO, *disguised as*
CAMBIO.

GRUMIO

130   Here's no knavery! See, to beguile the old folks, how the young
folks lay their heads together!
Master, master, look about you! Who goes there, ha!

HORTENSIO

Peace, Grumio! it is the rival of my love.
Petruchio, stand by a while.

GRUMIO

135   A proper stripling and an amorous!

HORTENSIO
Wait a minute, Petruchio, I must go with you
110   because my treasure is in Baptista's house.
He has the jewel of my life in his stronghold—
his youngest daughter, the beautiful Bianca.
He keeps me away from her, and others—
her suitors and my rivals—
115   since he thinks it is impossible,
because of those faults I've told you about,
that Katherine will ever be married.
So Baptista's given this order:
no one will see or talk to Bianca
120   until Katherine the shrew has a husband.

GRUMIO
Katherine the shrew!
That's the worst possible nickname for a woman.

HORTENSIO
Now my friend, Petruchio, do me a favor
and introduce me—after I've disguised myself in proper clothing—
125   to old Baptista as a teacher
knowledgeable about music and able to teach Bianca.
By this little scheme, I can at least
be given permission to see her and time to win her
and court her without suspicion when we're alone.
        Enter GREMIO *and* LUCENTIO, *who is disguised*
        as Cambio.

GRUMIO *(sacrastically)*
130   Why, this is honest stuff! See how the young
folks put their heads together to fool the old folks.
Master, master—look! Who's that?

HORTENSIO
Quiet, Grumio! That's my rival for Bianca's love.
Petruchio, stand close by for a moment.

GRUMIO *(looking at Gremio, exclaims sarcastically)*
135   He's a handsome boy and a real lover!

GREMIO

    O, very well; I have perus'd the note.

    Hark you, sir; I'll have them very fairly bound,—

    All books of love, see that at any hand;

    And see you read no other lectures to her.

140   You understand me? Over and beside

    Signior Baptista's liberality,

    I'll mend it with a largess. Take your paper too;

    And let me have them very well perfum'd,

    For she is sweeter than perfume itself

145   To whom they go to. What will you read to her?

LUCENTIO

    Whate'er I read to her, I'll plead for you

    As for my patron, stand you so assur'd,

    As firmly as yourself were still in place;

    Yea, and perhaps with more successful words

150   Than you, unless you were a scholar, sir.

GREMIO

    O this learning, what a thing it is!

GRUMIO

    O this woodcock, what an ass it is!

PETRUCHIO

    Peace, sirrah!

HORTENSIO

    Grumio, mum! God save you, Signior Gremio.

GREMIO

155   And you are well met, Signior Hortensio.

    Trow you whither I am going? To Baptista Minola.

    I promis'd to inquire carefully

    About a schoolmaster for the fair Bianca;

    And by good fortune I have lighted well

160   On this young man, for learning and behaviour

    Fit for her turn, well read in poetry

    And other books, good ones, I warrant ye.

HORTENSIO

    'Tis well; and I have met a gentleman

GREMIO
　　Very well, I've read the reading list.
　　Listen, sir, I want all the books to have pretty covers.
　　And all the books must be about love. That's important.
　　See that you don't talk to her about anything else.
140　I think you understand me. Besides
　　Signior Baptista's good wages,
　　I'll add on a gift. Take the list, too.
　　I'll see that the sheets are nicely perfumed
　　since she is sweeter than perfume itself—
145　the girl they're going to. What will you read to her?

LUCENTIO
　　Whatever I read to her, I'll court her for you,
　　my patron—you can be as certain of that
　　as if you yourself were still present.
　　Yes, I'll do that and perhaps with more winning words
150　than you would use, unless you were a scholar, sir.

GREMIO
　　O, knowledge is a wonderful thing!

GRUMIO *(Aside)*
　　O, this fool is such an ass!

PETRUCHIO
　　Quiet, servant!

HORTENSIO
　　Grumio, hush! *(coming forward)* Good day to you, Signior Gremio!

GREMIO
155　Nice to see you, Signior Hortensio.
　　So you know where I'm going? To Baptista Minola.
　　I promised to search
　　for a schoolmaster for beautiful Bianca,
　　and with good luck, I happened to find
160　this young man. In knowledge and bearing
　　he's exactly right for her. He's well read in poetry
　　and other books—good ones, too, I'll bet.

HORTENSIO
　　That's good. I've met a gentleman, too,

Hath promis'd me to help me to another,
165   A fine musician, to instruct our mistress;
So shall I no whit be behind in duty
To fair Bianca, so belov'd of me.

GREMIO
Belov'd of me; and that my deeds shall prove.

GRUMIO
And that his bags shall prove.

HORTENSIO
170   Gremio, 'tis now no time to vent our love.
Listen to me, and if you speak me fair,
I'll tell you news indifferent good for either.
Here is a gentleman whom by chance I met,
Upon agreement from us to his liking,
175   Will undertake to woo curst Katherine,
Yea, and to marry her, if her dowry please.

GREMIO
So said, so done is well.
Hortensio, have you told him all her faults?

PETRUCHIO
I know she is an irksome brawling scold.
180   If that be all, masters, I hear no harm.

GREMIO
No, say'st me so, friend? What countryman?

PETRUCHIO
Born in Verona, old Antonio's son.
My father dead, my fortune lives for me;
And I do hope good days and long to see.

GREMIO
185   O sir, such a life with such a wife, were strange!
But if you have a stomach, to't i' God's name;
You shall have me assisting you in all.
But will you woo this wild-cat?

PETRUCHIO
                      Will I live?

---

174 *agreement* Hortensio means Petruchio will court Kate if the expenses he incurs while wooing her are paid.

who has promised me to help find a teacher—
165   a fine musician who can teach our lady love—
so I won't be lagging in my duty
to beautiful Bianca, my dearly beloved.

GREMIO
My dearly beloved—my actions will prove that.

GRUMIO *(to himself)*
And his moneybags will prove that.

HORTENSIO
170   Gremio, this isn't the time to talk about our love.
Listen to me, and if you're being honest with me,
I'll tell you some news that's good for us both.
    (Presents Petruchio.)
Here is a gentleman whom I met by chance.
If we agree to what he asks,
175   he says he'll try to court the shrewish Katherine—
yes, even marry her if he likes her dowry.

GREMIO
If he does as he says, that would be good.
Hortensio, have you told him about all her faults?

PETRUCHIO
I know she's an irritating, quarrelsome shrew.
180   If that's all, gentlemen, I'm not discouraged.

GREMIO
No! You really mean that, my friend? Where are you from?

PETRUCHIO
I was born in Verona. I'm old Antonio's son.
My father is dead now, my fortune still is to be made,
and I hope to live a good, long life.

GREMIO
185   O, sir, such a life with such a wife is most unlikely!
But if you have the desire to try, go to it, by God.
I'll help you in every possible way.
But will you really court this wildcat?

PETRUCHIO
Will I live?

GRUMIO

190   Will he woo her? Ay, or I'll hang her.

PETRUCHIO

Why came I hither but to that intent?
Think you a little din can daunt mine ears?
Have I not in my time heard lions roar?
Have I not heard the sea, puff'd up with winds,
195   Rage like an angry boar chafed with sweat?
Have I not heard great ordnance in the field,
And heaven's artillery thunder in the skies?
Have I not in a pitched battle heard
Loud 'larums, neighing steeds, and trumpets' clang?
200   And do you tell me of a woman's tongue,
That gives not half so great a blow to hear
As will a chestnut in a farmer's fire?
Tush, tush! fear boys with bugs.

GRUMIO

For he fears none.

GREMIO

205   Hortensio, hark.
This gentleman is happily arriv'd,
My mind presumes, for his own good and ours.

HORTENSIO

I promis'd we would be contributors
And bear his charge of wooing, whatsoe'er.

GREMIO

210   And so we will, provided that he win her.

GRUMIO

I would I were as sure of a good dinner.
Enter TRANIO *brave, and* BIONDELLO.

TRANIO

Gentlemen, God save you. If I may be bold,
Tell me, I beseech you, which is the readiest way
To the house of Signior Baptista Minola?

GRUMIO *(to himself)*
190   Listen to him—will he court her? Yes, or I'll hang her.

PETRUCHIO
Why did I come here except to do that?
Do you think a little noise can frighten me?
Haven't I heard lions roaring in my day?
Haven't I heard the sea, swelled by winds,
195   rage like a hot, angry boar?
Haven't I heard the big cannons in battles
and heaven's gunfire thunder in the skies?
Haven't I heard in the heat of battle
the call to arms, neighing horses, and the clang of trumpets?
200   And you tell me about a woman's sharp tongue
that doesn't sound as half as loud
as a chestnut cracking in a farmer's fire?
Nonsense, nonsense. Go frighten boys with goblins.

GRUMIO *(to himself)*
Because they don't scare him.

GREMIO
205   Listen, Hortensio,
this gentleman has arrived at a good moment,
I think—both for us and for him.

HORTENSIO
I promised we would chip in
and pay the expenses for his courting, whatever the cost.

GREMIO
210   And we'll do just that, provided he marry her.

GRUMIO *(to himself)*
I wish I were as sure of a good dinner.
    Enter TRANIO *(as Lucentio), very well
    dressed, and* BIONDELLO.

TRANIO
Gentlemen, God bless you! If I may be so bold to ask,
please tell me which is the quickest way
to Singior Baptista Minola's house?

BIONDELLO
215   He that has the two fair daughters? Is't he you mean?

TRANIO
Even he, Biondello.

GREMIO
Hark you, sir; you mean not her to—

TRANIO
Perhaps, him and her, sir; what have you to do?

PETRUCHIO
Not her that chides, sir, at any hand, I pray.

TRANIO
220   I love no chiders, sir. Biondello, let's away.

LUCENTIO
Well begun, Tranio.

HORTENSIO
Sir, a word ere you go;
Are you a suitor to the maid you talk of, yea or no?

TRANIO
And if I be, sir, is it any offence?

GREMIO
225   No; if without more words you will get you hence.

TRANIO
Why, sir, I pray, are not the streets as free
For me as for you?

GREMIO
But so is not she.

TRANIO
For what reason, I beseech you?

GREMIO
230   For this reason, if you'll know,
That she's the choice love of Signior Gremio.

HORTENSIO
That she's the chosen of Signior Hortensio.

BIONDELLO

215   The man who has two lovely daughters—is that the one you mean?

TRANIO

That's the one, Biondello.

GREMIO

Listen, sir—the girl—you don't mean to—

TRANIO

Perhaps the girl and Signior Baptista, sir. What business is it of yours?

PETRUCHIO

You don't have any plans for the shrew, at any rate, I hope.

TRANIO

220   I don't care for shrews, sir. Biondello, let's go.

LUCENTIO *(Aside)*

That was a nice start, Tranio.

HORTENSIO

Sir, I'd like a word with you before you go:
are you a suitor of the girl you spoke of—yes or no?

TRANIO

And if I am a suitor, sir, is that a crime?

GREMIO

225   No, not if you leave Padua without another word.

TRANIO

Why is that, sir? Aren't these streets just as free
to me as they are to you?

GREMIO

But not her.

TRANIO

Why, may I ask?

GREMIO

230   For this reason, if you want to know:
she's my chosen love.

HORTENSIO

She's my chosen love!

TRANIO

    Softly, my masters! If you be gentlemen,

    Do me this right: hear me with patience.

235   Baptista is a noble gentleman,

    To whom my father is not all unknown;

    And were his daughter fairer than she is,

    She may more suitors have, and me for one.

    Fair Leda's daughter had a thousand wooers;

240   Then well one more may fair Bianca have;

    And so she shall. Lucentio shall make one,

    Though Paris came in hope to speed alone.

GREMIO

    What! this gentleman will out-talk us all.

LUCENTIO

    Sir, give him head; I know he'll prove a jade.

PETRUCHIO

245   Hortensio, to what end are all these words?

HORTENSIO

    Sir, let me be so bold as ask you,

    Did you yet ever see Baptista's daughter?

TRANIO

    No, sir; but hear I do that he hath two,

    The one as famous for a scolding tongue

250   As is the other for beauteous modesty.

PETRUCHIO

    Sir, sir, the first's for me; let her go by.

GREMIO

    Yea, leave that labour to great Hercules;

    And let it be more than Alcides' twelve.

PETRUCHIO

    Sir, understand you this of me in sooth:

255   The youngest daughter, whom you hearken for,

    Her father keeps from all access of suitors,

    And will not promise her to any man

    Until the elder sister first be wed.

    The younger then is free and not before.

---

239 *Leda's daughter* Helen, daughter of Leda and the Greek god Zeus. Paris took Helen away from her husband to Troy, causing the Trojan War.   252 *Hercules* or Alcides, a Greek hero, performed twelve great labors to free himself.

TRANIO
    Relax, gentlemen! If you're gentlemen,
    grant me this right—listen to me with patience.
235   Baptista is a noble gentleman
    to whom my father is not a complete stranger.
    And if his daughter were lovelier than she is,
    she still could have more suitors—me for one.
    Lovely Leda's daughter had a thousand suitors.
240   Then certainly lovely Bianca can have one more.
    And so she will. Lucentio will be one,
    even if Paris showed up hoping to court her without rivals.

GREMIO
    Really! This gentleman will out-talk us all!

LUCENTIO
    Sir, let him talk. I know he'll fade in the stretch.

PETRUCHIO
245   Hortensio, what's all the point to this talk?

HORTENSIO
    Sir, let me be so bold as to ask you
    if you've ever seen Baptista's daughter?

TRANIO
    No, sir, but I hear that he has two daughters,
    the one as renowned for her shrewish tongue
250   as the other one is for her beauty and modesty.

PETRUCHIO
    Sir, the oldest daughter is mine; pass her by.

GREMIO
    Yes, leave that labor to great Hercules, here.
    That will amount to more that Alcides' twelve labors.

PETRUCHIO
    Sir, understand this that I'll tell you honestly:
255   the youngest daughter, the one you're after,
    is kept away from all suitors by her father
    who refuses to let any man marry her
    until his eldest daughter is married first.
    Then the younger one is free to marry, and only then.

TRANIO

260   If it be so, sir, that you are the man
       Must stead us all, and me amongst the rest,
       And if you break the ice and do this feat,
       Achieve the elder, set the younger free
       For our access, whose hap shall be to have her
265   Will not so graceless be to be ingrate.

HORTENSIO

       Sir, you say well, and well you do conceive;
       And since you do profess to be a suitor,
       You must, as we do, gratify this gentleman,
       To whom we all rest generally beholding.

TRANIO

270   Sir, I shall not be slack; in sign whereof,
       Please ye we may contrive this afternoon
       And quaff carouses to our mistress' health;
       And do as adversaries do in law,
       Strive mightily, but eat and drink as friends.

GRUMIO and BIONDELLO

275   O excellent motion! Fellows, let's be gone.

HORTENSIO

       The motion's good indeed, and be it so.
       Petruchio, I shall be your *ben venuto.*
           [*Exeunt.*]

Act II, Scene i: [*Padua. A room in Baptista's house.*]
Enter KATHERINA *and* BIANCA.

BIANCA

       Good sister, wrong me not, nor wrong yourself,
       To make a bondmaid and a slave of me.
       That I disdain; but for these other gawds,
       Unbind my hands, I'll pull them off myself,
5   Yea, all my raiment, to my petticoat;
       Or what you will command me will I do,
       So well I know my duty to my elders.

TRANIO

260   If that's so, sir, then you are the man
who must help us all—me included.
And if you break the ice and are able to
win the eldest daughter and set the younger one free
so we can court her, whoever is lucky enough to gain her love

265   will not be so ungracious as to be ungrateful.

HORTENSIO

Sir, that's well said, and you state the situation well.
And since you say that you're a suitor,
you must, like us, reward this gentleman
to whom we all remain in debt.

TRANIO

270   Sir, I won't duck my share—and to show you that I mean it,
if it suits you, let's spend the afternoon
drinking from deep-bottomed cups to our ladies' healths,
and do just as attorneys do:
try to beat the other fellow in court, but eat and drink like friends.

GRUMIO and BIONDELLO *(together)*

275   That's a wonderful idea! Gentlemen, let's go.

HORTENSIO

It's a good idea and let's do it.
Petruchio, I'll be your host.
    They exit.

Act II, Scene i: Padua. A room in Baptista's house.
Enter KATHERINE *and* BIANCA, *with her hands tied.*

BIANCA

Dear sister, don't abuse me or abuse yourself
by making me a servant and a slave.
I despise that. But as for these other ornaments,
untie my hands, and I'll pull them off myself.

5   Yes, all my clothing, down to my petticoat.
Or whatever you order me to do, I will,
to show you how well I know my duty to my elders.

KATHERINA
   Of all thy suitors, here I charge thee, tell
   Whom thou lov'st best; see thou dissemble not.

BIANCA
10   Believe me, sister, of all the men alive
   I never yet beheld that special face
   Which I could fancy more than any other.

KATHERINA
   Minion, thou liest. Is't not Hortensio?

BIANCA
   If you affect him, sister, here I swear
15   I'll plead for you myself, but you shall have him.

KATHERINA
   O then, belike, you fancy riches more.
   You will have Gremio to keep you fair.

BIANCA
   Is it for him you do envy me so?
   Nay then you jest, and now I well perceive
20   You have but jested with me all this while.
   I prithee, sister Kate, untie my hands.

KATHERINA
   If that be jest, then all the rest was so.
      [*Strikes her.*]
      Enter BAPTISTA.

BAPTISTA
   Why, how now, dame! whence grows this insolence?
   Bianca, stand aside. Poor girl! she weeps.
25   Go ply thy needle; meddle not with her.
   For shame, thou hilding of a devilish spirit,
   Why dost thou wrong her that did ne'er wrong thee?
   When did she cross thee with a bitter word?

KATHERINA
   Her silence flouts me, and I'll be reveng'd.
      [*Flies after Bianca.*]

KATHERINE
    I demand that you tell me which one of all your suitors
    you love best—and don't lie to me!

BIANCA
10   Believe me, sister, of all the men I've seen,
    I've never yet seen that special face
    which attracted me more than any other.

KATHERINE
    You spoiled brat, you're lying! It's Hortensio, isn't it?

BIANCA
    If you like him, sister, I swear here and now
15   that I'll try to win him for your husband.

KATHERINE
    O, then perhaps you're more partial to wealth:
    you'll marry Gremio to keep you pretty.

BIANCA
    Is it because of him that you hate me so much?
    No, you're joking. Now I see that
20   you've just been joking all this time.
    Please, sister Kate, untie my hands.

KATHERINE
    If this is a joke, then so was everything else.
        (Hits Bianca.)
        Enter BAPTISTA.

BAPTISTA
    What's this, woman? What's the cause of this insolence?
    Bianca, stand aside. Poor girl, she's crying! *(He unties her hands.)*
25   Go and do your sewing. Stay out of Katherine's way.
    (To Katherine) Shame on you, you wretch, you devil!
    Why do you hurt her when she's never hurt you?
    When did she ever anger you with a bitter word?

KATHERINE
    Her silence insults me, and I'll have my revenge!
        (Runs after Bianca.)

BAPTISTA

30   What, in my sight. Bianca, get thee in.
            [*Exit Bianca.*]

KATHERINA

What, will you not suffer me? Nay, now I see
She is your treasure, she must have a husband;
I must dance bare-foot on her wedding-day
And for your love to her lead apes in hell.

35   Talk not to me; I will go sit and weep
Till I can find occasion of revenge.
            [*Exit.*]

BAPTISTA

Was ever gentleman thus griev'd as I?
But who comes here?
            Enter GREMIO, LUCENTIO *in the habit of a mean*
            man; PETRUCHIO *with* HORTENSIO *as a*
            musician; and TRANIO, *with his boy,*
            BIONDELLO, *bearing a lute and books.*

GREMIO

Good morrow, neighbour Baptista.

BAPTISTA

40   Good morrow, neighbour Gremio. God save you, gentlemen!

PETRUCHIO

And you, good sir! Pray, have you not a daughter
Call'd Katherina, fair and virtuous?

BAPTISTA

I have a daughter, sir, call'd Katherina.

GREMIO

You are too blunt; go to it orderly.

PETRUCHIO

45   You wrong me, Signior Gremio; give me leave.
I am a gentleman of Verona, sir,
That, hearing of her beauty and her wit,
Her affability and bashful modesty,
Her wondrous qualities and mild behaviour,

---

33 *dance bare-foot* older unmarried sisters were expected to do this at the weddings of their younger sisters.   34 *lead apes in hell* proverbial fate of old maids.

BAPTISTA

30   What—before my very eyes? Bianca, hurry to your room.
          Exit BIANCA.

KATHERINE

      So, you try to stop me? Well, now I see
      that she's your treasure. She must have a husband,
      while I dance barefoot on her wedding day,
      and on account of your love for her, I must lead apes in hell.

35   Don't speak to me! I'll go sit and cry
      until I can find an opportunity for revenge.
          She exits.

BAPTISTA

      Was there ever a man so faced with troubles as I am?
      But who is this approaching?
          *Enter GREMIO; LUCENTIO, disguised as Cambio, in the
          clothes of a lowerclass man; PETRUCHIO; HORTENSIO,
          disguised as Licio, a musician; TRANIO, disguised as
          Lucentio; and the servant BIONDELLO, carrying a lute and
          books.*

GREMIO

      Good morning, neighbor Baptista.

BAPTISTA

40   Good morning, neighbor Gremio. Bless you, gentlemen!

PETRUCHIO

      And you, too, sir. Don't you have a daughter
      named Katherine, lovely and virtuous?

BAPTISTA

      I have a daughter, sir, named Katherine.

GREMIO

      You're being too blunt—use a little more tact.

PETRUCHIO

45   You're wrong, Signior Gremio; let me continue.
          (To Baptista.)
      I am a gentleman from Verona, sir,
      who, hearing of Katherine's beauty and wit,
      her pleasant temper and shy modesty,
      her wonderful qualities and mild manners,

50   Am bold to show myself a forward guest
      Within your house, to make mine eye the witness
      Of that report which I so oft have heard.
      And, for an entrance to my entertainment,
      I do present you with a man of mine,
                    [*Presenting Hortensio.*]
55   Cunning in music and the mathematics,
      To instruct her fully in those sciences,
      Whereof I know she is not ignorant.
      Accept of him, or else you do me wrong:
      His name is Licio, born in Mantua.

BAPTISTA
60   You're welcome, sir; and he, for your good sake.
      But for my daughter Katherine, this I know,
      She is not for your turn, the more my grief.

PETRUCHIO
      I see you do not mean to part with her,
      Or else you like not of my company.

BAPTISTA
65   Mistake me not; I speak but as I find.
      Whence are you, sir? What may I call your name?

PETRUCHIO
      Petruchio is my name; Antonio's son,
      A man well known throughout all Italy.

BAPTISTA
      I know him well; you are welcome for his sake.

GREMIO
70   Saving your tale, Petruchio, I pray,
      Let us, that are poor petitioners, speak too.
      Baccare! you are marvellous forward.

PETRUCHIO
      O, pardon me, Signior Gremio; I would fain be doing.

GREMIO
      I doubt it not, sir; but you will curse your wooing. Neighbour,
75   this is a gift very grateful, I am sure of it. To express the like

50 decided to be so bold as to present myself as an eager guest
at your house, to witness for myself
that which I've so often heard reported.
And to pay my admission fee,
I present you with a servant of mine
  HORTENSIO *steps forward.*
55 who is knowledgeable in music and mathematics.
He'll instruct her well in those sciences
of which I know she's not ignorant.
Accept him or you'll hurt my feelings.
His name is Licio, from Mantua.

BAPTISTA
60 You are welcome, sir, and your servant, too, for your sake.
But as for my daughter, Katherine, I know this—
she won't suit you, much to my regret.

PETRUCHIO
I see you don't want the woman to leave home,
or else you don't like me.

BAPTISTA
65 Don't misunderstand me, sir. I'm telling you the truth.
Where are you from, sir? What is your name?

PETRUCHIO
My name is Petruchio, son of Antonio,
a man well known throughout Italy.

BAPTISTA
I'm very familiar with his name; you're welcome for his sake.

GREMIO
70 With all due respect to your story, Petruchio, please
let us poor petitioners speak, too.
Back off! You're amazingly eager.

PETRUCHIO
Pardon me, Signior Gremio. I just want to get moving.

GREMIO
I don't doubt it, sir, but you'll regret your courting. Neighbor,
Petruchio's gift is very nice, I'm sure. And to express my own

kindness, myself, that have been more kindly beholding to you than any, freely give unto you this young scholar [*presenting Lucentio*], that hath been long studying at Rheims; as cunning in Greek, Latin, and other languages, as the other in music and
80   mathematics. His name is Cambio; pray, accept his service.

BAPTISTA

A thousand thanks, Signior Gremio. Welcome, good Cambio [*To Tranio.*] But, gentle sir, methinks you walk like a stranger. May I be so bold to know the cause of your coming?

TRANIO

Pardon me, sir, the boldness is mine own,
85   That, being a stranger in this city here,
Do make myself a suitor to your daughter,
Unto Bianca, fair and virtuous.
Nor is your firm resolve unknown to me,
In the preferment of the eldest sister.
90   This liberty is all that I request,
That, upon knowledge of my parentage,
I may have welcome 'mongst the rest that woo,
And free access and favour as the rest;
And, toward the education of your daughters,
95   I here bestow a simple instrument,
And this small packet of Greek and Latin books.
If you accept them, then their worth is great.

BAPTISTA

Lucentio is your name; of whence, I pray?

TRANIO

Of Pisa, sir; son to Vincentio.

BAPTISTA
100   A mighty man of Pisa; by report
I know him well. You are very welcome, sir.
Take you the lute, and you the set of books.
You shall go see your pupils presently.
Holla, within!
                Enter a Servant.
105   Sirrah, lead these gentlemen

---

80 *Cambio* is Italian for exchange.

gratitude, I—who am more gratefully indebted to you
than anyone—freely give you this young scholar (LUCENTIO
steps forward) who has been studying at Rheims for a long time. He's
    knowledgeable
about Greek, Latin, and other languages, as well as about music and
80   mathematics. His name is Cambio. Please accept his service.

BAPTISTA

    A thousand thanks, Signior Gremio. Welcome, good Cambio. *(To
    Tranio)* But, sir, I think you look like a stranger to Padua. May
    I be so bold as to ask the reason you come here?

TRANIO

    Pardon me, sir; I'm the one who should be excused for being bold,
85   since, being a stranger here in this city,
    I'm making myself a suitor to your daughter,
    the lovely and virtuous Bianca.
    I know, too, about your firm decision
    to see the older sister married first.
90   The only liberty I ask is this:
    that once you know who my parents are,
    I may be welcome along with the rest of the suitors
    and be given the same free access and acceptance as the rest.
    And toward the education of your daughters,
95   I give you a simple instrument
    and this small package of Greek and Latin books.
        (BIONDELLO *steps forward with the lute and books.)*
    If you accept them, then they're worth a great deal.

BAPTISTA

    Your name is Lucentio? Where do you come from?

TRANIO

    From Pisa, sir. I'm the son of Vincentio.

BAPTISTA

100   A great man in Pisa; by reputation,
    I feel I almost know him. You are most welcome, sir.
    (To Hortensio) You take the lute, *(To Lucentio)* and you take the set
    of books.
    You'll see your pupils right now.
    Servant!
        Enter a SERVANT.
105   Servant, take these gentlemen

To my daughters; and tell them both,
These are their tutors. Bid them use them well.
　　　[*Exit Servant, with Lucentio and Hortensio,
　　　　　Biondello following.*]
We will go walk a little in the orchard,
And then to dinner. You are passing welcome,
110　And so I pray you all to think yourselves.

PETRUCHIO
Signior Baptista, my business asketh haste,
And every day I cannot come to woo.
You knew my father well, and in him me,
Left solely heir to all his lands and goods,
115　Which I have bettered rather than decreas'd.
Then tell me, if I get your daughter's love,
What dowry shall I have with her to wife?

BAPTISTA
After my death the one half of my lands,
And in possession twenty thousand crowns.

PETRUCHIO
120　And, for that dowry, I'll assure her of
Her widowhood, be it that she survive me,
In all my lands and leases whatsoever.
Let specialties be therefore drawn between us,
That covenants may be kept on either hand.

BAPTISTA
125　Ay, when the special thing is well obtain'd,
That is, her love; for that is all in all.

PETRUCHIO
Why, that is nothing; for I tell you, father,
I am as peremptory as she proud-minded;
And where two raging fires meet together
130　They do consume the thing that feeds their fury.
Though little fire grows great with little wind,
Yet extreme gusts will blow out fire and all;
So I to her, and so she yields to me,
For I am rough and woo not like a babe.

to my daughters and tell both of them
that these gentlemen are their tutors. Tell them to treat the gentlemen well.
> *Exit* SERVANT *with* LUCENTIO, HORTENSIO, *and*
> BIONDELLO *following behind.*
We'll go walk a little in the garden
and then go to dinner. You are most welcome,
110   and I hope you'll all think of yourselves that way.

PETRUCHIO
Signior Baptista, my business demands quick action,
and I can't come to court every day.
You knew my father well and through him, me.
I've been left the sole heir to all his land and possessions
115   which I've added to, rather than decreased.
So, tell me, if I win your daughter's love,
what dowry will I receive with my wife?

BAPTISTA
After my death, you'll receive half of my lands
and when you marry, twenty thousand crowns.

PETRUCHIO
120   And for that dowry, I'll guarantee her
rights to part of my estate—if she outlives me—
in all my lands and leases.
Let special contracts be drawn up between us
so that our vows may be kept by both of us.

BAPTISTA
125   Certainly; that is after another special thing is obtained—
I mean her love, for that means everything.

PETRUCHIO
Why, that's a mere detail. I tell you, sir,
that I'm as quick to have my way as she is stubborn;
and when two raging fires meet,
130   they consume the thing that feeds their rage.
Though a small fire grows large just by a small wind,
large gusts will totally extinguish a fire.
I'll be just like that wind to her, and so she'll give in to me,
for I'm rough and I don't court like a child.

BAPTISTA

135   Well mayst thou woo, and happy be thy speed!
    But be thou arm'd for some unhappy words.

PETRUCHIO

    Ay, to the proof; as mountains are for winds,
    That shake not, though they blow perpetually.
          Re-enter HORTENSIO, *with his head broke.*

BAPTISTA

    How now, my friend! why dost thou look so pale?

HORTENSIO

140   For fear, I promise you, if I look pale.

BAPTISTA

    What, will my daughter prove a good musician?

HORTENSIO

    I think she'll sooner prove a soldier.
    Iron may hold with her, but never lutes.

BAPTISTA

    Why, then thou canst not break her to the lute?

HORTENSIO

145   Why, no; for she hath broke the lute to me.
    I did but tell her she mistook her frets,
    And bow'd her hand to teach her fingering;
    When, with a most impatient devilish spirit,
    "Frets, call you these?" quoth she; "I'll fume with them;"
150   And, with that word, she struck me on the head,
    And through the instrument my pate made way;
    And there I stood amazed for a while,
    As on a pillory, looking through the lute;
    While she did call me rascal fiddler
155   And twangling Jack, with twenty such vile terms,
    As had she studied to misuse me so.

PETRUCHIO

    Now, by the world, it is a lusty wench!
    I love her ten times more than e'er I did.
    O, how I long to have some chat with her!

---

149 *fume* Katherine plays with the cliche "fret and fume."   153 *pillory* a wooden collar used on criminals for punishment.

BAPTISTA

135   Court her well, then, and more luck to you.
But be prepared for some unpleasant words.

PETRUCHIO

I will be shielded against the worst; like mountains are to the winds—
the mountains don't shake, though the winds blow all the time.
Enter HORTENSIO, *with his head injured.*

BAPTISTA

What happened, my friend? Why do you look so pale?

HORTENSIO

140   If I look pale, it's out of fear, I swear.

BAPTISTA

Well, will my daughter turn out to be a good musician?

HORTENSIO

I think she'll sooner turn out to be a soldier.
Iron may withstand her touch, but never lutes.

BAPTISTA

Why, then, can't you break her into playing the lute?

HORTENSIO

145   Why, no—she's broken the lute on my head.
I just told her that she was touching the wrong frets
and bent her hand to teach her the fingering
when, in a very impatient, devilish mood,
she said, "Do you call these frets? I'll fume with them."

150   And with that, she hit me on the head,
and my head pushed clear through the instrument.
There I stood for awhile, stunned,
as if a wooden collar were around my neck, and peered through the lute,
while she called me a rascal, a fiddler,

155   a twanging idiot, and twenty other terrible names
as if she had prepared them beforehand to abuse me.

PETRUCHIO

Well, I declare, that's a lively girl!
I love her ten times more than I did before.
O, how I long to have a chat with her!

BAPTISTA

160   Well, go with me and be not so discomfited.
       Proceed in practice with my younger daughter;
       She's apt to learn and thankful for good turns.
       Signior Petruchio, will you go with us,
       Or shall I send my daughter Kate to you?

PETRUCHIO

165   I pray you do. [*Exeunt all but Petruchio.*] I will
            attend her here,
       And woo her with some spirit when she comes.
       Say that she rail, why then I'll tell her plain
       She sings as sweetly as a nightingale.
       Say that she frown, I'll say she looks as clear
170   As morning roses newly wash'd with dew.
       Say she be mute and will not speak a word,
       Then I'll commend her volubility,
       And say she uttereth piercing eloquence.
       If she do bid me pack, I'll give her thanks,
175   As though she bid me stay by her a week.
       If she deny to wed, I'll crave the day
       When I shall ask the banns and when be married.
       But here she comes; and now, Petruchio, speak.
            Enter KATHERINA.
       Good morrow, Kate; for that's your name, I hear.

KATHERINA

180   Well have you heard, but something hard of hearing.
       They call me Katherina that do talk of me.

PETRUCHIO

       You lie, in faith; for you are call'd plain Kate,
       And bonny Kate, and sometimes Kate the curst;
       But Kate, the prettiest Kate in Christendom,
185   Kate of Kate Hall, my super-dainty Kate,
       For dainties are all Kates, and therefore, Kate,
       Take this of me, Kate of my consolation;
       Hearing thy mildness praised in every town,

---

177 *banns* are an announcement of a forthcoming marriage made three times in a church.   180 *heard* was spoken to sound like "hard" in Elizabethan days.   185 *Kate* a play on the word "cates" which are delicate tidbits.

BAPTISTA *(to Hortensio)*
160   Well, come with me and don't be so downcast.
Continue to teach my younger daughter—
she's willing to learn and grateful for any kindness.
Signior Petruchio, do you want to go with us,
or shall I send my daughter Kate to you?

PETRUCHIO
165   Please do that. *(Everyone except* PETRUCHIO *exits.)*
       I'll await her here
and court her with some spirit when she comes.
Suppose she scolds—why then I'll tell her flatly
that she sings as sweetly as a nightingale.
Suppose she frowns—I'll say that she looks as cheerful
170   as morning roses just washed with dew.
Suppose she's silent and refuses to speak a word—
then I'll praise her talkativeness
and say she speaks with keen eloquence.
If she tells me to leave, I'll thank her
175   as if she told me to stay by her side for a week.
If she refuses to marry me, I'll ask her what day
the banns should be spoken and when we should set the wedding.
But here she comes—now, Petruchio, speak.
       Enter KATHERINE.
Good morning, Kate—for that's your name, I hear.

KATHERINE
180   You've heard well, but you're a little hard of hearing:
Those who talk about me call me Katherine.

PETRUCHIO
You're lying, you know, for you're called plain Kate,
and fine Kate, and sometimes Kate the shrew.
But the prettiest Kate in the Christian world,
185   Kate of Kate-Hall, my superdainty Kate—
for dainties are all cates. So, Kate,
hear me speak, my consoler, Kate:
hearing your mildness praised in every town,

190

Thy virtues spoke of, and thy beauty sounded,
Yet not so deeply as to thee belongs,
Myself am mov'd to woo thee for my wife.

KATHERINA

Mov'd! in good time. Let him that mov'd you hither
Remove you hence. I knew you at the first
You were a moveable.

PETRUCHIO

195

Why, what's a moveable?

KATHERINA

A join'd-stool.

PETRUCHIO

Thou hast hit it; come, sit on me.

KATHERINA

Asses are made to bear, and so are you.

PETRUCHIO

Women are made to bear, and so are you.

KATHERINA

200

No such jade as you, if me you mean.

PETRUCHIO

Alas! good Kate, I will not burden thee;
For, knowing thee to be but young and light—

KATHERINA

Too light for such a swain as you to catch;
And yet as heavy as my weight should be.

PETRUCHIO

205

Should be! should—buzz!

KATHERINA

Well ta'en, and like a buzzard.

PETRUCHIO

O slow-wing'd turtle! shall a buzzard take thee?

KATHERINA

Ay, for a turtle, as he takes a buzzard.

---

189 *sounded* means both "spoken about" and "measured for depth." (Note the pun on "deeply" in the next line).   194 *moveable* is a (moveable) piece of furniture.   196 *join'd-stool* phrase to disparage something.   202 *light* means both "spirited" and "loose in

your virtues spoken of, and your beauty discussed—
190   yet not as highly praised as you deserve—
I'm moved to try to persuade you to be my wife.

KATHERINE
Moved! Well, let the person who moved you here
move you back again. I knew from the beginning
that you were a movable.

PETRUCHIO
195   Why, what's a movable?

KATHERINE
A stool made by a carpenter.

PETRUCHIO
There you have it—come sit on me.

KATHERINE
Asses are made to carry (burdens), and so are you.

PETRUCHIO
Women are made to carry (children), and so are you.

KATHERINE
200   Not an old nag like you, if you're talking about me.

PETRUCHIO
Come, good Kate, I won't burden you
because knowing that you are young and slender—

KATHERINE
Too slender for a rube like you to catch,
and yet as heavy as I should be.

PETRUCHIO
205   Should be! Should—buzz!

KATHERINE
Well spoken—and just like an idiot.

PETRUCHIO
O, you slow-moving turtledove—will a hawk overtake you?

KATHERINE
Yes, he'll mistake me for a turtledove when I'm really a hawk.

---

morals.''   205 *buzz* Petruchio is picking up on Katherine's "be" (bee). A buzz is also a scandal—like Kate's statement that she is a "light" woman.   207 *buzzard* Petruchio means a hawk.

PETRUCHIO
Come, come, you wasp; i'faith, you are too angry.

KATHERINA
210   If I be waspish, best beware my sting.

PETRUCHIO
My remedy is then, to pluck it out.

KATHERINA
Ay, if the fool could find it where it lies.

PETRUCHIO
Who knows not where a wasp does wear his sting?
In his tail.

KATHERINA
215   In his tongue.

PETRUCHIO
Whose tongue?

KATHERINA
Yours, if you talk of tales: and so farewell.

PETRUCHIO
What, with my tongue in your tail?
Nay, come again,
220   Good Kate; I am a gentleman—

KATHERINA
                          That I'll try.
          [*She strikes him.*]

PETRUCHIO
I swear I'll cuff you, if you strike again.

KATHERINA
So may you lose your arms.
If you strike me, you are no gentleman;
225   And if no gentleman, why then no arms.

PETRUCHIO
A herald, Kate? O, put me in thy books!

---

209 *wasp* Petruchio turns the meaning once again to play on the word "buzzer" or buzzing insect. 218 *tongue in your tail* Petruchio turns Katherine's comment into a sexual suggestion. 226 *book* coats of arms were registered and recorded in books. Petruchio is also asking for Katherine's favor ("put in your good books").

PETRUCHIO
　Come, come, you wasp. Really, you're too angry.

KATHERINE
210　If I'm waspish, you'd better beware of my sting.

PETRUCHIO
　My response then would be to remove your sting.

KATHERINE
　Yes, if you could find where it lies, you fool.

PETRUCHIO
　Who doesn't know where a wasp keeps its sting?
　In his tail.

KATHERINE
215　In his tongue.

PETRUCHIO
　Whose tongue?

KATHERINE
　Yours, if you tell tales. So, goodbye.

PETRUCHIO
　What, with my tongue in your tail?
　Really, try again.
220　Good Kate, I'm a gentleman.

KATHERINE
　I'll see if that's so.
　　　(She hits him.)

PETRUCHIO
　I swear, I'll hit you if you hit me again.

KATHERINE
　Go ahead, if you want to lose your arms.
　If you hit me, then you're no gentleman,
225　and if you're no gentleman, why then you don't have a coat of arms.

PETRUCHIO
　So you're a scholar of heraldy, Kate? O, put me in your heralds' books.

KATHERINA
What is your crest? A coxcomb?

PETRUCHIO
A combless cock, so Kate will be my hen.

KATHERINA
No cock of mine; you crow too like a craven.

PETRUCHIO
230   Nay, come, Kate, come; you must not look so sour.

KATHERINA
It is my fashion, when I see a crab.

PETRUCHIO
Why, here's no crab; and therefore look not sour.

KATHERINA
There is, there is.

PETRUCHIO
Then show it me.

KATHERINA
235   Had I a glass, I would.

PETRUCHIO
What, you mean my face?

KATHERINA
Well aim'd of such a young one.

PETRUCHIO
Now, by Saint George, I am too young for you.

KATHERINA
Yet you are wither'd.

PETRUCHIO
240   'Tis with cares.

KATHERINA
I care not.

PETRUCHIO
Nay, hear you, Kate. In sooth you scape not so.

---

227 *crest* heraldic symbol.   227 *coxcomb* a fool's cap.

KATHERINE
What's your crest? A coxcomb?

PETRUCHIO
I'll be a tame cock if you'll be my hen, Kate.

KATHERINE
You won't be any cock of mine. You crow too much like a timid rooster.

PETRUCHIO
230   Now come, Kate, come. You must not look so sour.

KATHERINE
I'm like that when I see a crab apple.

PETRUCHIO
Why, there's no crab apple here, so don't look sour.

KATHERINE
Yes there is.

PETRUCHIO
Then show it to me.

KATHERINE
235   I would if I had a mirror.

PETRUCHIO
What? Do you mean my face?

KATHERINE
That's a nice guess from such a youngster.

PETRUCHIO
By Saint George, I'm too young for you.

KATHERINE
Yet you're wrinkled.

PETRUCHIO
240   That's from worry.

KATHERINE
That's not my worry. *(Starts to leave.)*

PETRUCHIO
Not so fast, Kate. You won't get away so easily.

KATHERINA
I chafe you, if I tarry. Let me go.

PETRUCHIO
No, not a whit; I find you passing gentle.
245 'Twas told me you were rough and coy and sullen.
And now I find report a very liar;
For thou art pleasant, gamesome, passing courteous,
But slow in speech, yet sweet as spring-time flowers.
Thou canst not frown, thou canst not look askance,
250 Nor bit the lip, as angry wenches will,
Nor hast thou pleasure to be cross in talk,
But thou with mildness entertain'st thy wooers,
With gentle conference, soft and affable.
Why does the world report that Kate doth limp?
255 O sland'rous world! Kate like the hazel-twig
Is straight and slender, and as brown in hue
As hazel nuts and sweeter than the kernels.
O, let me see thee walk. Thou dost not halt.

KATHERINA
Go, fool, and whom thou keep'st command.

PETRUCHIO
260 Did ever Dian so become a grove
As Kate this chamber with her princely gait?
O, be thou Dian, and let her be Kate;
And then let Kate be chaste and Dian sportful!

KATHERINA
Where did you study all this goodly speech?

PETRUCHIO
265 It is extempore, from my mother-wit.

KATHERINA
A witty mother! witless else her son.

PETRUCHIO
Am I not wise?

KATHERINA
Yes; keep you warm.

---

260 *Dian* or Diana, the Roman goddess of hunting and virginity.   268 *Yes . . . warm* Kate is alluding to a proverb that says even fools have enough intelligence to keep themselves warm.

KATHERINE
I'll harrass you if I stay. Let me go.

PETRUCHIO
No, not a bit. I find you very gentle.
245   I heard that you were rough, aloof, and sullen,
and now I see that these reports are lies.
You are pleasant, sporting, very courteous,
perhaps slow to speak, yet sweet as springtime flowers.
You can't even frown, you can't look scornfully
250   or bite your lip as angry women do.
And you don't take pleasure in rough talk.
You receive your suitors with mildness
and gentle conversation, soft and friendly.
Why does everyone say that Kate limps?
255   O slanderous world! Kate is like the hazel twig,
straight and slender, and as brown in color
as are hazelnuts, and sweeter than the kernels.
O, let me see you walk—why, you don't limp!

KATHERINE
Go, fool, and save those commands for your servants.

PETRUCHIO
260   Did Diana ever set off a grove
as Kate does this chamber with her beautiful walk?
O, you be Diana and let Diana be Kate,
and then let Kate be chaste and Diana be sporting.

KATHERINE
Where did you learn all this fine talk?

PETRUCHIO
265   It's all extemporaneous, from my mother wit.

KATHERINE
She kept her wit, and left none to her son.

PETRUCHIO
I'm not wise?

KATHERINE
Yes, wise enough to keep yourself warm.

PETRUCHIO
Marry, so I mean, sweet Katherina, in thy bed;
270   And therefore, setting all this chat aside,
Thus in plain terms: your father hath consented
That you shall be my wife; your dowry 'greed on;
And, will you, nill you, I will marry you.
Now, Kate, I am a husband for your turn;
275   For, by this light whereby I see thy beauty,
Thy beauty, that doth make me like thee well,
Thou must be married to no man but me;
        Re-enter BAPTISTA, GREMIO, *and* TRANIO.
For I am he am born to tame you Kate,
And bring you from a wild Kate to a Kate
280   Conformable as other household Kates.
Here comes your father. Never make denial;
I must and will have Katherina to my wife.

BAPTISTA
Now, Signior Petruchio, how speed you with my daughter?

PETRUCHIO
How but well, sir? How but well?
285   It were impossible I should speed amiss.

BAPTISTA
Why, how now, daughter Katherina! In your dumps?

KATHERINA
Call you me daughter? Now I promise you
You have show'd a tender fatherly regard,
To wish me wed to one half lunatic;
290   A mad-cap ruffian and a swearing Jack,
That thinks with oaths to face the matter out.

PETRUCHIO
Father, 'tis thus: yourself and all the world,
That talk'd of her, have talk'd amiss of her.
If she be curst, it is for policy,
295   For she's not froward, but modest as the dove;
She is not hot, but temperate as the morn;
For patience she will prove a second Grissel,

---

279 *wild Kate* a play on the word "wildcat."   297 *Grissel* the patient wife in Boccaccio's
Decameron and in Chaucer's "Clerk's Tale."

PETRUCHIO
    Really, that's just what I mean to do, sweet Katherine—in your bed.
270   So, putting all this chatting aside,
    I'll tell you this in plain language: your father has agreed
    that you will be my wife, your dowry is settled,
    and whether you want to or not, I'm going to marry you.
    Now, Kate, I'm just the husband to suit you
275   because, by this light that reveals your beauty—
    beauty that makes me like you very much—
    you must be married to no man except me.
        Enter BAPTISTA, GREMIO, *and* TRANIO.
    Because I'm the man born to tame you, Kate,
    and change you from a wild Kate to a Kate
280   as agreeable as any other housewife Kate.
    Here comes your father. Don't try to fight it—
    I must and will have you to be my wife.

BAPTISTA
    Now, Signior Petruchio, how are you getting on with my daughter?

PETRUCHIO
    How else but well, sir? How else but well?
285   It would be impossible that I should not get along well with her.

BAPTISTA
    What's wrong, daughter Katherine? Are you sulking?

KATHERINE
    You call me your daughter? Well, I swear,
    you have shown me tender, fatherly respect
    to wish me to marry a man who's half a lunatic,
290   a crazy rascal, and a swearing scoundrel
    who thinks he can bluff his way through anything with oaths.

PETRUCHIO
    Sir, it's like this: you and everyone else
    that have spoken of her have mistaken what she's like.
    If she is shrewish, that's just a front
295   because she's not willful but modest as the dove.
    She is not hot-tempered but as cool as the morning.
    As for patience, she will turn out to be another Grissel

And Roman Lucrece for her chastity;
And to conclude, we have 'greed so well together
300   That upon Sunday is the wedding-day.

KATHERINA
I'll see thee hang'd on Sunday first.

GREMIO
Hark, Petruchio; she says she'll see thee hang'd first.

TRANIO
Is this your speeding? Nay, then, good night our part!

PETRUCHIO
Be patient, gentlemen; I choose her for myself.
305   If she and I be pleas'd, what's that to you?
'Tis bargain'd 'twixt us twain, being alone,
That she shall still be curst in company.
I tell you, 'tis incredible to believe
How much she loves me. O, the kindest Kate!
310   She hung about my neck; and kiss on kiss
She vied so fast, protesting oath on oath,
That in a twink she won me to her love.
O, you are novices! 'Tis a world to see,
How tame, when men and women are alone,
315   A meacock wretch can make the curstest shrew.
Give me thy hand, Kate. I will unto Venice,
To buy apparel 'gainst the wedding-day.
Provide the feast, father, and bid the guests;
I will be sure my Katherina shall be fine.

BAPTISTA
320   I know not what to say; but give me your hands.
God send you joy, Petruchio! 'Tis a match.

GREMIO and TRANIO
Amen, say we. We will be witnesses.

PETRUCHIO
Father, and wife, and gentlemen, adieu.
I will to Venice; Sunday comes apace.
325   We will have rings and things and fine array;

---

298 *Lucrece* A Roman woman who killed herself after she was raped. Shakespeare wrote a poem, *The Rape of Lucrece,* about her.

and like the Roman Lucrece for her chastity.
So, to conclude, we're in such agreement with one another
300   that we've set the wedding for next Sunday.

KATHERINE
I'll see you hanged on Sunday first.

GREMIO
Listen, Petruchio, she said she'd see you hanged first.

TRANIO
Is this the headway you've made? Well, then, farewell to our suits!

PETRUCHIO
Be patient, gentlemen. I'm choosing her for myself.
305   If she and I are satisfied, what difference does that make to you?
We settled between us when we were alone
that she should always be shrewish when other people are around.
I tell you, it's hard to believe
how much she loves me. O, kindest Kate!
310   She put her arms around my neck and kissed
me faster and faster, swearing she loved me again and again,
so that in a twinkling, she'd made me fall in love with her.
O, you are novices! It's a wonder to see
when men and women are alone how tame
315   a timid wretch can make the shrillest shrew.
Give me your hand, Kate. I'll go to Venice
to buy clothes for our wedding.
You set up the feast, father-in-law, and invite the guests.
I want to be sure my Katherine will look fine.

BAPTISTA
320   I don't know what to say. Well, give me your hands.
God bring you joy, Petruchio, you and Katherine will be married.

GREMIO and TRANIO *(together)*
We say amen to that; we'll be witnesses.

PETRUCHIO
Father and wife and gentlemen: goodbye.
I'm off for Venice. Sunday isn't far off.
325   We must have rings and things and fine clothing.

And kiss me, Kate, "we will be married o' Sunday."
[*Exeunt Petruchio and Katherina severally.*]

GREMIO
Was ever match clapp'd up so suddenly?

BAPTISTA
Faith, gentlemen, now I play a merchant's part,
And venture madly on a desperate mart.

TRANIO
330   'Twas a commodity lay fretting by you.
'Twill bring you gain, or perish on the seas.

BAPTISTA
The gain I seek is, quiet in the match.

GREMIO
No doubt but he hath got a quiet catch.
But now, Baptista, to your younger daughter.
335   Now is the day we long have looked for.
I am your neighbour, and was suitor first.

TRANIO
And I am one that love Bianca more
Than words can witness, or your thoughts can guess.

GREMIO
Youngling, thou canst not love so dear as I.

TRANIO
340   Greybeard, thy love doth freeze.

GREMIO
                But thine doth fry.
Skipper, stand back! 'Tis age that nourisheth.

TRANIO
But youth in ladies' eyes that flourisheth.

BAPTISTA
Content you, gentlemen; I will compound this strife.
345   'Tis deeds must win the prize; and he of both
That can assure my daughter greatest dower
Shall have my Bianca's love.
Say, Signior Gremio, what can you assure her?

---

330 *fretting* means both "bothering" and "rotting away."

Kiss me, Kate; we'll be married on Sunday.
Exit PETRUCHIO *and* KATHERINE.

GREMIO

Was there ever a match made so quickly?

BAPTISTA

In truth, gentlemen, now I play the part of a merchant
and gamble like a madman on a risky deal.

TRANIO

330   You're dealing in a commodity that was rotting away in the warehouse.
It will bring you a profit or else be lost at sea.

BAPTISTA

The profit I'm looking for in the marriage is quiet.

GREMIO

There's no doubt but that he has caught a quiet catch.
But now, Baptista, about your younger daughter:
335   this is the day we've long been waiting for.
I'm your neighbor and I was the first suitor.

TRANIO

And I'm the one that loves Bianca, more
than words can express or thoughts can guess.

GREMIO

Youngster, you can't love her as much as I do.

TRANIO

340   Old man, your love is cold.

GREMIO

But yours is too hot.
Stand back, whippersnapper! It's age that brings prosperity.

TRANIO

But it's youth that's most highly valued by ladies.

BAPTISTA

Stop fighting, gentlemen; I'll settle this argument.
345   It's deeds that will win the prize, and whichever one of you
can guarantee my daughter the largest wedding gift
will have Bianca's love.
So, tell me, Signior Gremio, what can you promise her?

GREMIO
First, as you know, my house within the city
350   Is richly furnished with plate and gold,
Basins and ewers to lave her dainty hands;
My hangings all of Tyrian tapestry;
In ivory coffers I have stuff'd my crowns,
In cypress chests my arras counterpoints,
355   Costly apparel, tents, and canopies,
Fine linen, Turkey cushions boss'd with pearl,
Valance of Venice gold in needle-work,
Pewter and brass and all things that belongs
To house or housekeeping. Then, at my farm
360   I have a hundred milch-kine to the pail,
Six score fat oxen standing in my stalls,
And all things answerable to this portion.
Myself am struck in years, I must confess;
And if I die to-morrow, this is hers,
365   If whilst I live she will be only mine.

TRANIO
That "only" came well in. Sir, list to me.
I am my father's heir and only son.
If I may have your daughter to my wife,
I'll leave her houses three or four as good,
370   Within rich Pisa walls, as any one
Old Signior Gremio has in Padua;
Besides two thousand ducats by the year
Of fruitful land, all which shall be her jointure.
What, have I pinch'd you, Signior Gremio?

GREMIO
375   [*Aside*.] Two thousand ducats by the year of land!
(My land amounts not to so much in all,)
That she shall have; besides an argosy
That now is lying in Marseilles' road.
What, have I chok'd you with an argosy?

TRANIO
380   Gremio, 'tis known my father hath no less

---

372 *ducats* gold coins.

GREMIO

First, as you know, my house in the city
350   is filled with silverware and gold.
I have basins and pitchers to wash her dainty hands.
My hangings are all purple tapestries;
I've stuffed my money in ivory coffers.
In my cypress chests, I have my French tapestries,
355   expensive clothing, bed spreads and canopies.
I have delicate linens, Turkish cushions embroidered with pearl,
bed drapes from Venice done in gold stitchery,
pewter and brass, and everything that
a house or housekeeper should have. Then, at my farm,
360   I have a hundred cows who give milk that I sell,
one hundred twenty fat oxen standing in their stalls,
and everything else fits this scale of operations I just described.
I must confess that I'm old.
So if I die tomorrow, all of this is hers.
365   And while I live, she will be my only concern and heir.

TRANIO

That "only" is well to the point. Sir, listen to me:
I am my father's heir and his only son.
If your daughter marries me,
I'll leave her three or four houses
370   in rich Pisa as good as any that
old Signior Gremio has in Padua.
Besides that, I'll give her two thousand ducats every year
from fertile land—all of that will be her settlement.
Well, are you feeling the heat, Signior Gremio?

GREMIO *(to himself)*
375   Two thousand ducats a year from your land!
The price of my land doesn't even total that much!
     (To Tranio)
Well, she'll have that, besides a merchant ship
that's now docked at Marseilles' harbor.
Well, have I choked you with the ship?

TRANIO
380   Gremio, it's well known that my father has no less

Than three great argosies, besides two galliases
And twelve tight galleys. These I will assure her,
And twice as much, whate'er thou off'rest next.

GREMIO

Nay, I have off'red all, I have no more;
385 And she can have no more than all I have.
If you like me, she shall have me and mine.

TRANIO

Why, then the maid is mine from all the world,
By your firm promise; Gremio is out-vied.

BAPTISTA

I must confess your offer is the best;
390 And, let your father make her the assurance,
She is your own; else, you must pardon me,
If you should die before him, where's her dower?

TRANIO.

That's but a cavil. He is old, I young.

GREMIO

And may not young men die, as well as old?

BAPTISTA

395 Well, gentlemen,
I am thus resolv'd: on Sunday next you know
My daughter Katherine is to be married.
Now, on the Sunday following, shall Bianca
Be bride to you, if you make this assurance;
400 If not, to Signior Gremio.
And so, I take my leave, and thank you both.
                    [*Exit.*]

GREMIO

Adieu, good neighbour. Now I fear thee not.
Sirrah young gamester; your father were a fool
To give thee all, and in his waning age
405 Set foot under thy table. Tut, a toy!
An old Italian fox is not so kind, my boy.
                    [*Exit.*]

than three big ships, besides two large galleys
and twelve well-built galleys. I'll guarantee her those
and twice as much as whatever you offer next.

GREMIO

385 No, I've offered everything—I don't have anything more,
and she can't have more than everything I have.
If you prefer me, she will have me and all I own.

TRANIO

Then the girl is mine and no one else's
according to your firm promise. I've outbid Gremio.

BAPTISTA

I must confess, your offer is the best.
390 If you have your father guarantee her the settlement,
then she's yours. Otherwise, you'll excuse me for saying so,
where is her settlement if you should die before your father?

TRANIO

That's just a detail. He is old; I'm young.

GREMIO

And can't young men die just as quickly as old men?

BAPTISTA

395 Well, gentlemen,
I've decided this. You know that on next Sunday,
my daughter Katherine is to be married.
Now, on the following Sunday, Bianca will
marry you if you make that guarantee.
400 If not, she'll marry Signior Gremio.
And with that, I'll leave and thank both of you.
        Exit.

GREMIO

Goodbye, good neighbor. Now I'm not afraid of you.
Foolish young gambler, your father would have to be a fool
to give you everything in his old age
405 and become your dependent. Nonsense, what rubbish!
An old Italian fox is not so generous, my boy.
        Exit.

TRANIO
    A vengeance on your crafty withered hide!
    Yet I have fac'd it with a card of ten.
    'Tis in my head to do my master good.
410   I see no reason but suppos'd Lucentio
    Must get a father, call'd "suppos'd Vincentio";
    And that's a wonder. Fathers commonly
    Do get their children; but in this case of wooing,
    A child shall get a sire, if I fail not of my cunning.
        [*Exit.*]

Act III, Scene i: [*Padua. Baptista's house.*] *Enter* LUCENTIO,
HORTENSIO, *and* BIANCA.

LUCENTIO
    Fiddler, forbear; you grow too forward, sir.
    Have you so soon forgot the entertainment
    Her sister Katherine welcom'd you withal?

HORTENSIO
    But, wrangling pedant, this is
5   The patroness of heavenly harmony.
    Then give me leave to have prerogative;
    And when in music we have spent an hour,
    Your lecture shall have leisure for as much.

LUCENTIO
    Preposterous ass, that never read so far
10   To know the cause why music was ordain'd!
    Was it not to refresh the mind of man
    After his studies or his usual pain?
    Then give me leave to read philosophy,
    And while I pause, serve in your harmony.

HORTENSIO
15   Sirrah, I will not bear thee braves of thine.

BIANCA
    Why, gentlemen, you do me double wrong
    To strive for that which resteth in my choice.

---

411 *get* Tranio makes a pun on the double meaning of get: "to find," and "to father"
or "beget."   9 *preposterous* putting secondary things first. The Greek philosopher Aristotle
said study should come before music.

TRANIO

    Damn your crafty, wrinkled hide!

    Still, I've bluffed with a low card.

    I think I know how to help my master.

410   I see no other way out except to get the sham Lucentio

    a father who will be called the sham Vincentio.

    And that's amazing—fathers generally

    sire their own children. But in this case of courting,

    a child will produce a father, if my cunning doesn't fail me.

        Exit.

Act III, Scene i: Padua. Baptista's house. Enter LUCENTIO,
HORTENSIO, *and* BIANCA.

LUCENTIO

    Fiddler, ease off; you're getting too eager, sir.

    Have you so quickly forgotten the reception

    with which her sister Katherine greeted you?

HORTENSIO

    But, you quarrelsome pedant, this is

5   the patroness of heavenly harmony.

    So let me go first,

    and after we've spent an hour with music,

    you can give just as much time for your lesson.

LUCENTIO

    You turned-around fool, you're not even well-read enough

10   to know the reason why music was created!

    Wasn't the reason to refresh man's mind

    after studying or usual work?

    Therefore, let me lecture in philosophy,

    and whenever I stop, present your tunes.

HORTENSIO

15   Servant, I won't stand for these impudent speeches of yours.

BIANCA

    Why, gentlemen, you both do me wrong

    by trying to decide that which is up to me.

I am no breeching scholar in the schools.
I'll not be tied to hours nor 'pointed times,
20   But learn my lessons as I please myself.
And, to cut off all strife, here sit we down;
Take you your instrument, play you the whiles;
His lecture will be done ere you have tun'd.

HORTENSIO
You'll leave his lecture when I am in tune?

LUCENTIO
25   That will be never; tune your instrument.

BIANCA
Where left we last?

LUCENTIO
Here, madam:
    "Hic ibat Simois; hic est Sigeia tellus;
    Hic steterat Priami regia celsa senis."

BIANCA
30   Construe them.

LUCENTIO
"Hic ibat," as I told you before, *"Simois,"* I am Lucentio, *"hic est,"* son unto Vincentio of Pisa, *"Sigeia tellus,"* disguised thus to get your love; *"Hic steterat,"* and that Lucentio that comes a-wooing, *"Priami,"* is my man Tranio, *"regia,"* bearing my
35   port, *"celsa senis,"* that we might beguile the old pantaloon.

HORTENSIO
Madam, my instrument's in tune.

BIANCA
Let's hear. O fie! the treble jars.

LUCENTIO
Spit in the hole, man, and tune again.

BIANCA
Now let me see if I can construe it:
40   *"Hic ibat Simois,"* I know you not, *"hic est Sigeia tellus,"* I trust you not; *"Hic steterat Priami,"* take heed he hear us not, *"regia,"* presume not, *"celsa senis,"* despair not.

28-29 *Hic . . . senis* a quote from the Roman poet Ovid's *Heriodes*. Sigeia was the site of many battles in the Trojan War.

I'm no schoolboy ready for the teacher's whip.
I won't be tied to a schedule or appointments;
20   I'll learn my lessons when it suits me.
So, to end the argument, we'll sit down here.
(To Hortensio) You, take your instrument and play in the meanwhile.
His lesson will be finished before you've even tuned up.

HORTENSIO
You'll stop studying his lesson when I have tuned up?

LUCENTIO
25   That will never happen; go tune your instrument.

BIANCA
Where did we stop last time?

LUCENTIO
Here, madam:
    Here flowed the Simois; here is the Sigeian land;
    Here stood ancient Priam's towering palace.

BIANCA
30   Translate that.

LUCENTIO
    Hic ibat means as I told you before. *Simois,* I am Lucentio. *Hic est,* son of Vincentio of Pisa. *Sigeia tellus,* disguised like this to win your love. *Hic steterat,* and the Lucentio who is courting you, *Priami,* is my servant Tranio, *regia,* acting my
35   part, *celsa senis,* that we might trick the old pantaloon.

HORTENSIO
Madam, my instrument is in tune.

BIANCA
Let's hear. O, heavens, the treble note is jarring!

LUCENTIO
Give it another try, man, and tune it again.

BIANCA
Now let me see if I can translate it.
40   *Hic ibat Simois,* I don't know you. *Hic est Sigeia tellus,* I don't trust you. *Hic steterat Priami,* be careful he doesn't overhear us. *Regia,* don't overstep your boundaries. *Celsa senis,* don't despair.

HORTENSIO
Madam, 'tis now in tune.

LUCENTIO
All but the base.

HORTENSIO
45   The base is right; 'tis the base knave that jars.
[*Aside.*] How fiery and forward our pedant is!
Now, for my life, the knave doth court my love:
Pedascule, I'll watch you better yet.

BIANCA
In time I may believe, yet I mistrust.

LUCENTIO
50   Mistrust it not; for, sure, Aeacides
Was Ajax, call'd so from his grandfather.

BIANCA
I must believe my master; else, I promise you,
I should be arguing still upon that doubt.
But let it rest. Now, Licio, to you.
55   Good master, take it not unkindly, pray,
That I have been thus pleasant with you both.

HORTENSIO [*to Lucentio.*]
You may go walk, and give me leave a while.
My lessons make no music in three parts.

LUCENTIO
Are you so formal, sir? Well, I must wait,
60   [*Aside.*] And watch withal; for, but I be deceiv'd,
Our fine musician groweth amorous.

HORTENSIO
Madam, before you touch the instrument,
To learn the order of my fingering,
I must begin with rudiments of art;
65   To teach you gamut in a briefer sort,
More pleasant, pithy, and effectual,
Than hath been taught by any of my trade;
And there it is in writing, fairly drawn.

---

50 *Aeacides* Ajax, a Greek warrior who fought against the Trojans. A reference to Ajax
appears in the line of Ovid's text following the passage Hortensio previously quoted.

HORTENSIO
Madam, it's tuned up now.

LUCENTIO
Everything but the bass notes.

HORTENSIO
45   The low notes are in tune, it's just the low rascal that's jarring.
(To himself) How hot-blooded and eager our pedant is!
I'd swear on my life that the rascal is courting my love.
Little pedant, I'll keep a closer watch on you than before.

BIANCA
In time I may believe you, yet now I have doubts.

LUCENTIO
50   Don't doubt me. Aeacides
was definitely called Ajax—named that for his grandfather.

BIANCA
I must believe my teacher. Otherwise, I swear to you
that I would still argue the question.
But let it go. *(To Hortensio)* Now, Licio, I'll learn from you.
55   Good teacher, please don't be offended, I beg you,
that I've been so light-hearted with both of you.

HORTENSIO *(to Lucentio)*
You can take a walk and leave me alone for a bit.
My lessons don't have music for three voices.

LUCENTIO
You want to be so formal, sir? *(To himself)* Well, I must wait
60   and watch, too, because unless I'm deceived,
our fine musician is falling in love.

HORTENSIO
Madam, before you touch the instrument
to learn where to put your fingers,
I must begin with the basics of the art
65   to teach you a scale of a shorter kind,
more pleasant, succinct, and effective
than has been taught by any of my fellow music teachers.
And there it is in writing, nicely written.

BIANCA
Why, I am past my gamut long ago.

HORTENSIO
70   Yet read the gamut of Hortensio.

BIANCA [*Reads.*]
"*Gamut* I am, the ground of all accord,
   A re, to plead Hortensio's passion.
B mi, Bianca, take him for thy lord,
   C fa ut, that loves with all affection.
75   *D sol re,* one clef, two notes have I.
   E la mi, show pity, or I die."
Call you this gamut? Tut, I like it not:
Old fashions please me best; I am not so nice,
To change true rules for odd inventions.
         Enter a MESSENGER.

MESSENGER
80   Mistress, your father prays you leave your books
And help to dress your sister's chamber up.
You know to-morrow is the wedding-day.

BIANCA
Farewell, sweet masters both; I must be gone.
         [*Exeunt Bianca and Messenger.*]

LUCENTIO
Faith, mistress, then I have no cause to stay.
         [*Exit.*]

HORTENSIO
85   But I have cause to pry into this pedant.
Me thinks he looks as though he were in love;
Yet if thy thoughts, Bianca, be so humble
To cast thy wand'ring eyes on every stale,
Seize thee that list. If once I find thee ranging,
90   Hortensio will be quit with thee by changing.
         [*Exit.*]

BIANCA
Why, I learned the scales a long time ago.

HORTENSIO
70   Still, read Hortensio's scale.

BIANCA *(Reads)*
    Gamut, I am the scale, the beginning of all harmony.
      A re, to urge Hortensio's passion;
    B mi, Bianca, take him as your husband;
      C fa ut, who loves you with all his heart;
75   *D sol re,* I have one clef and two notes,
      E la mi, show me mercy or I'll die.
    Do you call this a scale? Nonsense, I don't like it.
    Old-fashioned things please me the best. I'm not so whimsical
    as to change true rules for strange inventions.
      Enter a MESSENGER.

MESSENGER
80   Mistress, your father asks you to leave your books
    and help decorate your sister's room.
    You know tomorrow is her wedding day.

BIANCA
    Goodbye, both of you sweet teachers. I must go.
      Exit BIANCA *and* MESSENGER.

LUCENTIO
    Well then, mistress, I have no reason to stay.
      Exit.

HORTENSIO
85   But I have reason to investigate this pedant.
    I thought he looked as though he were in love.
    Yet if your affections, Bianca, can stoop so low
    so that you cast your wandering eye on every decoy,
    let whoever wants you have you. If I once find you straying,
90   I'll leave you by changing lovers.
      Exit.

Scene ii: [Padua. Before Baptista's house.] Enter, BAPTISTA,
GREMIO, TRANIO, KATHERINA, BIANCA, LUCENTIO,
and others, attendants.

BAPTISTA [*To Tranio.*]
    Signior Lucentio, this is the 'pointed day,
    That Katherina and Petruchio should be married,
    And yet we hear not of our son-in-law.
    What will be said? What mockery will it be,
5   To want the bridegroom when the priest attends
    To speak the ceremonial rites of marriage!
    What says Lucentio to this shame of ours?

KATHERINA
    No shame but mine. I must, forsooth, be forc'd
    To give my hand oppos'd against my heart
10   Unto a mad-brain rudesby full of spleen,
    Who woo'd in haste and means to wed at leisure.
    I told you, I, he was a frantic fool,
    Hiding his bitter jests in blunt behaviour;
    And, to be noted for a merry man,
15   He'll woo a thousand, 'point the day of marriage,
    Make friends, invite, yes, and proclaim the banns,
    Yet never means to wed where he hath woo'd.
    Now must the world point at poor Katherina,
    And say, "Lo, there is mad Petruchio's wife,
20   If it would please him come and marry her!"

TRANIO
    Patience, good Katherina, and Baptista too.
    Upon my life, Petruchio means but well,
    Whatever fortune stays him from his word.
    Though he be blunt, I know him passing wise;
25   Though he be merry, yet withal he's honest.

KATHERINA
    Would Katherina had never seen him though!
        [*Exit weeping, followed by Bianca and others.*]

Act III, Scene ii: Padua. Before Baptista's house. Enter BAPTISTA, GREMIO, TRANIO, KATHERINE, BIANCA, LUCENTIO, *and other guests, as well as servants.*

BAPTISTA *(to Tranio)*
Signior Lucentio, this is the scheduled day
for Katherine and Petruchio to be married,
and yet I haven't heard from my son-in-law.
What will people say? What a cruel joke it will be
5   if the bridegroom is missing when the priest appears
to say the ceremonial wedding ritual!
What do you say, Lucentio, about this embarrassment?

KATHERINE
No one has been embarrassed except me. Really, I'm to be forced
to marry against my will
10   a crazy, rude fellow, full of crazy impulses,
who courted with such speed, and means to be married in his own
      good time.
I told you that he was a mad fool,
hiding his bitter jokes in crude behavior.
And to be known as a jolly fellow,
15   he'll court a thousand women, set the marriage date,
provide the feast, invite guests, and have the banns read—
yet he never intends to marry the one he's courted.
Now everyone in the world will point at poor Katherine
and say, "Look! There's crazy Petruchio's wife—
20   if he wanted to come and marry her."

TRANIO
Be patient, good Katherine and you, too, Baptista.
I swear on my life that Petruchio has only good intentions,
whatever might be keeping him from keeping his word.
He might be rough, but I know he's sensible.
25   He might be a joker, yet, nevertheless, he's truthful.

KATHERINE
Yet, I wish that I had never seen him!
    Exit weeping, followed by BIANCA *and others.*

BAPTISTA
> Go, girl, I cannot blame thee now to weep;
> For such an injury would vex a very saint,
> Much more a shrew of thy impatient humour.
>> *Enter* BIONDELLO.

BIONDELLO
30
> Master, master! news, and such old news as you
> never heard of!

BAPTISTA
> Is it new and old too? How may that be?

BIONDELLO
> Why, is it not news to hear of Petruchio's coming?

BAPTISTA
> Is he come?

BIONDELLO
> Why, no, sir.

BAPTISTA
35
> What then?

BIONDELLO
> He is coming.

BAPTISTA
> When will he be here?

BIONDELLO
> When he stands where I am and sees you there.

TRANIO
> But say, what to thine old news?

BIONDELLO
40
> Why, Petruchio is coming in a new hat and an old jerkin; a pair
> of old breeches thrice turn'd; a pair of boots that have been
> candle-cases, one buckled, another lac'd; an old rusty sword ta'en
> out of the town-armoury, with a broken hilt, and chapeless; with
> two broken points; his horse hipp'd with an old mothy saddle
45
> and stirrups of no kindred, besides, possess'd with the glanders
> and like to mose in the chine, troubled with the lampass, infected

---

41 *thrice turned* turned inside out three times to hide signs of wear.   44 *points* laces that
tied a man's hose to his breeches.

BAPTISTA
> Go, girl. I can't blame you for crying now,
> for an insult like you've received would irritate even a saint,
> much less a shrew with your impatient temper.
>> *Enter* BIONDELLO.

BIONDELLO
30 > Master, master! News! Old news and news you've
> not yet heard.

BAPTISTA
> News that's both new and old? How can that be?

BIONDELLO
> Why, isn't it news to know that Petruchio is coming?

BAPTISTA
> Has he arrived?

BIONDELLO
> Why, no, sir.

BAPTISTA
35 > What then?

BIONDELLO
> He is coming.

BAPTISTA
> When will he be here?

BIONDELLO
> When he stands where I am and sees you there.

TRANIO
> But then tell us, what's your old news?

BIONDELLO
40 > Why, Petruchio is coming in a new hat and an old coat; a pair
> of old pants turned inside out three times; a pair of boots that have been
> candleholders, one buckled, the other laced; an old rusty sword taken
> out of the town armory with a broken hilt and no metal tip on the end
> of the scabbard, and with
> two broken laces. His horse has a dislocated hip, is wearing a moth-eaten
> saddle
45 > and stirrups that don't match; it also has an inflamed jaw
> and a runny nose. It's bothered by a swollen mouth, infected

with the fashions, full of windgalls, sped with spavins, rayed with
the yellows, past cure of the fives, stark spoil'd with the staggers,
begnawn with the bots, sway'd in the back and shoulder-shotten,
50   nearlegg'd before, and with a half-check'd bit and a head-stall
of sheep's leather which, being restrain'd to keep him from
stumbling, hath been often burst and now repaired with knots;
one girth six times piec'd, and a woman'd crupper of velure, which
hath two letters for her name fairly set down in studs, and here
55   and there piec'd with packthread.

BAPTISTA
Who comes with him?

BIONDELLO
O, sir, his lackey, for all the world caparison'd like the horse;
with a linen stock on one leg and a kersey boot-hose on the other,
gart'red with a red and blue list; an old hat and the humour of
60   forty fancies prick'd in't for a feather: a monster, a very monster
in apparel, and not like a Christian footboy or a gentleman's
lackey.

TRANIO
'Tis some odd humour pricks him to this fashion;
Yet oftentimes he goes but mean-apparell'd.

BAPTISTA
65   I am glad he's come, howsoe'er he comes.

BIONDELLO
Why, sir, he comes not.

BAPTISTA
Didst thou not say he comes?

BIONDELLO
Who? That Petruchio came?

BAPTISTA
Ay, that Petruchio came.

BIONDELLO
70   No, sir; I say his horse comes, with him on his back.

with swollen glands, has tumors on its lower legs, tumors on its upper leg, is filthy

from jaundice, has an incurable case of swelling behind the ears, is completely shot from bad nerves,

is eaten up by worms and swaybacked; has a shoulder out of joint,

50 is knocked-kneed in front; has an improperly hooked bridle, and the bridle over its head

is made of sheep's leather, which has been frequently broken from being pulled to keep the horse from

stumbling, and now its been fixed by knotting the broken parts.

One belly strap has been fixed six times. The strap under the tail is made out of velvet, with

some woman's initials set in studs, and here

55 and there tied with cheap thread.

BAPTISTA
Who is with him?

BIONDELLO
O, sir! His servant is outfitted exactly like the horse.
He has a linen stocking on one leg and a rough boot sock on the other.
His garters are red and blue cloth hems. He's wearing an old hat that has

60 forty weird ornaments pinned on it instead of a feather. He's a monster, a real monster
in his dress—not at all like a Christian uniformed page or a gentleman's servant.

TRANIO
It's some strange mood that leads him to go around in this kind of clothing.
Yet, he often walks around in shabby clothing.

BAPTISTA
65 I'm glad he's coming, no matter what he looks like.

BIONDELLO
Why, sir, he's not coming.

BAPTISTA
Didn't you say he was coming?

BIONDELLO
Who? That Petruchio was coming?

BAPTISTA
Yes, that Petruchio was coming.

BIONDELLO
70 No, sir. I'm telling you his horse is coming, with him on the horse's back.

BAPTISTA
Why, that's all one.

BIONDELLO
Nay, by Saint Jamy,
I hold you a penny,
A horse and a man
75   Is more than one,
And yet not many.
Enter PETRUCHIO *and* GRUMIO.

PETRUCHIO
Come, where be these gallants? Who's at home?

BAPTISTA
You are welcome, sir.

PETRUCHIO
                And yet I come not well.

BAPTISTA
80   And yet you halt not.

TRANIO
                Not so well apparell'd
As I wish you were.

PETRUCHIO
Were it better, I should rush in thus.
But where is Kate? Where is my lovely bride?
85   How does my father? Gentles, methinks you frown;
And wherefore gaze this goodly company,
As if they saw some wondrous monument,
Some comet or unusual prodigy?

BAPTISTA
Why, sir, you know this is your wedding day.
90   First were we sad, fearing you would not come;
Now sadder, that you come so unprovided.
Fie, doff this habit, shame to your estate,
An eye-sore to our solemn festival!

---

79 *come* also means "walk." Baptista makes a joke on this meaning when he remarks that
Petruchio is not limping.

BAPTISTA
Why that's the same thing.

BIONDELLO
No, not by Saint Jamy.
I'll bet you a penny
That a horse and a man
75   Is more than one
And yet not many.
Enter PETRUCHIO *and* GRUMIO.

PETRUCHIO
Come, where are the fancy lords? Who's at home?

BAPTISTA
Welcome, sir.

PETRUCHIO
And yet I don't look well.

BAPTISTA
80   Still, you're not limping.

TRANIO
You're not as well dressed
as I wish you were.

PETRUCHIO
Even if I were better dressed, I would rush in like this.
But where is Kate? Where is my lovely bride?
85   How are you, father-in-law? Gentlemen, I think you're frowning.
And why is this nice group staring
as if they saw some amazing omen,
some comet, or unusual marvel?

BAPTISTA
Why, sir, you know this is your wedding day.
90   First we were sad because we were afraid that you wouldn't come.
Now we're sadder that you've come so poorly dressed.
For shame! Take off those clothes that are a disgrace to your position
and an eyesore to our solemn festival.

TRANIO

95 And tell us, what occasion of import
   Hath all so long detain'd you from your wife,
   And sent you hither so unlike yourself?

PETRUCHIO

   Tedious it were to tell, and harsh to hear.
   Sufficeth, I am come to keep my word,
   Though in some part enforced to digress;
100 Which, at more leisure, I will so excuse
   As you shall well be satisfied withal.
   But where is Kate? I stay too long from her.
   The morning wears, 'tis time we were at church.

TRANIO

   See not your bride in these unreverent robes.
105 Go to my chamber; put on clothes of mine.

PETRUCHIO

   Not I, believe me; thus I'll visit her.

BAPTISTA

   But thus, I trust, you will not marry her.

PETRUCHIO

   Good sooth, even thus; therefore ha' done with words.
   To me she's married, not unto my clothes.
110 Could I repair what she will wear in me,
   As I can change these poor accoutrements,
   'Twere well for Kate and better for myself.
   But what a fool am I to chat with you,
   When I should bid good morrow to my bride
115 And seal the title with a lovely kiss!
     [*Exeunt Petruchio and Grumio.*]

TRANIO

   He hath some meaning in his mad attire.
   We will persuade him, be it possible,
   To put on better ere he go to church.

BAPTISTA

   I'll after him, and see the event of this.
     [*Exeunt Baptista, Gremio, and attendants.*]

TRANIO

And tell us what important reason

95   has detained you so long from joining your wife

and sent you here dressed in a style so unlike yourself?

PETRUCHIO

It would be tedious to tell and boring to listen to.

Let it suffice that I've come to keep my promise,

though I'm forced to abandon part of my plan.

100   When we have more time, I'll explain all this

to your complete satisfaction.

But where is Kate? I've been apart from her for too long.

The morning is passing, and it's time we went to church.

TRANIO

Don't go to your bride in these ridiculous clothes.

105   Go to my room and put on some of my clothes.

PETRUCHIO

No, I won't. I'll see her dressed as I am.

BAPTISTA

But I trust you won't marry her in those clothes.

PETRUCHIO

So help me, just like this. So stop talking.

She's marrying me, not my clothes.

110   If I could repair what she'll wear out in me

as easily as I could change these shabby clothes,

it would be good for Kate and better for me.

But what a fool I am to chat with you

when I should be saying good morning to my bride

115   and seal my right to use that title with a loving kiss!

       Exit with GRUMIO.

TRANIO

He means something by wearing those crazy clothes.

We'll try to persuade him, if it's possible,

to put on something nicer before he goes to church.

BAPTISTA

I'll follow him and see what happens.

       Exit with GREMIO *and attendants.*

TRANIO

120 But to her love concerneth us to add
Her father's liking; which to bring to pass,
As I before imparted to your worship,
I am to get a man,—whate'er he be,
It skills not much, we'll fit him to our turn,—
125 And he shall be Vincentio of Pisa;
And make assurance here in Padua
Of greater sums than I have promised.
So shall you quietly enjoy your hope,
And marry sweet Bianca with consent.

LUCENTIO

130 Were it not that my fellow-schoolmaster
Doth watch Bianca's steps so narrowly,
'Twere good, methinks, to steal our marriage;
Which once perform'd, let all the world say no,
I'll keep mine own, despite of all the world.

TRANIO

135 That by degrees we mean to look into,
And watch our vantage in this business.
We'll over-reach the greybeard, Gremio,
The narrow prying father, Minola,
The quaint musician, amorous Licio,
140 All for my master's sake, Lucentio.
           Re-enter GREMIO.
Signior Gremio, came you from the church?

GREMIO

As willingly as e'er I came from school.

TRANIO

And is the bride and bridegroom coming home?

GREMIO

A bridegroom say you? 'Tis a groom indeed,
145 A grumbling groom, and that the girl shall find.

TRANIO

Curster than she? Why, 'tis impossible.

---

120 *But to her love* Some scholars believe part of the play is missing here, since Tranio switches
subjects so abruptly.

TRANIO

120 But to Bianca's love we should be concerned to add
her father's approval. So to bring that about,
as I told you before, my lord,
I'll find a man—who he is
doesn't really matter since we'll outfit him to serve our purpose—

125 and he'll be Vincentio from Pisa.
And he'll make settlement guarantees here in Padua
of larger sums than I promised to Baptista.
So you quietly fulfill your wish
and marry sweet Bianca with her father's consent.

LUCENTIO

130 If it weren't for the fact that my fellow teacher
closely watches every move Bianca makes,
I'd think it would be best to elope.
Then, once we're married, everyone in the world could try to stop us,
but I'd keep my love in spite of them.

TRANIO

135 We'll explore that more carefully
and guard our advantage in this business.
We'll best that greybeard, Gremio,
the suspicious and watchful father, Minola,
the clever musician, amorous Licio—

140 all for the sake of my master, Lucentio.
     Enter GREMIO.
Signior Gremio, have you just come from the church?

GREMIO

As eagerly as I ever came home from school.

TRANIO

And are the bride and groom coming home?

GREMIO

Did you say groom? He's a stable groom, indeed,
145 a grumbling groom, and the girl will find that out.

TRANIO

He's more of a shrew than she is? Why, that's impossible!

GREMIO
Why, he's a devil, a devil, a very fiend.

TRANIO
Why, she's a devil, a devil, the devil's dam.

GREMIO
Tut, she's a lamb, a dove, a fool to him!
150   I'll tell you, Sir Lucentio: when the priest
Should ask, if Katherina should be his wife,
"Ay, by gogs-wouns," quoth he; and swore so loud,
That, all-amaz'd, the priest let fall the book;
And, as he stoop'd again to take it up,
155   The mad-brain'd bridegroom took him such a cuff
That down fell priest and book, and book and priest.
"Now take them up," quoth he, "if any list."

TRANIO
What said the wench when he rose again?

GREMIO
Trembled and shook; for why, he stamp'd and swore
160   As if the vicar meant to cozen him.
But after many ceremonies done,
He calls for wine. "A health!" quoth he, as if
He'd been aboard, carousing to his mates
After a storm; quaff'd off the muscadel,
165   And threw the sops all in the sexton's face,
Having no other reason
But that his beard grew thin and hungerly,
And seem'd to ask him sops as he was drinking.
This done, he took the bride about the neck
170   And kiss'd her lips with such a clamorous smack
That at the parting all the church did echo.
And I seeing this, came thence for very shame,
And after me, I know, the rout is coming.
Such a mad marriage never was before.
175   Hark, hark! I hear the minstrels play.
                [*Music plays.*]

---

164 *muscadel* or muscatel, a sweet wine usually drunk at the end of a wedding
ceremony.   165 *sops* pieces of cake floating in the wine.   165 *sexton* a church official who
takes care of a church.

GREMIO
Why, he's a devil, a devil, a real demon!

TRANIO
Why, she's a devil, a devil, the devil's mother.

GREMIO
Nonsense, she's a lamb, a dove, a complete innocent compared to him!
150   I'll tell you, Sir Lucentio, when the priest
asked if Katherine would be his wife,
he said, "Ay, by God's wounds," and swore so loudly
that the priest, totally shocked, dropped the book.
And as he bent down to pick it up again,
155   this crazy bridegroom give him such a slap
that down fell the priest and book, and the book and priest.
"Now pick them up," he said, "if anyone wants to."

TRANIO
What did the woman say when he got up again?

GREMIO
She trembled and shook because he stomped and swore
160   as if the priest meant to cheat him out of his wedding.
But after all the ceremonies were completed,
he called for wine. "A toast!" he said, as if
he were on board ship, toasting his shipmates
after a storm. He guzzled off all the wine
165   and threw all the dregs in the sexton's face
for no other reason
than that his beard was thin and whispery
and seemed to beg for the dregs while he was drinking.
After he'd done this, he grabbed the bride around the neck
170   and kissed her lips with such a noisy smack
that when they were finished, the whole church echoed.
After I saw that, I left there out of embarrassment.
I know the crowd is at my heels.
There never before was such a crazy marriage!
175   Listen, listen! I hear the musicians playing.
        (Music plays.)

Re-enter PETRUCHIO, KATHERINA, BIANCA,
BAPTISTA, HORTENSIO, GRUMIO, *and Train*.

PETRUCHIO
 Gentlemen and friends, I thank you for your pains.
 I know you think to dine with me to-day,
 And have prepar'd great store of wedding cheer;
 But so it is, my haste doth call me hence,
180 And therefore here I mean to take my leave.

BAPTISTA
 Is't possible you will away to-night?

PETRUCHIO
 I must away to-day, before night come.
 Make it no wonder; if you knew my business,
 You would entreat me rather go than stay.
185 And, honest company, I thank you all
 That have beheld me give away myself
 To this most patient, sweet, and virtuous wife.
 Dine with my father, drink a health to me,
 For I must hence; and farewell to you all.

TRANIO
190 Let us entreat you stay till after dinner.

PETRUCHIO
 It may not be.

GREMIO
    Let me entreat you.

PETRUCHIO
 It cannot be.

KATHERINA
    Let me entreat you.

PETRUCHIO
195 I am content.

KATHERINA
 Are you content to stay?

Enter PETRUCHIO, KATHERINE, BIANCA, BAPTISTA,
HORTENSIO, GRUMIO, *and* TRANIO, *guests.*

PETRUCHIO
    Gentlemen and friends, I thank you for your efforts.
    I know you had planned to eat with me today
    and had prepared a great banquet for the wedding feast.
    But it so happens that something urgent calls me away,
180   and therefore, I must say goodbye.

BAPTISTA
    Do you really mean you're leaving tonight?

PETRUCHIO
    I must leave today, before night falls.
    Don't be surprised. If you knew my business,
    you would beg me to go rather than to stay.
185   So, my good fellows, I thank everyone
    who saw me give myself
    to this most patient, sweet, and virtuous wife.
    Go eat with my father-in-law, and drink a toast to me
    since I must leave. Goodbye to you all.

TRANIO
190   We beg you to stay until after dinner.

PETRUCHIO
    I can't.

GREMIO
    Let me beg you.

PETRUCHIO
    It's not possible.

KATHERINE
    Let me beg you.

PETRUCHIO
195   I am satisfied.

KATHERINE
    You mean you'll be satisfied to stay?

PETRUCHIO

I am content you shall entreat me stay;
But yet not stay, entreat me how you can.

KATHERINA

Now, if you love me, stay.

PETRUCHIO

200   Grumio, my horse.

GRUMIO

Ay, sir, they be ready; the oats have eaten the horses.

KATHERINA

Nay, then,
Do what thou canst, I will not go to-day;
No, nor to-morrow, not till I please myself.
205 The door is open, sir; there lies your way;
You may be jogging while your boots are green.
For me, I'll not be gone till I please myself.
'Tis like you'll prove a jolly surly groom,
That take it on you at the first so roundly.

PETRUCHIO

210 O Kate, content thee; prithee, be not angry.

KATHERINA

I will be angry. What hast thou to do?
Father, be quiet; he shall stay my leisure.

GREMIO

Ay, marry, sir, now it begins to work.

KATHERINA

Gentlemen, forward to the bridal dinner.
215 I see a woman may be made a fool,
If she had not a spirit to resist.

PETRUCHIO

They shall go forward, Kate, at thy command.
Obey the bride, you that attend on her.
Go to the feast, revel and domineer,
220 Carouse full measure to her maidenhead,
Be mad and merry, or go hang yourselves;

---

206 *You . . . green* proverbial phrase used to push unwanted guests out the door.

PETRUCHIO
I'm satisfied that you beg me to stay,
but I won't stay, no matter how you beg me.

KATHERINE
If you love me, let's stay.

PETRUCHIO
200 Grumio, get my horse!

GRUMIO
Yes, sir, they're ready. The horses are stuffed with their oats.

KATHERINE
Well, then,
do what you want. I'm not leaving today—
no, not tomorrow, either—until I want to go.
205 The door is open, sir; that's the road you're taking.
You might as well be trotting along while your boots are clean.
As for me, I won't leave until I want to.
It's likely that you'll prove an arrogant, surly groom
when you take charge like this at the very start.

PETRUCHIO
210 O, Kate, be content. Please don't be angry.

KATHERINE
I will be angry—what have you to to say about it?
Father, be quiet. He will wait until I'm ready to go.

GREMIO
Yes, indeed, sir—now you'll see some action.

KATHERINE
Gentlemen, let's go inside to the wedding feast.
215 I see a woman may be made a fool
if she doesn't have the spirit to put her foot down.

PETRUCHIO
They will go inside, Kate, at your command.
Obey the bride, those of you who wait on her.
Go to the feast, enjoy yourselves, and kick up your heels.
220 Toast a full cup to her virginity,
be crazy or merry, or go hang yourselves.

But for my bonny Kate, she must with me.
Nay, look not big, nor stamp, nor stare, nor fret;
I will be master of what is mine own.
225   She is my goods, my chattels; she is my house,
My household stuff, my field, my barn,
My horse, my ox, my ass, my any thing;
And here she stands, touch her whoever dare,
I'll bring mine action on the proudest he
230   That stops my way in Padua. Grumio,
Draw forth thy weapon, we are beset with thieves;
Rescue thy mistress, if thou be a man.
Fear not, sweet wench, they shall not touch thee, Kate;
I'll buckler thee against a million.
    [*Exeunt Petruchio, Katherina, and Grumio.*]

BAPTISTA
235   Nay, let them go, a couple of quiet ones.

GREMIO
Went they not quickly, I should die with laughing.

TRANIO
Of all mad matches never was the like.

LUCENTIO
Mistress, what's your opinion of your sister?

BIANCA
That, being mad herself, she's madly mated.

GREMIO
240   I warrant him, Petruchio is Kated.

BAPTISTA
Neighbours and friends, though bride and bridegroom wants
For to supply the places at the table,
You know there wants no junkets at the feast.
Lucentio, you shall supply the bridegroom's place;
245   And let Bianca take her sister's room.

TRANIO
Shall sweet Bianca practise how to bride it?

But as for my good Kate, she must go with me.
No, don't look so angry, don't stomp you feet, or swagger or fret.
I will be master of what is mine.
225 She is my goods, my holdings. She is my house,
my household stuff, my field, my barn,
my horse, my ox, my ass, my anything.
And here she stands, whoever dares to touch her.
I'll bring a lawsuit against even the proudest man if he
230 tries to keep me here in Pauda. Grumio,
draw your weapon; we're surrounded by thieves.
Rescue your mistress, if you're a man.
Don't be afraid, sweet woman—they'll never touch you, Kate.
I'll shield you from a million of them.
    Exit PETRUCHIO, KATHERINE, *and* GRUMIO.

BAPTISTA
235 No, let them go, quiet couple that they are.

GREMIO
If they hadn't left as quickly as they did, I would have died from laughing.

TRANIO
Of all the crazy couples, there never was one like these two.

LUCENTIO
Lady, what's your opinion of your sister?

BIANCA
I think that being crazy herself, she's married a crazy man.

GREMIO
240 I guarantee you, Petruchio has already caught Kate's temper.

BAPTISTA
Neighbors and friends, though the bride and groom aren't here
to take their places at the table,
you know there's no lack of sweetmeats at the feast.
Lucentio, you will fill the bridegroom's place,
245 and let Bianca take her sister's place.

TRANIO
Is Bianca being allowed to practice how to act as a bride?

BAPTISTA
      She shall, Lucentio. Come, gentlemen, let's go.
            [*Exeunt.*]

Act IV, Scene i: [*Petruchio's country house.*] *Enter* GRUMIO.

GRUMIO
      Fie, fie on all tired jades, on all mad masters, and all foul ways!
      Was ever man so beaten? Was ever man so ray'd? Was ever man
      so weary? I am sent before to make a fire, and they are coming
      after to warm them. Now, were not I a little pot and soon hot,
5   my very lips might freeze to my teeth, my tongue to the roof of
      my mouth, my heart in my belly, ere I should come by a fire to
      thaw me; but I, with blowing the fire, shall warm myself; for,
      considering the weather, a taller man than I will take cold. Holla,
      ho! Curtis.
            Enter CURTIS.

CURTIS
10   Who is that calls so coldly?

GRUMIO
      A piece of ice. If thou doubt it, thou mayst slide from my shoulder
      to my heel with no greater a run but my head and my neck. A
      fire, good Curtis.

CURTIS
      Is my master and his wife coming, Grumio?

GRUMIO
15   O, ay, Curtis, ay; and therefore fire, fire; cast on no water.

CURTIS
      Is she so hot a shrew as she's reported?

GRUMIO
      She was, good Curtis, before this frost; but thou know'st, winter
      tames man, woman, and beast; for it hath tam'd my old master
      and my new mistress and myself, fellow Curtis.

CURTIS
20   Away, you three-inch fool! I am no beast.

---

4 *a little pot and soon hot* is a proverb meaning that small people have quick
tempers.   20 *three-inch fool* Curtis is commenting on Grumio's shortness and also making
a phallic joke.

BAPTISTA

She is, Lucentio. Come, gentlemen, let's go.
They exit.

Act IV, Scene i: Petruchio's country house. Enter GRUMIO.

GRUMIO

Damn all tired nags, all crazy masters, and all muddy roads!
Was there ever a man as beaten as I've been? Was there ever a man as
    muddy? Was there ever a man
as weary? I'm sent ahead to make a fire, and they'll arrive
later to warm themselves. Well, if I wasn't a little kettle and quick to
    get boiling mad,
5   my lips might freeze to my teeth, my tongue to the roof of
my mouth, my heart in my belly before I could reach a fire to
thaw myself. But I, by blowing the fire, will warm myself.
Considering the weather, a tougher man than I am would catch
    cold. Hello,
  hello! Curtis!
      Enter CURTIS.

CURTIS

10   Who is calling in that shaking voice?

GRUMIO

A piece of ice. If you doubt my word, you can slide from my shoulder
to my heel with no more of a running start than my head and neck. A
fire, good Curtis.

CURTIS

Are my master and his wife coming, Grumio?

GRUMIO

15   O, yes, Curtis, yes. Therefore, make a fire, a fire. Don't throw any water
on it.

CURTIS

Is she as hot-tempered a shrew as she's reported to be?

GRUMIO

She was, good Curtis, before this frost. But you know that winter
tames man, woman, and beast. And it has tamed my old master,
my new mistress, and me, fellow Curtis.

CURTIS

20   Go away, you three-inch fool! I'm not an animal.

GRUMIO

Am I but three inches? Why, thy horn is a foot; and so long am I at the least. But wilt thou make a fire, or shall I complain on thee to our mistress, whose hand, she being now at hand, thou shalt soon feel, to thy cold comfort, for being slow in thy hot

25   office?

CURTIS

I prithee, good Grumio, tell me, how goes the world?

GRUMIO

A cold world, Curtis, in every office but thine; and therefore fire. Do thy duty and have thy duty, for my master and mistress are almost frozen to death.

CURTIS

30   There's fire ready; and therefore, good Grumio, the news.

GRUMIO

Why, "Jack, boy! ho! boy!" and as much news as thou wilt.

CURTIS

Come, you are so full of cony-catching!

GRUMIO

Why, therefore fire; for I have caught extreme cold. Where's the cook? Is supper ready, the house trimm'd, rushes strew'd,

35   cobwebs swept; the servingmen in their new fustian, the white stockings, and every officer his wedding garment on? Be the jacks fair within, the gills fair without, the carpets laid, and every thing in order?

CURTIS

All ready; and therefore, I pray thee, news.

GRUMIO

40   First, know, my horse is tired; my master and mistress fall'n out.

CURTIS

How?

GRUMIO

Out of their saddles into the dirt; and thereby hangs a tale.

---

21 *horn* was the sign of a cuckold (a man whose wife was an adultress).   31 *Jack . . . boy!* a line from a familiar song.   36 *jacks* means both a "male servant" and a "leather drinking cup."   37 *gills* means both "female servants" and a "metal drinking cup smaller than a jack."

GRUMIO

So I'm just three inches? Why, your horn is a foot long, and I'm
at least that long. But will you make a fire, or shall I complain about
you to our mistress, whose hand—and she's coming shortly—you
shall soon feel to your cold discomfort if you're slow
25   about your job of making a fire?

CURTIS

I beg you, good Grumio, tell me what's going on in the world.

GRUMIO

A cold world, Curtis, in every respect except yours and therefore, make
    a fire.
Do your duty, and receive your reward because my master and mistress are
almost frozen to death.

CURTIS

30   The fire is ready. Therefore, good Grumio, let's have the news.

GRUMIO

Why, "Jack, boy! Ho, boy!" and whatever news you want.

CURTIS

Come on, you're too full of mischief.

GRUMIO

Well then, make a fire, because I'm extremely cold. Where's the
cook? Is supper ready, the house tidy, rushes scattered on the floor,
35   the cobwebs swept away, all the menials in their best working clothes
    and white
stockings, and every servant with his wedding uniform on? Are the men
inside tidy, the maids well dressed, the tableclothes laid, and everything
in order?

CURTIS

Everything is ready. Therefore, please tell me the news.

GRUMIO

40   First, I'll tell you that my horse is tired. And my master and mistress
    have had a falling out.

CURTIS

    What?

GRUMIO

Out of their saddles and into the dirt—and thereby hangs a tale.

CURTIS
Let's ha't, good Grumio.

GRUMIO
Lend thine ear.

CURTIS
45   Here.

GRUMIO
There.
[*Strikes him.*]

CURTIS
This is to feel a tale, not to hear a tale.

GRUMIO
And therefore 'tis call'd a sensible tale; and this cuff was but to knock at your ear, and beseech list'ning. Now I begin: *Imprimis*,
50   we came down a foul hill, my master riding behind my mistress,—

CURTIS
Both of one horse?

GRUMIO
What's that to thee?

CURTIS
Why, a horse.

GRUMIO
Tell thou the tale. But hadst thou not cross'd me, thou shouldst
55   have heard how her horse fell and she under her horse; thou shouldst have heard in how miry a place, how she was bemoil'd, how he left her with the horse upon her, how he beat me because her horse stumbled, how she waded through the dirt to pluck him off me, how he swore, how she pray'd that never pray'd before,
60   how I cried, how the horses ran away, how her bridle was burst, how I lost my crupper, with many things of worthy memory, which now shall die in oblivion and thou return unexperienc'd to thy grave.

CURTIS
By this reck'ning he is more shrew than she.

---

48 *sensible* means both "reasonable" and "able to be sensed or felt."

CURTIS
Let's hear it, good Grumio.

GRUMIO
Then lend an ear.

CURTIS
45   Here it is.

GRUMIO
There.
(Strikes him.)

CURTIS
This is feeling a tale, not hearing one.

GRUMIO
And that's why it's called a sensible tale. That blow was just to
knock at your ear and beg you to listen. Now I'll start: first,
50   we came down a muddy hill, my master riding behind my mistress—

CURTIS
Both of them on one horse?

GRUMIO
What's that to you?

CURTIS
Why, a horse.

GRUMIO
Then you tell the story. But if you hadn't interrupted, you would
55   have heard how her horse fell, and she fell under the horse. You
would have heard how muddy the place was where she fell, how she was
   covered in mud,
how he let her lie there with the horse on top of her, how he beat me
   because
her horse had stumbled, how she waded through the mud to pull him
off of me, how he swore, how she prayed when she'd never prayed before,
60   how I cried, how the horses ran away, how her bridle broke,
and how I lost my horse's tail strap. All this and many other memorable
   things
will now die unheard and you go to your
grave none the wiser.

CURTIS
By your tale, he's more of a shrew than she is.

GRUMIO

65   Ay; and that thou and the proudest of you all shall find when
he comes home. But what talk I of this? Call forth Nathaniel,
Joseph, Nicholas, Philip, Walter, Sugarsop and the rest; let their
heads be slickly comb'd, their blue coats brush'd and their garters
of an indifferent knit; let them curtsy with their left legs and not
70   presume to touch a hair of my master's horsetail till they kiss their
hands. Are they all ready?

CURTIS

They are.

GRUMIO

Call them forth.

CURTIS

Do you hear, ho? You must meet my master to countenance my
75   mistress.

GRUMIO

Why, she hath a face of her own.

CURTIS

Who knows not that?

GRUMIO

Thou, it seems, that calls for company to countenance her.

CURTIS

I call them forth to credit her.
Enter four or five SERVINGMEN.

GRUMIO

80   Why, she comes to borrow nothing of them.

NATHANIEL

Welcome home, Grumio!

PHILIP

How now, Grumio!

JOSEPH

What, Grumio!

NICHOLAS

Fellow Grumio.

---

74 *countenance* means both "show respect to" and "face."

GRUMIO

65   Yes, and you and the proudest one of the servants will find that out when
     he comes home. But why am I talking about this? Call Nathaniel,
     Joseph, Nicholas, Philip, Walter, Sugarsop, and the rest. See that their
     hair is slickly combed, their blue coats brushed, and that they're
     wearing proper garters.
     See that they bow with their left legs and don't

70   dare touch a hair of my master's horse's tail until they have kissed their
     lord's and lady's hands. Is everyone ready?

CURTIS
     They are.

GRUMIO
     Call them here.

CURTIS
     Did you hear that? Come! You must meet my master to present my

75   mistress with a respectful face.

GRUMIO
     Why, she has a face of her own.

CURTIS
     Who doesn't know that?

GRUMIO
     You, it seems, who ask for the servants to face her.

CURTIS
     I summoned them to pay their respects to her.

GRUMIO

80   Why, she hasn't come here to borrow anything from them!
          Enter four or five SERVINGMEN.

NATHANIEL
     Welcome home, Grumio!

PHILIP
     How are you doing, Grumio!

JOSEPH
     What's up, Grumio!

NICHOLAS
     My good fellow, Grumio.

NATHANIEL

85   How now, old lad?

GRUMIO

Welcome, you; how now, you; what, you; fellow, you;—and thus much for greeting. Now, my spruce companions, is all ready, and all things neat?

NATHANIEL

All things is ready. How near is our master?

GRUMIO

90   E'en at hand, alighted by this; and therefore be not—Cock's passion, silence! I hear my master.

Enter PETRUCHIO *and* KATHERINA.

PETRUCHIO

Where be these knaves? What, no man at door
To hold my stirrup nor to take my horse!
Where is Nathaniel, Gregory, Philip?

ALL SERVANTS

95   Here, here, sir; here, sir.

PETRUCHIO

Here, sir! here, sir! here, sir, here, sir!
You logger-headed and unpolish'd grooms!
What, no attendance? No regard? No duty?
Where is the foolish knave I sent before?

GRUMIO

100   Here, sir; as foolish as I was before.

PETRUCHIO

You peasant swain! You whoreson malthorse drudge!
Did I not bid thee meet me in the park,
And bring along these rascal knaves with thee?

GRUMIO

Nathaniel's coat, sir, was not fully made,
105   And Gabriel's pumps were all unpink'd i' th' heel;
There was no link to colour Peter's hat,
And Walter's dagger was not come from sheathing;
There were none fine but Adam, Ralph, and Gregory;

---

101 *malthorse* a type of slow and heavy workhorse used on a brewery treadmill.   106 *link* or torch; the soot from torches was used to blacken hats.

NATHANIEL
85   How are you, old lad!

GRUMIO
    Welcome to you; how are you doing, what's up with you; my good fellow
        to you; and that's
    all for greetings. Now my, tidy friends, is everything ready and
    everything prepared?

NATHANIEL
    Everything is ready. How near is our master?

GRUMIO
90   He's nearly here; dismounted by now. Therefore, don't be—by God,
    quiet! I hear my master.
               Enter PETRUCHIO *and* KATHERINE.

PETRUCHIO
    Where are those rascals? What! No man at the door,
    to hold my stirrup or take my horse?
    Where is Nathaniel, Gregory, and Philip?

ALL SERVANTS
95   Here, here, sir. Here, sir.

PETRUCHIO
    Here, sir! Here, sir! Here, sir! Here, sir!
    You blockheaded and clumsy grooms!
    What, no service? No respect? Not doing your duty?
    Where is that foolish rascal I sent ahead of me?

GRUMIO
100   Here, sir. Just as foolish as I was before.

PETRUCHIO
    You peasant rustic! You worthless brewery horse!
    Didn't I tell you to meet me outside
    and bring along those rascally scamps with you?

GRUMIO
    Nathaniel's coat was not completely finished,
105   and Gabriel's shoes were not decorated with punched holes at the heel.
    There was no torch to color Peter's hat,
    and Walter's dagger scabbard hasn't been repaired, yet.
    No one was presentable, except Adam, Ralph, and Gregory.

The rest were ragged, old, beggarly;
110   Yet, as they are, here are they come to meet you.

PETRUCHIO
Go, rascals, go, and fetch my supper in.
[*Exeunt Servants.*]
[*Singing.*] "Where is the life that late I led"—
Where are those—Sit down, Kate, and welcome.—
Soud, soud, soud, soud!
Re-enter SERVANTS, *with supper.*
115   Why, when, I say?—Nay, good sweet Kate, be merry.—
Off with my boots, you rogues! You villains, when?
[*Sings.*] "It was the friar of order grey,
As he forth walked on his way:"—
Out, you rogue! you pluck my foot awry.
120   Take that, and mend the plucking off the other.
[*Strikes him.*]
Be merry, Kate.—Some water, here; what, ho!
Enter one with water.
Where's my spaniel Troilus? Sirrah, get you hence,
And bid my cousin Ferdinand come hither;
One, Kate, that you must kiss, and be acquainted with.
125   Where are my slippers? Shall I have some water?
Come, Kate, and wash, and welcome heartily.
You whoreson villain! Will you let it fall?
[*Strikes him.*]

KATHERINA
Patience, I pray you; 'twas a fault unwilling.

PETRUCHIO
A whoreson beetle-headed, flap-ear'd knave!
130   Come, Kate, sit down; I know you have a stomach.
Will you give thanks, sweet Kate; or else shall I?
What's this? Mutton?

1. SERVANT
Ay.

PETRUCHIO
Who brought it?

---

112 *Where . . . led* line from an old ballad.   114 *Soud* the meaning of the word is debated. Some scholars believe it is an exclamation expressing impatience. Others believe the word really should read "food."   117-18 *It . . . way* a line from another old

The rest were ragged, old, and looked like beggars.
110　Yet, even with their flaws, they come here to meet you.

PETRUCHIO
　　Go, rascals, go and bring my supper.
　　　　Exit SERVANTS.
　　(*Sings*) "Where is the life that late I led?"
　　Where are those?— Sit down, Kate. Welcome.
　　Food, food, food, food!
　　　　Enter SERVANTS *with supper.*
115　Well, when are you going to bring it in?—No, good, sweet Kate, be
　　　　happy—
　　Take off my boots, you rascals, you peasants! Service!
　　　　(*Sings*)"It was a friar of the grey brotherhood,
　　　　　　who walked onward on his way."—
　　Stop, you rascal! You're pulling my foot the wrong way!
120　Take that, and do better with pulling the other foot!
　　　　(*Strikes him.*)
　　Be happy, Kate. Bring some water, here. Speed it up!
　　　　A SERVANT *enters carrying water.*
　　Where's my spaniel, Troilus? Servant, go
　　and tell my cousin Ferdinand to come here.
　　　　Exit SERVANT.
　　He's a person, Kate, that you must kiss and get to know.
125　Where are my slippers? Will you give me some water?
　　Come, Kate, and wash. You're heartily welcome.
　　You shiftless peasant! So you'll drop it, will you?
　　　　(*Strikes him.*)

KATHERINE
　　Please show a little patience. He didn't mean to drop it.

PETRUCHIO
　　A shiftless, stupid, floppy-eared rascal!
130　Come, Kate, sit down. I know you have an appetite.
　　Will you say grace, sweet Kate, or should I?
　　What's this? Mutton?

FIRST SERVANT
　　Yes.

PETRUCHIO
　　Who brought it?

---

song.   129 *beetle-headed* a beetle was a wooden mallet.   130 *stomach* means both
"appetite" and "hot temper."

PETER.

135   I.

PETRUCHIO
'Tis burnt; and so is all the meat.
What dogs are these. Where is the rascal cook?
How durst you, villains, bring it from the dresser,
And serve it thus to me that love it not?
140   There, take it to you, trenchers, cups, and all.
              [*Throws the meat, etc., about the stage.*]
You heedless joltheads and unmanner'd slaves!
What, do you grumble? I'll be with you straight.

KATHERINA
I pray you, husband, be not so disquiet.
The meat was well, if you were so contented.

PETRUCHIO
145   I tell thee, Kate, 'twas burnt and dried away,
And I expressly am forbid to touch it,
For it engenders choler, planteth anger;
And better 'twere that both of us did fast,
Since, of ourselves, ourselves are choleric,
150   Than feed it with such over-roasted flesh.
Be patient; to-morrow 't shall be mended.
And, for this night, we'll fast for company.
Come, I will bring thee to thy bridal chamber.
              [*Exeunt.*]
              Re-enter SERVANTS *severally.*

NATHANIEL
Peter, didst ever see the like?

PETER
155   He kills her in her own humour.
              Re-enter CURTIS, *a servant.*

GRUMIO
Where is he?

PETER

135   I did.

PETRUCHIO

It's burnt. And so is all the rest of the meat.
These fellows are dogs! Where is that rascal of a cook?
How dare you, you peasants, bring it from the sideboard
and serve it like this to me when I dislike it?

140   There! Take it away—the platters, cups, everything!
        (Throws the meat and dishes about.)
You dim-witted idiots and uncouth slaves!
What! Are you griping? I'll settle your hash right now!

KATHERINE

Please, husband, don't get so upset.
The meat was tasty, if you had just been willing to try it.

PETRUCHIO

145   I tell you, Kate, it was burnt and completely dry.
And I'm specifically forbidden to eat dry meat
since it brings about bad temper and raises anger.
So it would be better if both of us fasted,
since we ourselves are hot-tempered,

150   rather than feed our tempers with that burned meat.
Be patient. Tomorrow we'll make up for it.
Tonight we'll fast together.
Come, I'll take you to your bridal room.
        Exit.
        Enter several SERVANTS *from different directions.*

NATHANIEL

Peter, did you ever see the likes of that?

PETER

155   He's taming her with her own medicine.
        Enter CURTIS *and a* SERVANT.

GRUMIO

Where is he?

CURTIS

    In her chamber, making a sermon of continency to her;
    And rails, and swears, and rates, that she, poor soul,
    Knows not which way to stand, to look, to speak,
160   And sits as one new-risen from a dream.
    Away, away! for he is coming hither.
          [*Exeunt.*]
          Re-enter PETRUCHIO.

PETRUCHIO

    Thus have I politicly begun my reign,
    And 'tis my hope to end successfully.
    My falcon now is sharp and passing empty;
165   And till she stoop she must not be full-gorg'd,
    For then she never looks upon her lure.
    Another way I have to man my haggard,
    To make her come and know her keeper's call,
    That is, to watch her, as we watch these kites
170   That bate and beat and will not be obedient.
    She eat no meat to-day, nor none shall eat;
    Last night she slept not, nor to-night she shall not;
    As with the meat, some undeserved fault
    I'll find about the making of the bed;
175   And here I'll fling the pillow, there the bolster,
    This way the coverlet, another way the sheets.
    Ay, and amid this hurly I intend
    That all is done in reverend care of her;
    And in conclusion she shall watch all night;
180   And if she chance to nod I'll rail and brawl
    And with the clamour keep her still awake.
    This is a way to kill a wife with kindness,
    And thus I'll curb her mad and headstrong humour.
    He that knows better how to tame a shrew,
185   Now let him speak; 'tis charity to show.
          [*Exit.*]

---

164 *falcon* a hawk trained to hunt.   165 *stoop* means both "obey" and "a falcon's swoop
to seize prey."   166 *lure* bait that a falconer uses to get the falcon to return.   169 *kites*
small hawks.   172 *last night* this seems to be a mistake. This scene occurs the night of the
wedding.   185 *show* pronounced to rhyme with "shrew" in Shakespeare's day.

CURTIS
    In her room, giving her a sermon on abstaining.
    And he rants and swears and rates so much that she, poor soul,
    doesn't know which way to stand, or look, or speak.
160   She sits like someone just awakened from a dream.
    Hide, hide! He's coming here.
         They exit.
         Enter PETRUCHIO.

PETRUCHIO
    I have begun my reign shrewdly
    and I hope to end successfully.
    My falcon is now starved and very empty,
165   and until she's tamed, she must not have a full meal
    because then she'll never be tempted by the bait.
    I have another way to tame my unruly female hawk,
    to make her come and recognize her keeper's command,
    and that is to keep her up, like a kite is kept from sleeping
170   when it flutters and beats its wings and won't obey.
    She ate no meat today, and she won't be given any.
    She didn't sleep last night, and she won't tonight.
    As I did with the meat, I'll pretend to find something wrong
    with the way the bed is made.
175   I'll fling a pillow here, a bolster there;
    toss the coverlet this way, the sheets in another direction.
    Yes, and while I'm creating all this fuss, I'll pretend
    that I'm doing it all out of respectful care for her.
    In short, she'll be up all night;
180   and if she should start to nod off, I'll rant and rave
    and keep her awake with the noise.
    This is the way to kill a wife with kindness,
    and the way I'll tame her crazy, headstrong temper.
    The man who knows how to tame a shrew better than this,
185   let him speak now—it would be an act of kindness to tell how.
         Exit.

Scene ii: [*Padua. Before Baptista's house.*] *Enter* TRANIO, *as*
LUCENTIO, *and* HORTENSIO, *as* LICIO.

TRANIO
    Is't possible, friend Licio, that Mistress Bianca
    Doth fancy any other but Lucentio?
    I tell you, sir, she bears me fair in hand.

HORTENSIO
    Sir, to satisfy you in what I have said,
5   Stand by and mark the manner of his teaching.
        Enter BIANCA *and* LUCENTIO, *as* CAMBIO.

LUCENTIO
    Now, mistress, profit you in what you read?

BIANCA
    What, master, read you? First resolve me that.

LUCENTIO
    I read that I profess, the Art to Love.

BIANCA
    And may you prove, sir, master of your art!

LUCENTIO
10   While you, sweet dear, prove mistress of my heart!

HORTENSIO
    Quick proceeders, marry! Now, tell me, I pray,
    You that durst swear that your mistress Bianca
    Lov'd none in the world so well as Lucentio.

TRANIO
    O despiteful love! Unconstant womankind!
15   I tell thee, Licio, this is wonderful.

HORTENSIO
    Mistake no more; I am not Licio,
    Nor a musician, as I seem to be;
    But one that scorn to live in this disguise
    For such a one as leaves a gentleman
20   And makes a good of such a cullion.
    Know, sir, that I am call'd Hortensio.

---

8 *Art to Love* a treatise on love by the Roman poet Ovid.

Act IV, Scene ii: Padua. Before Baptista's house. Enter TRANIO *and* HORTENSIO.

TRANIO
Is it possible, my friend Licio, that Lady Bianca
can like anyone except Lucentio?
I tell you, sir, she seems to lead me on.

HORTENSIO
Sir, to assure you that what I said was true,
5   stand aside and watch how he conducts himself when he teaches.
(They stand aside.)
Enter BIANCA *and* LUCENTIO.

LUCENTIO
Now, my lady, do you learn anything from what you read?

BIANCA
What are you reading, master? First tell me that.

LUCENTIO
I read what I preach, *The Art to Love.*

BIANCA
And may you prove to be a master of your art, sir!

LUCENTIO
10   While you, my dear sweet, prove yourself mistress of my heart.

HORTENSIO
Fast workers, indeed! Now what do you say, I ask you—
you who dared swear that your lady Bianca
loved no one in the world as well as Lucentio?

TRANIO
O spiteful love! Fickle women!
15   I tell you, Licio, this is shocking!

HORTENSIO
Don't be fooled, anymore. I'm not Licio,
or a musician, as I appear to be,
but someone who despises keeping up this disguise
for a woman who deserts a gentleman
20   and worships such a crude fellow.
Sir, know that my name is Hortensio.

TRANIO
Signior Hortensio, I have often heard
Of your entire affection to Bianca;
And since mine eyes are witness of her lightness,
25   I will with you, if you be so contented,
Forswear Bianca and her love for ever.

HORTENSIO
See, how they kiss and court! Signior Lucentio,
Here is my hand, and here I firmly vow
Never to woo her more, but do forswear her,
30   As one unworthy all the former favours
That I have fondly flatter'd her withal.

TRANIO
And here I take the like unfeigned oath,
Never to marry with her though she would entreat.
Fie on her! see, how beastly she doth court him!

HORTENSIO
35   Would all the world but he had quite forsworn!
For me, that I may surely keep mine oath,
I will be married to a wealthy widow,
Ere three days pass, which hath as long lov'd me
As I have lov'd this proud disdainful haggard.
40   And so farewell, Signior Lucentio.
Kindness in women, not their beauteous looks,
Shall win my love; and so I take my leave,
In resolution as I swore before.
        [*Exit.*]

TRANIO
Mistress Bianca, bless you with such grace
45   As 'longeth to a lover's blessed case!
Nay, I have ta'en you napping, gentle love,
And have forsworn you with Hortensio.

BIANCA
Tranio, you jest; but have you both forsworn me?

TRANIO
Mistress, we have.

TRANIO
>   Signior Hortensio, I've often heard
>   about your complete devotion to Bianca.
>   And since I witnessed for myself her fickleness,
25 I'll join with you, if you're agreeable,
>   in swearing off Bianca and her love forever.

HORTENSIO
>   Look at how they're kissing and courting. Signior Lucentio,
>   here's my hand, and here I swear
>   never to court her again. I reject her
30 as someone who is unworthy of all the respect
>   that I foolishly paid her in everything before.

TRANIO
>   And here I'll take the same sincere vow
>   never to marry her, even though she begged me.
>   Damn her! Just look at how blatantly she courts him.

HORTENSIO
35 If only she had just one lover!
>   As for me, so that I may be sure to keep my vow,
>   I'll marry a wealthy widow
>   before three days have gone by. She has loved me as long
>   as I've loved this proud, uppity, untamed hawk.
40 Well, goodbye, Signior Lucentio.
>   Now kindness in women, not a beautiful appearance,
>   will win my love. So, I'll leave you
>   with the vow I just swore to you.
>   *Exit.*

TRANIO *(to Bianca)*
>   Lady Bianca, may you be blessed with the kind of grace
45 as suits a lover's happy state!
>   Oh yes, I've seen your love-play, gentle lover,
>   and I've forsaken you, as has Hortensio.

BIANCA
>   Tranio, you're joking. Have both of you really deserted me?

TRANIO
>   We have, lady.

LUCENTIO

50   Then we are rid of Licio.

TRANIO

I'faith, he'll have a lusty widow now,
That shall be woo'd and wedded in a day.

BIANCA

God give him joy!

TRANIO

Ay, and he'll tame her.

BIANCA

55   He says so, Tranio.

TRANIO

Faith, he is gone unto the taming-school.

BIANCA

The taming-school! What, is there such a place?

TRANIO

Ay, mistress, and Petruchio is the master;
That teacheth tricks eleven and twenty long,
60   To tame a shrew and charm her chattering tongue.
            Enter BIONDELLO.

BIONDELLO

O master, master, I have watch'd so long
That I am dog-weary; but at last I spied
An ancient angel coming down the hill,
Will serve the turn.

TRANIO

65   What is he, Biondello?

BIONDELLO

Master, a *mercatante*, or a pedant,
I know not what; but formal in apparel,
In gait and countenance surely like a father.

LUCENTIO

And what of him, Tranio?

---

59 *tricks eleven and twenty long* this may be a reference to the card game trentuno, where
a player who took thirty-one tricks won the game.   63 *angel* is an old, valued coin.

LUCENTIO

50 Then we're rid of Licio.

TRANIO

Yes, really. He'll marry a lively widow, now,
whom he'll court and marry in the same day.

BIANCA

God make him happy!

TRANIO

Yes, if he'll tame her.

BIANCA

55 He says he will, Tranio.

TRANIO

Indeed, he's gone to the taming school.

BIANCA

The taming school! What! Is there such a place?

TRANIO

Yes, lady, and Petruchio is the teacher
who teaches winning tricks
60 to tame a shrew and quiet her nagging tongue.
        Enter BIONDELLO.

BIONDELLO

O master, master! I've been watching for so long
that I'm dead-tired, but I finally spotted
a trusty old soul coming down the hill
who will do the trick.

TRANIO

65 Who is he, Biondello?

BIONDELLO

Master, either a merchant or a teacher,
I'm not sure. But he dresses formally,
and in the way he carries himself and behaves, he's just like a father.

LUCENTIO

And what do you plan to do, Tranio?

TRANIO

70 If he be credulous and trust my tale,
 I'll make him glad to seem Vincentio,
 And give assurance to Baptista Minola,
 As if he were the right Vincentio.
 Take in your love, and then let me alone.
  [*Exeunt Lucentio and Bianca.*]
  Enter a PEDANT.

PEDANT

75 God save you, sir!

TRANIO

     And you sir! you are welcome.
 Travel you far on, or are you at the farthest?

PEDANT

 Sir, at the farthest for a week or two;
 But then up farther, and as far as Rome;
80 And so to Tripoli, if God lend me life.

TRANIO

 What countryman, I pray?

PEDANT

    Of Mantua.

TRANIO

 Of Mantua, sir? Marry, God forbid!
 And come to Padua, careless of your life?

PEDANT

85 My life, sir! How, I pray? for that goes hard.

TRANIO

 'Tis death for any one in Mantua
 To come to Padua. Know you not the cause?
 Your ships are stay'd at Venice, and the Duke,
 For private quarrel 'twixt your Duke and him,
90 Hath publish'd and proclaim'd it openly.
 'Tis might marvel, but that you are but newly come,
 You might have heard it else proclaim'd about.

TRANIO

70   If he's trusting and believes my story,
     I'll make him happy to pretend to be Vincentio
     and give guarantees to Baptista Minola
     just as if he were the real Vincentio.
     Take your lover inside and leave me to see to this business.
          Exit LUCENTIO *and* BIANCA.
          Enter PEDANT.

PEDANT

75   God bless you, sir!

TRANIO

     And you, too, sir! Greetings.
     Are you traveling farther, or have you reached your destination?

PEDANT

     Sir, I'll stay here for a week or two,
     but then I'll go on as far as Rome
80   and then to Tripoli, if I live that long.

TRANIO

     Where are you from, if I may ask?

PEDANT

     From Mantua.

TRANIO

     From Mantua, sir! Indeed, God forbid!
     And you came to Padua, so recklessly risking your life?

PEDANT

85   My life, sir! What do you mean? That's rough news!

TRANIO

     It's death for anyone in Mantua
     to come to Padua. Don't you know the reason?
     Your ships are kept at Venice and the duke—
     because of a private quarrel between your duke and him—
90   has decreed and publicly issued the order.
     It's amazing you haven't heard, except that you just arrived.
     Otherwise, you might have heard it proclaimed somewhere.

PEDANT

    Alas! sir, it is worse for me than so;

    For I have bills for money by exchange

95   From Florence, and must here deliver them.

TRANIO

    Well, sir, to do you courtesy,

    This will I do, and this I will advise you.

    First, tell me, have you ever been at Pisa?

PEDANT

    Ay, sir, in Pisa have I often been,

100   Pisa renowned for grave citizens.

TRANIO

    Among them know you one Vincentio?

PEDANT

    I know him not, but I have heard of him;

    A merchant of incomparable wealth.

TRANIO

    He is my father, sir; and, sooth to say,

105   In count'nance somewhat doth resemble you.

BIONDELLO [*Aside.*]

    As much as an apple doth an oyster, and all one.

TRANIO

    To save your life in this extremity,

    This favour will I do you for his sake;

    And think it not the worst of all your fortunes

110   That you are like to Sir Vincentio.

    His name and credit shall you undertake,

    And in my house you shall be friendly lodg'd.

    Look that you take upon you as you should;

    You understand me, sir? So shall you stay

115   Till you have done your business in the city.

    If this be court'sy, sir, accept of it.

PEDANT

    O sir, I do; and will repute you ever

    The patron of my life and liberty.

PEDANT
Alas, sir, it's even worse in my case
because I have bills for money from deals
95   in Florence and must deliver them here.

TRANIO
Well, sir, to do you a favor
I'll do this and explain this to you—
but first, tell me, have you ever been in Pisa?

PEDANT
Yes, sir. I've often been in Pisa,
100   Pisa, famous for dignified citizens.

TRANIO
Among those citizens, do you know one named Vincentio?

PEDANT
I don't personally know him, but I've heard of him.
He's a merchant of unmatched wealth.

TRANIO
He's my father, sir. And to tell you the truth,
105   you somewhat resemble him in your bearing.

BIONDELLO *(to himself)*
As much as an apple resembles an oyster, and that's beside the point.

TRANIO
To save your life when you're faced with this danger,
I'll do you a favor, for his sake—
and don't think it the worst of misfortunes
110   that you look like Sir Vincentio.
You'll assume his name and position
and be nicely settled in my house.
Be sure you act your role as you should!
You get my meaning, sir? You can keep your part
115   until you've finished your business in the city.
If you take this to be a favor, sir, please accept my offer.

PEDANT
O sir, I do. And I'll esteem you forever
as the benefactor who gave me my life and freedom.

TRANIO

Then go with me to make the matter good.

120   This, by the way, I let you understand;

My father is here look'd for every day,

To pass assurance of a dow'r in marriage

'Twixt me and one Baptista's daughter here.

In all these circumstances I'll instruct you.

125   Go with me to clothe you as becomes you.

[*Exeunt.*]

Scene iii: [*A room in Petruchio's house.*] *Enter* KATHERINA *and* GRUMIO.

GRUMIO

No, no, forsooth; I dare not for my life.

KATHERINA

The more my wrong, the more his spite appears.

What, did he marry me to famish me?

Beggars, that come unto my father's door,

5   Upon entreaty have a present alms;

If not, elsewhere they meet with charity;

But I, who never knew how to entreat,

Nor never needed that I should entreat,

Am starv'd for meat, giddy for lack of sleep,

10   With oaths kept waking, and with brawling fed;

And that which spites me more than all these wants,

He does it under name of perfect love,

As who should say, if I should sleep or eat,

'Twere deadly sickness or else present death.

15   I prithee go and get me some repast;

I care not what, so it be wholesome food.

GRUMIO

What say you to a neat's foot?

KATHERINA

'Tis passing good; I prithee let me have it.

GRUMIO

I fear it is too choleric a meat.

20   How say you to a fat tripe finely broil'd?

---

19 *choleric* Grumio refers to the Elizabethan belief that certain foods affected certain temperaments.

TRANIO

    Then come with me to settle the matter.

120   And I'll tell you this as we walk along:

    my father is expected here any day now

    to give guarantees on a marriage settlement

    between myself and a daughter of a certain Baptista.

    I'll tell you everything about the situation.

125   Come with me so that you can be dressed as is proper for you.

        They exit.

Act IV, Scene iii: A room in Petruchio's house. Enter KATHERINE
and GRUMIO.

GRUMIO

    No, no, truly I can't, for fear of my life.

KATHERINE

    The more he does to hurt me, the more malicious he becomes.

    Really, did he marry me to starve me to death?

    Beggars who come to my father's door

5   received some money immediately when they asked,

    or if not, found charity elsewhere.

    But I, who never learned to beg

    and never needed to beg,

    I am starved for food, dizzy from lack of sleep,

10   kept awake by swearing, and fed with fighting.

    And the thing which irks me more than all the rest of my hungers

    is that he does all this under the guise of the deepest love,

    as if to say, if I should sleep or eat,

    that would mean fatal sickness or even immediate death.

15   I beg you, go and get me some food.

    I don't care what it is, just so long as it's nourishing.

GRUMIO

    What do you say to a calf's foot?

KATHERINE

    That would be wonderful. Please let me have it.

GRUMIO

    I'm afraid it's a kind of meat that will make you hot-tempered.

20   What do you say to a fat tripe, broiled nicely?

KATHERINA

I like it well; good Grumio, fetch it me.

GRUMIO

I cannot tell; I fear 'tis choleric.
What say you to a piece of beef and mustard?

KATHERINA

A dish that I do love to feed upon.

GRUMIO

25   Ay, but the mustard is too hot a little.

KATHERINA

Why then, the beef, and let the mustard rest.

GRUMIO

Nay then, I will not; you shall have the mustard,
Or else you get no beef of Grumio.

KATHERINA

Then both, or one, or any thing thou wilt.

GRUMIO

30   Why then, the mustard without the beef.

KATHERINA

Go, get thee gone, thou false deluding slave,
    [*Beats him.*]
That feed'st me with the very name of meat.
Sorrow on thee and all the pack of you,
That triumph thus upon my misery!
35   Go, get thee gone, I say.
      Enter PETRUCHIO *and* HORTENSIO, *with meat.*

PETRUCHIO

How fares my Kate? What, sweeting, all amort!

HORTENSIO

Mistress, what cheer?

KATHERINA

      Faith, as cold as can be.

PETRUCHIO

Pluck up thy spirits; look cheerfully upon me.

KATHERINE

I'd like that very much. Grumio, go get it for me.

GRUMIO

I'm not sure; I'm afraid it might make you temperamental.
What do you say to a piece of beef with mustard?

KATHERINE

That's a dish I love to eat.

GRUMIO

25   Yes, but the mustard is a little too hot.

KATHERINE

Well then, just give me the beef and leave out the mustard.

GRUMIO

Oh no I won't. You'll take the mustard,
or else you won't get any beef from Grumio.

KATHERINE

Then give me both, or just one, or whatever you want.

GRUMIO

30   Well then, I'll give you the mustard without the beef.

KATHERINE

Go on, go away, you false, lying slave.
    (Beats him.)
You feed me with just the name of food.
Bad luck to you and the whole lot of you
who delight in my misery!
35   Go, go away, I said.
    Enter PETRUCHIO *and* HORTENSIO *with food.*

PETRUCHIO

How are you doing, my Kate? What, my sweet? All down in the mouth?

HORTENSIO

Mistress, how are you?

KATHERINE

Actually, I'm not feeling too well.

PETRUCHIO

Take heart. Give me a smile.

40   Here, love, thou see'st how diligent I am
       To dress thy meat myself and bring it thee.
       I am sure, sweet Kate, this kindness merits thanks.
       What, not a word? Nay, then thou lov'st it not;
       And all my pains is sorted to no proof.
45   Here, take away this dish.

KATHERINA
    I pray you, let it stand.

PETRUCHIO
    The poorest service is repaid with thanks,
    And so shall mine, before you touch the meat.

KATHERINA
    I thank you, sir.

HORTENSIO
50   Signior Petruchio, fie! you are to blame.
       Come, Mistress Kate, I'll bear you company.

PETRUCHIO
    [*Aside.*] Eat it up all, Hortensio, if thou lovest me.
    Much good do it unto thy gentle heart!
    Kate, eat apace. And now, my honey love,
55   Will we return unto thy father's house
       And revel it as bravely as the best,
       With silken coats and caps and golden rings,
       With ruffs and cuffs and farthingales and things,
       With scarfs and fans and double change of brav'ry,
60   With amber bracelets, beads, and all this knav'ry.
       What, hast thou din'd? The tailor stays thy leisure,
       To deck thy body with his ruffling treasure.
          Enter TAILOR.
    Come, tailor, let us see these ornaments;
    Lay forth the gown.
          Enter HABERDASHER.
65   What news with you, sir?

HABERDASHER
    Here is the cap your worship did bespeak.

---

s.d. *haberdasher* is a hatmaker.

40   Here, love, you see how thoughtful I am
to prepare your food myself and bring it to you?
I'm sure, sweet Kate, that my thoughtfulness deserves a thank you.
What—not one word? Well, then, you must not like it,
and all my effort has been worthless.

45   Here, take this dish away.

KATHERINE
Please, leave it here!

PETRUCHIO
The most trifling favor is given thanks.
Mine will be, too, before you touch the food.

KATHERINE
I thank you, sir.

HORTENSIO
50   Signior Petruchio, for shame! You're the one to blame.
Come on, Mistress Kate, I'll keep you company.

PETRUCHIO *(Aside)*
Eat it all up, Hortensio, if you want to please me.
I hope it does your gentle heart good!
(To Kate) Kate, dig in. And now, my sweet love,

55   we'll return to your father's house
and party in as fine clothing as the best of them,
with such coats and caps and golden rings,
with stiff collars, cuffs, hooped petticoats, and things,
with scarfs, fans, and extra fancy clothing,

60   with amber bracelets, beads, and all sorts of trinkets.
What! Finished eating already? The tailor is waiting for you at your convenience
to cover you with his pretty ruffled treasures.
       Enter TAILOR.
Come, tailor, let's see your pretty wares.
Lay out the gown.
       Enter HABERDASHER.

65   What news do you bring, sir?

HABERDASHER
Here is the cap you ordered, your worship.

PETRUCHIO
Why, this was moulded on a porringer;
A velvet dish. Fie, fie! 'tis lewd and filthy.
Why, 'tis a cockle or a walnut-shell,
70   A knack, a toy, a trick, a baby's cap.
Away with it! come, let me have a bigger.

KATHERINA
I'll have no bigger; this doth fit the time,
And gentlewomen wear such caps as these.

PETRUCHIO
When you are gentle, you shall have one too,
75   And not till then.

HORTENSIO [*Aside.*]
That will not be in haste.

KATHERINA
Why, sir, I trust I may have leave to speak;
And speak I will. I am no child, no babe.
Your betters have endur'd me say my mind,
80   And if you cannot, best you stop your ears.
My tongue will tell the anger of my heart,
Or else my heart concealing it will break,
And rather than it shall, I will be free
Even to the uttermost, as I please, in words.

PETRUCHIO
85   Why, thou say'st true; it is a paltry cap,
A custard-coffin, a bauble, a silken pie.
I love thee well in that thou lik'st it not.

KATHERINA
Love me or love me not, I like the cap;
And it I will have, or I will have none.
[*Exit Haberdasher.*]

PETRUCHIO
90   Thy gown? Why, ay. Come, tailor, let us see't.
O mercy, God! what masquing stuff is here?
What's this? A sleeve? 'Tis like a demi-cannon.

---

92 *demi-cannon* is a large cannon and a type of sleeve that was tapered from the shoulder
to the waist.

PETRUCHIO
  Why, this was shaped on top of a soup bowl!
  It's a velvet dish. For shame, for shame! This is repulsive and disgusting.
  Why, it's a mollusk or a walnut shell,
70 a knickknack, a piece of fluff, a plaything, a baby's cap—
  take it away! Come, bring me a bigger one.

KATHERINE
  I don't want a bigger one. This one is fashionable,
  and ladies wear caps like this.

PETRUCHIO
  When you're a lady, you'll have one, too—
75 and not until then.

HORTENSIO *(to himself)*
  That won't be too soon.

KATHERINE
  Why, sir, I trust that I have permission to speak,
  and speak I will. I'm not a child or a baby.
  Better people than you have listened to me speak my mind,
80 and if you can't, you better plug your ears.
  I must voice my anger when I feel it,
  or else break my heart concealing it.
  Rather than do that, I'll speak freely,
  even to an extreme, if I choose.

PETRUCHIO
85 Really, you're right. It's a shabby cap,
  a custard cup, a bauble, a silk meat pie.
  I love you for not liking it.

KATHERINE
  Whether you love me or not, I like the cap,
  and I'll have it or nothing.
          Exit HABERDAHSER.

PETRUCHIO
90 Your gown? Why, yes. Come, tailor, let's see it.
  O my God! What kind of masquerade costume is that?
  What's this—a sleeve? It's like a big cannon.

What, up and down, carv'd like an apple-tart?
Here's snip and nip and cut and slish and slash,
95   Like to a censer in a barber's shop.
Why, what, i' devil's name, tailor, call'st thou this?

HORTENSIO [*Aside.*]
I see she's like to have neither cap nor gown.

TAILOR
You bid me make it orderly and well,
According to the fashion and the time.

PETRUCHIO
100   Marry, and did; but if you be rememb'red,
I did not bid you mar it to the time.
Go, hop me over every kennel home,
For you shall hop without my custom, sir.
I'll none of it. Hence! make your best of it.

KATHERINA
105   I never saw a better-fashion'd gown,
More quaint, more pleasing, nor more commendable.
Belike you mean to make a puppet of me.

PETRUCHIO
Why, true; he means to make a puppet of thee.

TAILOR
She says your worship means to make a puppet of her.

PETRUCHIO
110   O monstrous arrogance! Thou liest, thou thread, thou thimble,
Thou yard, three-quarters, half-yard, quarter, nail!
Thou flea, thou nit, thou winter-cricket thou!
Brav'd in mine own house with a skein of thread?
Away, thou rag, thou quantity, thou remnant,
115   Or I shall so be-mete thee with thy yard
As thou shalt think on prating whilst thou liv'st!
I tell thee, I, that thou hast marr'd her gown.

TAILOR
Your worship is deceiv'd; the gown is made
Just as my master had direction.
120   Grumio gave order how it should be done.

---

115 *be-mete* means both "measure" and "beat."

What! Carved everywhere like an apple tart?
Here's a snip, there a nip, a cut, a slish, a slash—
95   like an incense burner in a barber's shop.
Why, what in the devil do you call this, tailor?

HORTENSIO *(to himself)*
I see she's not likely to get either a cap or a gown.

TAILOR
You told me to make it neatly and well,
according to what is fashionable and in style.

PETRUCHIO
100   Indeed, I did. But if you recall,
I did not tell you to ruin it for all time.
Go and jump over every gutter on your way home,
for you'll have to get along without my business, sir.
I won't have any of this. Go away. Take this as you please.

KATHERINE
105   I never saw a better-made dress,
more elegant, more pleasing, or more commendable.
You probably want to make me a puppet.

PETRUCHIO
Why, that's the truth—he wants to make you a puppet.

TAILOR
She said you, your worship, wanted to make a puppet of her.

PETRUCHIO
110   O you monstrously arrogant man! You're lying, you thread, you thimble,
you yard, three quarters, half, quarter, sixteenth of a yard!
You flea, you louse egg, you winter cricket, you!
Defied in my own house by a coil of thread!
Go away you rag, you fragment, you scrap,
115   or I'll beat you so badly with your yardstick
that you'll never forget your stupid remark while you live!
I'm telling you, you ruined her dress.

TAILOR
You're mistaken, your worship. The dress was made
just as you told my master to make it.
120   Grumio gave me orders how to do it.

GRUMIO
I gave him no order; I gave him the stuff.

TAILOR
But how did you desire it should be made?

GRUMIO
Marry, sir, with needle and thread.

TAILOR
But did you not request to have it cut?

GRUMIO
125   Thou hast fac'd many things.

TAILOR
I have.

GRUMIO
Face not me; thou hast brav'd many men, brave not me; I will
neither be fac'd nor brav'd. I say unto thee, I bid thy master cut
out the gown; but I did not bid him cut it to pieces; *ergo*, thou liest.

TAILOR
130   Why, here is the note of the fashion to testify.

PETRUCHIO
Read it.

GRUMIO
The note lies in's throat, if he say I said so.

TAILOR
[*Reads.*]*"Imprimis*, a loose-bodied gown"*—

GRUMIO
Master, if ever I said loose-bodied gown, sew me in the skirts of
135   it, and beat me to death with a bottom of brown thread. I said
a gown.

PETRUCHIO
Proceed.

TAILOR
[*Reads.*] "With a small compass'd cape"—

---

125 *fac'd* means both "defiantly opposed" and "trimmed."   127 *brav'd* means both
"defied" and "elegantly made."   134 *loose-bodied gown* a dress for home wear. But a
pun on the word "loose" also implies that the dress is for a prostitute.

GRUMIO
    I didn't give him any orders; I just gave him the stuff to make it.

TAILOR
    But how did you want it made?

GRUMIO
    Indeed, sir, with a needle and thread.

TAILOR
    But didn't you ask for me to cut it?

GRUMIO
125   You've cut lots of clothes.

TAILOR
    Yes, I have.

GRUMIO
    Well don't cut me. You've dressed many men in fancy clothes; don't
        defy me. I won't
    be cut or defied. I tell you, I told your master to cut
    out the gown, but I did not tell him to cut it to pieces. Therefore,
        you're lying.

TAILOR
130   Why, here's a written order for the dress design to back me up.

PETRUCHIO
    Read it.

GRUMIO
    The note is a calculating liar if it says I said so.

TAILOR *(Reads)*
    "First, a loose-fitting dress."

GRUMIO
    Master, if I ever said a loose-fitting dress, sew me up in the skirts of
135   it, and beat me to death with a spool of brown thread. I said
    a gown.

PETRUCHIO
    Go on.

TAILOR *(Reads)*
    "With a small, circular cape."

GRUMIO
    I confess the cape.

TAILOR
140   [*Reads.*] "With a trunk sleeve"—

GRUMIO
    I confess two sleeves.

TAILOR
    [*Reads.*] "The sleeves curiously cut."

PETRUCHIO
    Ay, there's the villainy.

GRUMIO
    Error i' th' bill, sir; error i' th' bill. I commanded the sleeves
145   should be cut out and sew'd up again; and that I'll prove upon
    thee, though thy little finger be armed in a thimble.

TAILOR
    This is true that I say; an I had thee in place where, thou shouldst
    know it.

GRUMIO
    I am for thee straight. Take thou the bill, give me thy mete-yard,
150   and spare not me.

HORTENSIO.
    God-a-mercy, Grumio! then he shall have no odds.

PETRUCHIO
    Well, sir, in brief, the gown is not for me.

GRUMIO
    You are i' th' right, sir; 'tis for my mistress.

PETRUCHIO
    Go, take it up unto thy master's use.

GRUMIO
155   Villain, not for thy life! Take up my mistress' gown for thy
    master's use!

PETRUCHIO
    Why, sir, what's your conceit in that?

---

144 *bill* means both "a written order" and a kind of weapon.   156 *use* Grumio plays on
the meaning of use "to have sex with."

GRUMIO
I agree that's what I said about the cape.

TAILOR *(Reads)*
140   "With a full sleeve."

GRUMIO
I admit to ordering two sleeves.

TAILOR *(Reads)*
"The sleeves cut with fine details."

PETRUCHIO
Yes, there's the villainy.

GRUMIO
Error in the note, sir; error in the note! I ordered that the sleeves
145   should be cut out and sewed up again, and I'll fight you to prove
it, even if your little finger is armored in a thimble.

TAILOR
What I told you was the truth—and if we were in the right place, you'd
find that out.

GRUMIO
I'm ready for you right now. You take the note and give me your yardstick
150   and don't pull any punches.

HORTENSIO
Heavens, Grumio! Then he won't have a chance.

PETRUCHIO
Well, sir, in short: I don't think the dress suits me.

GRUMIO
You're right there, sir; it's for my lady.

PETRUCHIO
Go and pick it up for your master to use however he can.

GRUMIO
155   Don't you dare, you rascal! Pick up my lady's dress for your
master to use?

PETRUCHIO
What notion is bothering you, sir?

GRUMIO

O, sir, the conceit is deeper than you think for.
Take up my mistress' gown to his master's use!
160   O, fie, fie, fie!

PETRUCHIO

[*Aside.*] Hortensio, say thou wilt see the tailor paid.—
Go take it hence; be gone, and say no more.

HORTENSIO

Tailor, I'll pay thee for thy gown tomorrow;
Take no unkindness of his hasty words.
165   Away! I say; commend me to thy master.
       [*Exit Tailor.*]

PETRUCHIO

Well, come, my Kate; we will unto your father's
Even in these honest mean habiliments.
Our purses shall be proud, our garments poor,
For 'tis the mind that makes the body rich;
170   And as the sun breaks through the darkest clouds,
So honour peereth in the meanest habit.
What, is the jay more precious than the lark,
Because his feathers are more beautiful?
Or is the adder better than the eel,
175   Because his painted skin contents the eye?
O, no, good Kate; neither art thou the worse
For this poor furniture and mean array.
If thou account'st it shame, lay it on me;
And therefore frolic. We will hence forthwith,
180   To feast and sport us at thy father's house.
Go, call my men, and let us straight to him,
And bring our horses unto Long-lane end.
There will we mount, and thither walk on foot.
Let's see; I think 'tis now some seven o'clock,
185   And well we may come there by dinner-time.

KATHERINA

I dare assure you, sir, 'tis almost two;
And 'twill be supper-time ere you come there.

GRUMIO
    O, sir, the meaning is deeper than you think.
    To pick up my lady's gown so his master can use her as he likes?
160   O shame, shame, shame!

PETRUCHIO *(to Hortensio privately)*
    Hortensio, see that the tailor is paid.
    (To Tailor) Go, and take the dress. Go, and not another word.

HORTENSIO *(privately to Tailor)*
    Tailor, I'll pay you for the dress tomorrow.
    Don't resent his hot-tempered words.
165   Go, I said! Say hello to your master for me.
             Exit TAILOR.

PETRUCHIO
    Well, come, my Kate. We'll go to your father's
    just in these decent, simple clothes.
    Our purses will be rich if our clothes are poor
    because it's the mind that makes the body rich.
170   And just as the sun breaks through the darkest clouds,
    so honor shines through the crudest clothing.
    Why, is the jay more treasured than the lark
    because his feathers are more beautiful?
    Or is the adder better than the eel
175   because his colorful skin is nice to look at?
    No, good Kate. And neither are you any the worse
    for your simple outfit and cheap dress.
    If you are embarrassed, blame it on me.
    So, be happy. We'll leave here at once
180   to feast and enjoy ourselves at your father's house.
    (To Grumio) Go call my men, and let's set out for his house right now.
    Bring our horses to the end of Long Lane—
    we'll walk there and mount at that point.
    Let's see, I think it's now about seven o'clock,
185   and we'll probably be there about noon.

KATHERINE
    I assure you, sir, it's almost two,
    and it will be suppertime before we reach my father's house.

PETRUCHIO
  It shall be seven ere I go to horse.
  Look, what I speak, or do, or think to do,
190   You are still crossing it. Sirs, let't alone,
  I will not go to-day, and ere I do,
  It shall be what o'clock I say it is.

HORTENSIO
  [*Aside.*] Why, so this gallant will command the sun.
      [*Exeunt.*]

Scene iv: [*Padua. Before Baptista's house.*] *Enter* TRANIO, *and
the* PEDANT *dressed like* VINCENTIO.

TRANIO
  Sir, this is the house; please it you that I call?

PEDANT
  Ay, what else? And, but I be deceived,
  Signior Baptista may remember me,
  Near twenty years ago, in Genoa,
5   Where we were lodgers at the Pegasus.

TRANIO
  'Tis well; and hold your own, in any case,
  With such austerity as 'longeth to a father.
      Enter BIONDELLO.

PEDANT
  I warrant you. But, sir, here comes your boy;
  'Twere good he were school'd.

TRANIO
10   Fear you not him. Sirrah Biondello,
  Now do your duty throughly, I advise you.
  Imagine 'twere the right Vincentio.

BIONDELLO
  Tut, fear not me.

TRANIO
  But hast thou done thy errand to Baptista?

---

5 *Pegasus* a common name for an inn.

PETRUCHIO
    It will be seven before we leave.
    Whatever I say or do or plan to do,
190   you always contradict me. Gentlemen, forget it.
    I'm not leaving today. And before I do,
    it will be the time *I* say it is.

HORTENSIO *(Aside)*
    Why this lordly man will give the sun orders!
        They exit.

Act IV, Scene iv: Padua. Before Baptista's house. Enter TRANIO *and the* PEDANT, *dressed like Vincentio.*

TRANIO
    Sir, this is the house. Should I stop and knock?

PEDANT
    Certainly; why not? Unless I miss my guess,
    Signior Baptista may remember me
    from about twenty years ago in Genoa,
5   when we both stayed at the Pegasus.

TRANIO
    That's well acted. And play your part, doing everything
    with the dignity of a father.
        Enter BIONDELLO

PEDANT
    I promise you, I will. But sir, here comes your young servant—
    you'd better let him in on the secret.

TRANIO
10   Don't worry about him. My servant, Biondello,
    do your duty thoroughly now, I warn you.
    You must imagine he's the real Vincentio.

BIONDELLO
    Nonsense, don't worry about me.

TRANIO
    But have you run your errand to Baptista?

BIONDELLO

15   I told him that your father was at Venice,
And that you look'd for him this day in Padua.

TRANIO

Thou'art a tall fellow; hold thee that to drink.
Here comes Baptista; set your countenance, sir.
Enter BAPTISTA *and* LUCENTIO: PEDANT *booted
and bare-headed.*
Signior Baptista, you are happily met.

20   [*To the Pedant*.] Sir, this is the gentleman I told you of.
I pray you, stand good father to me now,
Give me Bianca for my patrimony.

PEDANT

Soft, son!
Sir, by your leave. Having come to Padua

25   To gather in some debts, my son Lucentio
Made me acquainted with a weighty cause
Of love between your daughter and himself;
And, for the good report I hear of you,
And for the love he beareth to your daughter

30   And she to him, to stay him not too long,
I am content, in a good father's care,
To have him match'd; and if you please to like
No worse than I, upon some agreement
Me shall you find ready and willing

35   With one consent to have her so bestow'd;
For curious I cannot be with you,
Signior Baptista, of whom I hear so well.

BAPTISTA

Sir, pardon me in what I have to say.
Your plainness and your shortness please me well.

40   Right true it is, your son Lucentio here
Doth love my daughter and she loveth him,
Or both dissemble deeply their affections;
And therefore, if you say no more than this,
That like a father you will deal with him

45   And pass my daughter a sufficient dower,

---

s.d. *booted and bare-headed* the Pedant is wearing boots as if he had just arrived from a
trip. He doffs his hat in courtesy to Baptista.

BIONDELLO

15   I told him that your father was in Venice
and that you expected him in Padua today.

TRANIO

You're a wonderful fellow—save this for a drink.
(Gives him a coin.) Here comes Baptista. Assume your proper style, sir.
    Enter BAPTISTA *and* LUCENTIO. PEDANT *is wearing*
      boots and not wearing a hat.
Signior Baptista, this is a fortunate meeting.
20   *(To the Pedant)* Sir, this is the gentleman I told you about.
I ask you to act like a good father to me, now.
Give me Bianca for my patrimony.

PEDANT

Slow down, son!
Sir, if you'll permit me to explain—having come to Padua
25   to collect some debts, my son Lucentio
told me about a serious case
of love between your daughter and himself.
And because of your good reputation
and his love for your daughter
30   and her love for him, I won't delay him too long.
I'm satisfied, like any good father,
to have him married. And if you're content to favor the marriage
as much as I am, then—after a marriage settlement has been made—
you'll find me ready and willing,
35   and with my hearty approval, to agree to her marriage to him.
For I can't be picky about the little details with you,
Signior Baptista, of whom I've heard so many good things.

BAPTISTA

Sir, please excuse me for what I'm going to say.
Your frankness and conciseness please me a great deal.
40   It's certainly true that your son Lucentio, here,
loves my daughter and that she loves him—
or they're both wonderful pretenders.
So, if you promise just this,
that you'll treat him like a father
45   and guarantee my daughter a sufficient marriage settlement,

The match is made, and all is done.
Your son shall have my daughter with consent.

TRANIO

I thank you, sir. Where, then, to you know best
We be affied and such assurance ta'en
50   As shall with either part's agreement stand?

BAPTISTA

Not in my house, Lucentio; for, you know,
Pitchers have ears, and I have many servants;
Besides, old Gremio is heark'ning still,
And happily we might be interrupted.

TRANIO

55   Then at my lodging, an it like you.
There doth my father lie; and there, this night,
We'll pass the business privately and well.
Send for your daughter by your servant here;
My boy shall fetch the scrivener presently.
60   The worst is this, that, at so slender warning,
You are like to have a thin and slender pittance.

BAPTISTA

It likes me well. Cambio, hie you home,
And bid Bianca make her ready straight;
And, if you will, tell what hath happened:
65   Lucentio's father is arriv'd in Padua,
And how she's like to be Lucentio's wife.
          [*Exit Lucentio.*]

BIONDELLO

I pray the gods she may with all my heart!

TRANIO

Dally not with the gods, but get thee gone.
          [*Exit Biondello.*]
Signior Baptista, shall I lead the way?
70   Welcome! one mess is like to be your cheer;
Come, sir; we will better it in Pisa.

I'll agree to the marriage, and it will be settled.
Your son will have my daughter with my blessings.

TRANIO
    I thank you, sir. Where, then, do you think it's best
    that we be formally engaged and give pledges
50   that will suit both parties?

BAPTISTA
    Not in my house, Lucentio. You know
    that pitchers have ears, and I have my servants.
    Besides, old Gremio is always eavesdropping,
    and perhaps we might be interrupted.

TRANIO
55   Then we'll do it at my house, if you like.
    That's where my father is staying, and there, tonight,
    we'll settle the business secretly and satisfactorily.
    Send your servant here to get your daughter.
       (He indicates Lucentio and winks at him.)
    My servant will fetch the notary immediately.
60   The worst you can expect is this: that at such short notice,
    you're likely to get a scanty, light meal.

BAPTISTA
    That suits me well. Cambio, hurry home
    and tell Bianca to get ready right away.
    And if you will, tell her what has happened—
65   that Lucentio's father has arrived in Padua
    and that she's likely to become Lucentio's wife.
       Exit LUCENTIO.

BIONDELLO
    I pray to the gods with all my heart that she may!

TRANIO
    Don't waste time with the gods, but get going.
       Exit BIONDELLO.
    Signior Baptista, shall I lead the way?
70   You are welcome, though one course is likely to be all the meal you'll get.
    Come, sir, we'll do better for you in Pisa.

BAPTISTA
> I follow you.
> > [*Exeunt omnes.*]
> > *Re-enter* LUCENTIO *and* BIONDELLO.

BIONDELLO
> Cambio!

LUCENTIO
> What say'st thou, Biondello?

BIONDELLO
75 You saw my master wink and laugh upon you?

LUCENTIO
> Biondello, what of that?

BIONDELLO
> Faith, nothing; but has left me here behind, to expound the
> meaning or moral of his signs and tokens.

LUCENTIO
> I pray thee, moralize them.

BIONDELLO
80 Then thus. Baptista is safe, talking with the deceiving father of
> a deceitful son.

LUCENTIO
> And what of him?

BIONDELLO
> His daughter is to be brought by you to the supper.

LUCENTIO
> And then?

BIONDELLO
85 The old priest of Saint Luke's church is at your command at all
> hours.

LUCENTIO
> And what of all this?

BIONDELLO
> I cannot tell. Expect they are busied about a counterfeit assurance;

BAPTISTA
I'll follow you.
  Exit.
  Enter LUCENTIO *and* BIONDELLO.

BIONDELLO
Cambio!

LUCENTIO
What did you want to say, Biondello?

BIONDELLO
75 You saw my "master" wink and laugh at you?

LUCENTIO
So what, Biondello?

BIONDELLO
Really, nothing—except that he has left me behind here to explain the meaning or significance of his signs and hints.

LUCENTIO
Please explain them.

BIONDELLO
80 It's like this. Baptista is taken care of, talking with the fake father of a fake son.

LUCENTIO
And what about him?

BIONDELLO
You're supposed to take his daughter to their supper.

LUCENTIO
And then?

BIONDELLO
85 The old priest at Saint Luke's church is ready and waiting for you at any time.

LUCENTIO
So what about all this?

BIONDELLO
I don't know—except that while they're busy with a fake marriage settlement,

take you assurance of her, *"cum privilegio ad imprimendum*
90   *solum."* To th' church! Take the priest, clerk, and some sufficient
honest witnesses.
  If this be not that you look for, I have no more to say,
  But bid Bianca farewell for ever and a day.

LUCENTIO
Hear'st thou, Biondello?

BIONDELLO
95   I cannot tarry. I knew a wench married in an afternoon as she
went to the garden for parsley to stuff a rabbit, and so may you,
sir; and so, adieu, sir. My master hath appointed me to go to Saint
Luke's, to bid the priest be ready to come against you come with
your appendix.
    [*Exit.*]

LUCENTIO
100   I may, and will, if she be so contented.
  She will be pleased; then wherefore should I doubt?
  Hap what hap may, I'll roundly go about her;
  It shall go hard if Cambio go without her.
    [*Exit.*]

Scene v: [*A public road.*] *Enter* PETRUCHIO, KATHERINA,
HORTENSIO, *and* Servants.

PETRUCHIO
Come on, a God's name; once more toward our father's.
  Good Lord, how bright and goodly shines the moon!

KATHERINA
The moon! the sun. It is not moonlight now.

PETRUCHIO
I say it is the moon that shines so bright.

KATHERINA
5   I know it is the sun that shines so bright.

PETRUCHIO
Now, by my mother's son, and that's myself,
  It shall be moon, or star, or what I list,

89-90 *cum privilegio ad imprimendum solum* a phrase giving a printer the sole rights to print.

you should settle with her on the exclusive right of
90   printing. Go to the church! Get the priest, a clerk, and enough
honest witnesses.
If this isn't the chance that you were looking for, I'll shut up.
But you might as well say goodbye to Bianca for forever.

LUCENTIO
Are you listening, Biondello?

BIONDELLO
95   I can't stay any longer. I knew a woman married in an afternoon as she
went to the garden to get parsley for stuffing for a rabbit. You could, too,
sir. So, goodbye, sir. My "master" has ordered me to go to Saint
Luke's to tell the priest to be prepared for you when you come with
your wife.
    Exit.

LUCENTIO
100   I may and will do that, if she is willing.
She will be pleased—so what am I doubting about?
Let what happens, happen. I'll go after her right now.
Only a disaster can keep Cambio from marrying her now.
    Exit.

Act IV, Scene v: A public road. Enter PETRUCHIO, KATE,
HORTENSIO, *and* SERVANTS.

PETRUCHIO
Come on, in God's name. Let's go once more to my father-in-law's.
Good Lord, how bright and well the moon is shining!

KATHERINE
The moon! You mean the sun; the moon isn't out now.

PETRUCHIO
I say it's the moon that's shining so brightly.

KATHERINE
5   I know it's the sun that's shining so brightly.

PETRUCHIO
Now, by my mother's son, and that means me,
it will be the moon, or a star, or whatever I please

Or ere I journey to your father's house.—
Go on, and fetch our horses back again.—
10   Evermore cross'd and cross'd; nothing but cross'd!

HORTENSIO
Say as he says, or we shall never go.

KATHERINA
Forward, I pray, since we have come so far,
And be it moon, or sun, or what you please.
An if you please to call it a rush-candle,
15   Henceforth I vow it shall be so for me.

PETRUCHIO
I say it is the moon.

KATHERINA
            I know it is the moon.

PETRUCHIO
Nay, then you lie; it is the blessed sun.

KATHERINA
Then, God be bless'd, it is the blessed sun;
20   But sun it is not, when you say it is not;
And the moon changes even as your mind.
What you will have it nam'd, even that it is;
And so it shall be so for Katherine.

HORTENSIO
Petruchio, go thy ways; the field is won.

PETRUCHIO
25   Well, forward, forward! thus the bowl should run,
And not unluckily against the bias.
But, soft! company is coming here.
      Enter VINCENTIO.
[*To Vincentio.*] Good morrow, gentle mistress;
   where away?
Tell me, sweet Kate, and tell me truly too,
30   Hast thou beheld a fresher gentlewoman?
Such war of white and red within her cheeks!
What stars do spangle heaven with such beauty,

---

14 *rush-candle* a candle made from a rush, coated with grease. 26 *bias* is lead in the side
of a bowling bowl that causes the ball to swerve when bowled properly.

before we go back to your father's house.

(To servants) Go and bring our horses back again.

10   I'm constantly contradicted and contradicted; nothing but contradicted.

HORTENSIO

Say what he says or we'll never get moving.

KATHERINE

Please, let's go on since we've come so far,

and let it be the moon or sun or whatever you want.

If you want to call it a rush candle,

15   I swear that from now on I'll call it that.

PETRUCHIO

I say it is the moon.

KATHERINE

I know it is the moon.

PETRUCHIO

Well then, you're lying; it's the blessed sun.

KATHERINE

Then, bless God, it's the blessed sun!

20   But it's not the sun when you say it isn't,

and the moon changes when you change your mind.

Whatever you want it to be called, it will be called exactly that,

and Kate will accept whatever you say.

HORTENSIO

Petruchio, go on; you've won the fight.

PETRUCHIO

25   Well, let's go, let's go! The bowling ball should roll like this

and not unluckily with a bad curve.

But wait a minute! Someone is approaching.

    Enter VINCENTIO.

(To Vincentio) Good day, gentle lady; where are you going?

Tell me, sweet Kate, and tell me the truth, too,

30   have you ever seen a more glowing gentlewoman?

Such a mix of white and red on her cheeks!

What stars sparkle in the heaven with the beauty

As those two eyes become that heavenly face?
Fair lovely maid, once more good day to thee.
35   Sweet Kate, embrace her for her beauty's sake.

HORTENSIO
'A will make the man mad, to make a woman of him.

KATHERINA
Young budding virgin, fair and fresh and sweet,
Whither away, or where is thy abode?
Happy the parents of so fair a child!
40   Happier the man, whom favourable stars
Allots thee for his lovely bed-fellow!

PETRUCHIO
Why, how now, Kate! I hope thou art not mad.
This is a man, old, wrinkled, faded, withered,
And not a maiden, as thou say'st he is.

KATHERINA
45   Pardon, old father, my mistaking eyes,
That have been so bedazzled with the sun
That every thing I look on seemeth green.
Now I perceive thou art a reverend father.
Pardon, I pray thee, for my mad mistaking.

PETRUCHIO
50   Do, good old grandsire; and withal make known
Which way thou travellest. If along with us,
We shall be joyful of thy company.

VINCENTIO
Fair sir, and you my merry mistress,
That with your strange encounter much amaz'd me,
55   My name is call'd Vincentio; my dwelling Pisa;
And bound I am to Padua, there to visit
A son of mine, which long I have not seen.

PETRUCHIO
What is his name?

VINCENTIO
                    Lucentio, gentle sir.

that those two eyes shine in her heavenly face?
Pretty, lovely lady, I say good day to you once again.

35   Sweet Kate, give her a hug for the sake of her beauty.

HORTENSIO
He will make the man mad if he tries to make a woman out of him.

KATHERINE
Young, blooming virgin, pretty and fresh and sweet,
where are you going, or where do you live?
The parents of such a pretty child must feel lucky.

40   The man whom good fortune lets have
you for his lovely mate will be even luckier.

PETRUCHIO
Why, what's wrong, Kate! I hope you're not crazy.
This is a man, old, wrinkled, faded, and withered
and not a girl as you said he was.

KATHERINE
45   Forgive me, old sir. My mistaken eyes
have been so dazzled by the sun
that everything I look at seems young.
Now I see that you are a venerable gentleman.
Please forgive me for my crazy mistake.

PETRUCHIO
50   Please do, good old gentleman. And now, tell us
which way you're traveling. If you're going our way,
we'd be happy to have your company.

VINCENTIO
Good sir, and you, my merry lady—
who shocked me so much by your strange greeting—

55   my name is Vincentio. I live in Pisa.
And I'm headed for Padua to visit
a son of mine there, whom I haven't seen in a long time.

PETRUCHIO
What's his name?

VINCENTIO
Lucentio, good sir.

PETRUCHIO

60   Happily met; the happier for thy son.
      And now by law, as well as reverend age,
      I may entitle thee my loving father.
      The sister to my wife, this gentlewoman,
      Thy son by this hath married. Wonder not,
65   Nor be not griev'd; she is of good esteem,
      Her dowry wealthy, and of worthy birth;
      Beside, so qualified as may beseem
      The spouse of any noble gentleman.
      Let me embrace with old Vincentio,
70   And wander we to see thy honest son,
      Who will of thy arrival be full joyous.

VINCENTIO

      But is this true, or is it else your pleasure,
      Like pleasant travellers, to break a jest
      Upon the company you overtake?

HORTENSIO

75   I do assure thee, father, so it is.

PETRUCHIO

      Come, go along, and see the truth hereof;
      For our first merriment hath made thee jealous.
          [*Exeunt all but Hortensio.*]

HORTENSIO

      Well, Petruchio, this has put me in heart.
      Have to my widow! and if she be froward,
80   Then hast thou taught Hortensio to be untoward.
          [*Exit.*]

Act V, Scene i: [*Padua. Before Lucentio's house.*] *Enter*
BIONDELLO, LUCENTIO, *and* BIANCA. GREMIO *is out
before.*

BIONDELLO

      Softly and swiftly, sir; for the priest is ready.

PETRUCHIO

60   This is a fortunate meeting—the more fortunate for your son.
    And now legally, as well as out of respect to your dignified age,
    I may call you my loving father.
    The sister to my wife—this lady here—
    has married your son by now. Don't be astonished
65   or sad. She is well-respected,
    her dowry is big, and she's from a good family.
    Besides that, she has qualities that are proper
    for the wife of any noble gentleman.
    Let me hug you, old Vincentio,
70   and let's go to see your honest son
    who will be delighted by your arrival.

VINCENTIO

    Is this true? Or else is it your idea of fun,
    like fun-loving travelers, to pull a trick
    on the people you overtake?

HORTENSIO

75   I assure you, father, it's as he said.

PETRUCHIO

    Come, go along with us, and see that it's true,
    since our first jokes made you suspicious.
        Exit all but HORTENSIO.

HORTENSIO

    Well, Petruchio, this has made me jealous.
    Onward to my widow! And if she's stubborn,
80   then you've taught Hortensio how to get his way.
        Exit.

Act V, Scene i: Padua. The street in front of Lucentio's house. Enter
BIONDELLO, LUCENTIO, *and* BIANCA; GREMIO *precedes the rest
and does not see the others.*

BIONDELLO

    Go quietly and quickly, sir. The priest is ready.

LUCENTIO

I fly, Biondello; but they may chance to need thee at home, therefore leave us.

[*Exeunt Lucentio and Bianca.*]

BIONDELLO

5   Nay, faith, I'll see the church a your back; and then come back to my master's as soon as I can.

[*Exit.*]

GREMIO

I marvel Cambio comes not all this while.

Enter PETRUCHIO, KATHERINA, VINCENTIO,
GRUMIO, *with* Attendants.

PETRUCHIO

Sir, here's the door, this is Lucentio's house.
My father's bears more toward the marketplace;
Thither must I, and here I leave you, sir.

VINCENTIO

10   You shall not choose but drink before you go.
I think I shall command your welcome here,
And, by all likelihood, some cheer is toward.

[*Knocks.*]

GREMIO

They're busy within; you were best knock louder.

PEDANT *looks out of the window.*

PEDANT

What's he that knocks as he would beat down the gate?

VINCENTIO

15   Is Signior Lucentio within, sir?

PEDANT

He's within, sir, but not to be spoken withal.

VINCENTIO

What if a man bring him a hundred pound or two, to make merry withal?

LUCENTIO
I'll rush, Biondello. But they may need you at home.
Therefore, leave us.
Exit with BIANCA.

BIONDELLO
No, I'll see you safely to the church and then go back
5   to my "master's" as fast as I can.
Exit.

GREMIO
I'm amazed that Cambio has not come yet.
Enter PETRUCHIO, KATE, VINCENTIO,
GRUMIO *and* ATTENDANTS.

PETRUCHIO
Sir, here's the door—this is Lucentio's house.
My father-in-law's house lies near the marketplace.
I must go there, so I'll leave you here, sir.

VINCENTIO
10   You must have a drink before you go.
I think I'll be able to guarantee your welcome here,
and it's likely that some entertainment will be available.
(Knocks.)

GREMIO
They're busy inside. You'd better knock louder.
PEDANT *looks out of the window.*

PEDANT
Who's knocking there as if he'd beat down the door?

VINCENTIO
15   Is Signior Lucentio at home, sir?

PEDANT
He's inside, sir, but you can't talk to him.

VINCENTIO
What if someone brought him a hundred or two hundred pounds to
entertain
with?

PEDANT

Keep your hundred pounds to yourself; he shall need none, so

20   long as I live.

PETRUCHIO

Nay, I told you your son was well beloved in Padua. Do you hear, sir? To leave frivolous circumstances, I pray you, tell Signior Lucentio that his father is come from Pisa and is here at the door to speak with him.

PEDANT

25   Thou liest. His father is come from Padua and is here looking out at the window.

VINCENTIO

Art thou his father?

PEDANT

Ay, sir, so his mother says, if I may believe her.

PETRUCHIO [*To Vincentio.*]

Why, how now, gentleman! Why, this is flat knavery, to take

30   upon you another man's name.

PEDANT

Lay hands on the villain. I believe 'a means to cozen somebody in this city under my countenance.

   Re-enter BIONDELLO.

BIONDELLO

I have seen them in the church together; God send 'em good shipping! But who is here? Mine old master Vincentio! Now we

35   are undone and brought to nothing.

VINCENTIO [*Seeing Biondello.*]

Come hither, crackhemp.

BIONDELLO

I hope I may choose, sir.

VINCENTIO

Come hither, you rogue. What, have you forgot me?

BIONDELLO

Forgot you? No, sir; I could not forget you, for I never saw you

40   before in all my life.

PEDANT

Keep your hundred pounds. He won't need any of that as
20   long as I'm alive.

PETRUCHIO

See, I told you that your son was well loved in Padua. You see,
sir? *(To Pedant)* To put aside trivial details, please tell Signior
Lucentio that his father has arrived from Pisa and is here outside
waiting to speak with him.

PEDANT

25   You're lying! His father has arrived from Padua and is here looking
out the window.

VINCENTIO

Are you his father?

PEDANT

Yes, sir, so his mother says—if I can believe her.

PETRUCHIO *(to Vincentio)*

Why, what's this, gentleman? Why, this is outright deception to assume
30   another man's name!

PEDANT

Grab that liar! I think he intends to cheat somebody
in this city pretending he's me.
          Enter BIONDELLO.

BIONDELLO *(to himself)*

I saw them to the church together. God give them good
luck! But who's this here? My old master, Vincentio! Now we're
35   done for, and our plan is ruined.

VINCENTIO

Come here, you gallows bird.

BIONDELLO

I hope I have some choice about that, sir.

VINCENTIO

Come here, you villain. Well? Have you forgotten me?

BIONDELLO

Forgotten you? No, sir. I can't forget you because I never saw you
40   before in my entire life.

VINCENTIO

What, you notorious villain, didst thou never see thy master's father, Vincentio?

BIONDELLO

What, my old worshipful old master? Yes, marry, sir; see where he looks out of the window.

VINCENTIO

45   Is't so, indeed?

[*Beats Biondello.*]

BIONDELLO

Help, help, help! here's a madman will murder me.

[*Exit.*]

PEDANT

Help, son! help, Signior Baptista!

[*Exit from above.*]

PETRUCHIO

Prithee, Kate, let's stand aside and see the end of this controversy.

[*They retire.*]

Re-enter PEDANT *below,* TRANIO, BAPTISTA,

and Servants.

TRANIO

Sir, what are you that offer to beat my servant?

VINCENTIO

50   What am I, sir! Nay, what are you, sir? O immortal gods! O fine villain! A silken doublet! a velvet hose! a scarlet cloak! and a copatain hat! O, I am undone! I am undone! While I play the good husband at home, my son and my servant spend all at the university.

TRANIO

55   How now! what's the matter?

BAPTISTA

What, is the man lunatic?

VINCENTIO
 What did you say, you outrageous villain! Have you never seen your master's
 father, Vincentio, before?

BIONDELLO
 What? My old, dignified, old master? Yes, indeed, sir—see him; he's looking out the window.

VINCENTIO
45 Is that so?
 (He beats Biondello.)

BIONDELLO
 Help, help, help! This madman here is trying to murder me.
 Exit.

PEDANT
 Help, son! Help, Signior Baptista!
 (Leaves window.)

PETRUCHIO
 Come, Kate, let's stand over here and see how this argument comes out.
 (They step aside.)
 Enter PEDANT *(below),* TRANIO, BAPTISTA,
 and SERVANTS.

TRANIO
 Sir, who are you that you dare to beat my servant?

VINCENTIO
50 Who am I, sir! Well! Who are you, sir? O immortal gods! O you well-dressed
 menial! Wearing a silken doublet! Velvet breeches! A scarlet cloak! And a
 tall, cone-shaped hat! O, I've been betrayed! I've been betrayed! While I act the
 careful manager at home, my son and my servant spend everything at the university!

TRANIO
55 What's wrong? What's the matter?

BAPTISTA
 Is the man mad?

TRANIO

Sir, you seem a sober ancient gentleman by your habit, but your words show you a madman. Why, sir, what 'cerns it you if I wear pearl and gold? I thank my good father, I am able to maintain it.

VINCENTIO

60   Thy father! O villain! he is a sailmaker in Bergamo.

BAPTISTA

You mistake, sir, you mistake, sir. Pray, what do you think is his name?

VINCENTIO

His name! as if I knew not his name! I have brought him up ever since he was three years old, and his name is Tranio.

PEDANT

65   Away, away, mad ass! his name is Lucentio; and he is mine only son, and heir to the lands of me, Signior Vincentio.

VINCENTIO

Lucentio! O, he hath murd'red his master! Lay hold on him, I charge you, in the Duke's name. O, my son, my son! Tell me, thou villain, where is my son Lucentio?

TRANIO

70   Call forth an officer.

[*Enter one with an officer.*]

Carry this mad knave to the gaol. Father Baptista, I charge you see that he be forthcoming.

VINCENTIO

Carry me to the gaol!

GREMIO

Stay, officer; he shall not go to prison.

BAPTISTA

75   Talk not, Signior Gremio; I say he shall go to prison.

GREMIO

Take heed, Signior Baptista, lest you be cony-catch'd in this business. I dare swear this is the right Vincentio.

TRANIO

Sir, you seem to be a dignified old gentleman from your manner, but you speak like a madman. Really, sir, why should it concern you if I wear pearls and gold? Thanks to my good father, I can afford it.

VINCENTIO

60   Your father! O you wretch! Your father is a sailmaker in Bergamo.

BAPTISTA

You're mistaken, sir; you're really mistaken, sir. Just what do you think his name is?

VINCENTIO

His name! As if I didn't know his name! I've raised him ever since he was three years old! His name is Tranio!

PEDANT

65   Go on, go on, you mad fool! His name is Lucentio, and he's my only son and heir to my lands—the lands of Signior Vincentio.

VINCENTIO

Lucentio! O, then he's murdered his master! Grab him, I order you in the duke's name. O my son, my son! Tell me, you wretch, where's my son Lucentio?

TRANIO

70   Call out an officer.
        Enter an OFFICER.
Take this mad rascal to the jail. Father Baptista, I leave it to you to see that he's available for trial.

VINCENTIO

Take me to jail?

GREMIO

Wait a minute, officer. You can't take him to prison.

BAPTISTA

75   Shut up, Signior Gremio. I say he will go to prison.

GREMIO

Beware, Signior Baptista, that you aren't tricked in this business. I dare swear to you that this is the real Vincentio.

PEDANT
Swear, if thou dar'st.

GREMIO
Nay, I dare not swear it.

TRANIO
80   Then thou wert best say that I am not Lucentio.

GREMIO
Yes, I know thee to be Signior Lucentio.

BAPTISTA
Away with the dotard! To the gaol with him!
    Re-enter BIONDELLO, *with* LUCENTIO *and*
    BIANCA.

VINCENTIO
Thus strangers may be hal'd and abus'd. O monstrous villain!

BIONDELLO
O! we are spoil'd and—yonder he is. Deny him, forswear him,
85   or else we are all undone.
    [*Exeunt Biondello, Tranio, and Pedant, as fast
    as may be.*]

LUCENTIO [*Kneeling.*]
Pardon, sweet father.

VINCENTIO
          Lives my sweet son?

BIANCA
Pardon, dear father.

BAPTISTA
          How hast thou offended?
90   Where is Lucentio?

LUCENTIO
Here's Lucentio,
Right son to the right Vincentio,
That have by marriage made thy daughter mine,
While counterfeit supposes blear'd thine eyne.

PEDANT
Swear if you dare.

GREMIO
No, I don't dare swear it.

TRANIO
80   Then maybe you'd dare say that I'm not Lucentio.

GREMIO
Yes, I know you're Signior Lucentio.

BAPTISTA
Take away that old fool. Take him to jail!

VINCENTIO
So, you let strangers be pestered and abused! O, you monstrous villain!
            Enter BIONDELLO, LUCENTIO, *and* BIANCA.

BIONDELLO
O, we're in for it! There he is—deny he is who he says he is, refuse to recognize him,
85   or else we'll all be caught.
            Exit BIONDELLO, TRANIO, *and* PEDANT *very quickly.*

LUCENTIO *(kneels)*
Forgive me, my sweet father.

VINCENTIO
Is my sweet son alive?

BIANCA
Forgive me, dear father.

BAPTISTA
What did you do wrong?
90   Where is Lucentio?

LUCENTIO
I'm Lucentio,
the real son to the real Vincentio
who has made your daughter mine by marrying her
while pretenders fooled your eyes.

GREMIO

95   Here's packing, with a witness, to deceive us all!

VINCENTIO

Where is that damned villain Tranio,
That fac'd and brav'd me in this matter so?

BAPTISTA

Why, tell me, is not this my Cambio?

BIANCA

Cambio is chang'd into Lucentio.

LUCENTIO

100   Love wrought these miracles. Bianca's love
Made me exchange my state with Tranio,
While he did bear my countenance in the town;
And happily I have arriv'd at last
Unto the wished haven of my bliss.

105   What Tranio did, myself enforc'd him to;
Then pardon him, sweet father, for my sake.

VINCENTIO

I'll slit the villain's nose, that would have sent me to the gaol.

BAPTISTA

But do you hear, sir? Have you married my daughter without
asking my good will?

VINCENTIO

110   Fear not, Baptista; we will content you, go to; but I will in to
be reveng'd for this villainy.
      [*Exit.*]

BAPTISTA

And I, to sound the depth of this knavery.
      [*Exit.*]

LUCENTIO

Look not pale, Bianca; thy father will not frown.
      [*Exeunt Lucentio and Bianca.*]

GREMIO

95 Here's scheming, blatant scheming, to fool everyone!

VINCENTIO

  Where is that damned rascal, Tranio,
  who defied me and betrayed me in this business?

BAPTISTA

  Why, tell me, isn't this my Cambio?

BIANCA

  Cambio has changed into Lucentio.

LUCENTIO

100 Love has brought about these miracles. Bianca's love
  has led me to change places with Tranio
  while he played my part in the town.
  And fortunately, I've at last reached
  my desired paradise.

105 What Tranio did, I myself forced him to do.
  So pardon him, sweet father, for my sake.

VINCENTIO

  I'll slit the wretch's nose. He wanted to send me to jail.

BAPTISTA

  But did you hear, sir? Did you marry my daughter without
  asking my permission?

VINCENTIO

110 Don't worry, Baptista. We'll see that you're satisfied; don't get upset.
   But I'll go inside and
  be revenged for this scheming.
    Exit.

BAPTISTA

  And I'll go in to get to the bottom of this scheming.
    Exit.

LUCENTIO

  Don't look pale, Bianca. Your father won't be upset.
    Exit LUCENTIO *and* BIANCA.

GREMIO

My cake is dough; but I'll in among the rest,

115   Out of hope of all but my share of the feast.
        [*Exit.*]

KATHERINA

Husband, let's follow, to see the end of this ado.

PETRUCHIO

First kiss me, Kate, and we will.

KATHERINA

What, in the midst of the street?

PETRUCHIO

What, art thou asham'd of me?

KATHERINA

120   No, sir, God forbid; but asham'd to kiss.

PETRUCHIO

Why, then let's home again. Come, sirrah, let's away.

KATHERINA

Nay, I will give thee a kiss; now pray thee, love, stay.

PETRUCHIO

Is not this well? Come, my sweet Kate:
Better once than never, for never too late.
        [*Exeunt.*]

Scene ii: [*Padua.Lucentio's house.*] *Enter* BAPTISTA,
VINCENTIO, GREMIO, *the* PEDANT, LUCENTIO,
BIANCA, PETRUCHIO, KATHERINA, HORTENSO, *and*
WIDOW, TRANIO, BIONDELLO, *and* GRUMIO; *the*
Servingmen with Tranio bringing in a banquet.

LUCENTIO

At last, though long, our jarring notes agree;
And time it is, when raging war is done,
To smile at scapes and perils overblown.
My fair Bianca, bid my father welcome,

5   While I with self-same kindness welcome thine.

GREMIO
My plan has failed, but I'll join the others,
hoping now only for my share of the feast.
Exit.

KATHERINE
Husband, let's follow the others to see what happens.

PETRUCHIO
First give me a kiss, Kate, and then we will.

KATHERINE
What! In the middle of the street?

PETRUCHIO
What! Are you ashamed of me?

KATHERINE
No, sir, God forbid! Just ashamed to kiss.

PETRUCHIO
Well then, let's go home again. Come, Grumio, let's go home.

KATHERINE
No, I'll give you a kiss. *(She kisses him)* Now, please, my love, stay.

PETRUCHIO
Isn't this better? Come, my sweet Kate.
Better late than never, and never too late to mend.
They exit.

*Act V, Scene ii: Padua, Lucentio's house. Enter BAPTISTA,
VINCENTIO, GREMIO, the PEDANT, LUCENTIO,
BIANCA, PETRUCHIO, KATHERINE, HORTENSIO, and
WIDOW, TRANIO, BIONDELLO, and GRUMIO;
SERVINGMEN enter with Tranio and bring in a dessert.*

LUCENTIO
At long last, we're all in accord,
and it's time, now that the heated war is finished,
to smile at past scrapes and dangers.
My lovely Bianca, welcome my father
while I, with equal kindness, welcome yours.

Brother Petruchio, sister Katherina,
And thou, Hortensio, with thy loving widow,
Feast with the best, and welcome to my house.
My banquet is to close our stomachs up,
10   After our great good cheer. Pray you, sit down;
For now we sit to chat as well as eat.

PETRUCHIO
Nothing but sit and sit, and eat and eat!

BAPTISTA
Padua affords this kindness, son Petruchio.

PETRUCHIO
Padua affords nothing but what is kind.

HORTENSIO
15   For both our sakes, I would that word were true.

PETRUCHIO
Now, for my life, Hortensio fears his widow.

WIDOW
Then never trust me, if I be afeard.

PETRUCHIO
You are very sensible, and yet you miss my sense.
I mean, Hortensio is afeard of you.

WIDOW
20   He that is giddy thinks the world turns round.

PETRUCHIO
Roundly replied.

KATHERINA
            Mistress, how mean you that?

WIDOW
Thus I conceive by him.

PETRUCHIO
Conceives by me! How likes Hortensio that?

HORTENSIO
25   My widow says, thus she conceives her tale.

---

9 *stomachs* Lucentio is punning on a second meaning of stomachs: "hot tempers."   16 *fears* means both "frightens" and "is frightened of."

Brother Petruchio, sister Katherine,
and you, Hortensio, with your loving widow,
feast with the best of them and welcome to my house.
My dessert is to seal our stomachs
10   after our wonderful reception. Please, sit down.
Now we'll sit to talk as well as eat.

PETRUCHIO
Nothing except sitting and sitting, and eating and eating!

BAPTISTA
Padua is famous for this type of kindness, my son Petruchio.

PETRUCHIO
Padua offers nothing except what is kind.

HORTENSIO
15   For both our sakes, I wish that was true.

PETRUCHIO
Well, I'd swear there's fear between Hortensio and his widow.

WIDOW
Never believe me again if I say I'm frightened.

PETRUCHIO
You're very sensible; and yet you misunderstood me:
I meant that Hortensio is frightened of you.

WIDOW
20   A dizzy man thinks the world is spinning.

PETRUCHIO
That's bluntly spoken.

KATHERINE
Madam, what do you mean by that?

WIDOW
Just what I conceived him to mean.

PETRUCHIO
Conceived by me! What do you think of that, Hortensio?

HORTENSIO
25   My widow said that she meant her statement as she said.

PETRUCHIO
Very well mended. Kiss him for that, good widow.

KATHERINA
"He that is giddy thinks the world turns round:"
I pray you, tell me what you meant by that.

WIDOW
Your husband, being troubled with a shrew,
30   Measures my husband's sorrow by his woe:
And now you know my meaning.

KATHERINA
A very mean meaning.

WIDOW
           Right, I mean you.

KATHERINA
And I am mean indeed, respecting you.

PETRUCHIO
35   To her, Kate!

HORTENSIO
To her, widow!

PETRUCHIO
A hundred marks, my Kate does put her down.

HORTENSIO
That's my office.

PETRUCHIO
Spoke like an officer. Ha' to thee, lad!
           [*Drinks to Hortensio.*]

BAPTISTA
40   How likes Gremio these quick-witted folks?

GREMIO
Believe me, sir, they butt together well.

BIANCA
Head, and butt! An hasty-witted body
Would say your head and butt were head and horn.

---

34 *mean* Kate is playing on another definition of mean: "gentle."   43 *horn* means both a "cuckold's horn" and "antlers to ram or butt."

PETRUCHIO
Nicely explained. Kiss him for that, good widow.

KATHERINE
"A dizzy man thinks the world is spinning."
Please tell me what you meant by that.

WIDOW
Your husband, pestered by a shrew,
30   judges my husband's trouble to be his own trouble.
Now you know what I meant.

KATHERINE
A very mean meaning.

WIDOW
Exactly—I meant you.

KATHERINE
And I am gentle, indeed, compared with you.

PETRUCHIO
35   Get her, Kate!

HORTENSIO
Get her, widow!

PETRUCHIO
I'll bet a hundred marks that my Kate lays her out.

HORTENSIO
That's my job.

PETRUCHIO
Spoken like a dedicated worker. Here's to you, lad.
(Drinks to Hortensio.)

BAPTISTA
40   How do you like these amusing people, Gremio?

GREMIO
Believe me, sir, they butt their heads together well.

BIANCA
Head and butt! A hasty person
might think your head and butt were head and horn.

VINCENTIO
   Ay, mistress bride, hath that awakened you?

BIANCA
45   Ay, but not frighted me; therefore I'll sleep again.

PETRUCHIO
   Nay, that you shall not; since you have begun,
   Have at you for a bitter jest or two!

BIANCA
   Am I your bird? I mean to shift my bush;
   And then pursue me as you draw your bow.
50   You are welcome all.
         [*Exeunt Bianca, Katherina, and Widow.*]

PETRUCHIO
   She hath prevented me. Here, Signior Tranio,
   This bird you aim'd at, though you hit her not;
   Therefore a health to all that shot and miss'd.

TRANIO
   O, sir, Lucentio slipp'd me like his greyhound,
55   Which runs himself and catches for his master.

PETRUCHIO
   A good swift simile, but something currish.

TRANIO
   'Tis well, sir, that you hunted for yourself;
   'Tis thought your deer does hold you at a bay.

BAPTISTA
   O ho, Petruchio! Tranio hits you now.

LUCENTIO
60   I thank thee for that gird, good Tranio.

HORTENSIO
   Confess, confess, hath he not hit you here?

PETRUCHIO
   'A has a little gall'd me, I confess;
   And, as the jest did glance away from me,
   'Tis ten to one it maim'd you two outright.

---

58 *deer* means both a "doe" and a "dear one."

VINCENTIO
So, madam bride, has that wakened you?

BIANCA
45   Yes, but not startled me, so I'll go to sleep again.

PETRUCHIO
Oh no you won't. Since you've started it,
watch out for a scalding joke or two.

BIANCA
So, I'm your prey? I'll change my perch, then,
and you can chase me as you're drawing your bow.
50   Everyone is welcome.
          Exit BIANCA *with* KATHERINE *and* WIDOW.

PETRUCHIO
She's outfoxed me. Here, Signior Tranio:
you aimed at that quarry, though you didn't bag her—
therefore, a toast to everyone who shot and missed.

TRANIO
O sir! Lucentio unleashed me, like his greyhound
55   which runs and catches for his master.

PETRUCHIO
A good, quick simile, but a little bit doggy.

TRANIO
It's a good thing that you hunt for yourself.
It's said that your deer has got you at a standoff.

BAPTISTA
Aha, Petruchio! Tranio got you there!

LUCENTIO
60   Thanks for that taunt, good Tranio.

HORTENSIO
Admit it, admit it! Didn't he get you with that one?

PETRUCHIO
He nicked me a little, I must admit.
And as the joke bounced away from me,
I'll bet ten to one that it hit you two squarely.

BAPTISTA

65 Now, in good sadness, son Petruchio,
I think thou hast the veriest shrew of all.

PETRUCHIO
Well, I say no; and therefore for assurance
Let's each one send unto his wife,
And he whose wife is most obedient
70 To come at first when he doth send for her,
Shall win the wager which we will propose.

HORTENSIO
Content. What is the wager?

LUCENTIO
Twenty crowns.

PETRUCHIO
Twenty crowns!
75 I'll venture so much of my hawk or hound,
But twenty times so much upon my wife.

LUCENTIO
A hundred then.

HORTENSIO
Content.

PETRUCHIO
A match! 'tis done.

HORTENSIO
80 Who shall begin?

LUCENTIO
That will I.
Go, Biondello, bid your mistress come to me.

BIONDELLO
I go.
[*Exit.*]

BAPTISTA
Son, I'll be your half, Bianca comes.

BAPTISTA
65 Now, in all seriousness, my son Petruchio,
I think you married the worst shrew of all.

PETRUCHIO
Well, I say I didn't. Therefore, to prove it,
let each one of us send for his wife.
The man whose wife is most obedient
70 to come at once when he sends for her
will win the bet I suggest.

HORTENSIO
Agreed. What are the stakes?

LUCENTIO
Twenty crowns.

PETRUCHIO
Twenty crowns!
75 I'd chance that much on my hawk or hound
but twenty times that much upon my wife.

LUCENTIO
A hundred then.

HORTENSIO
Agreed.

PETRUCHIO
It's a bet! Done.

HORTENSIO
80 Who should begin?

LUCENTIO
I will.
Go, Biondello, and tell your lady to come to me.

BIONDELLO
I'm going.
        Exit.

BAPTISTA
Son, I'll cover half your bet that Bianca comes.

LUCENTIO

85   I'll have no halves; I'll bear it all myself.
        Re-enter BIONDELLO.
    How now! what news?

BIONDELLO.
                Sir, my mistress sends you word
    That she is busy and she cannot come.

PETRUCHIO
    How! she is busy and she cannot come!
90   Is that an answer?

GREMIO
                Ay, and a kind one too.
    Pray God, sir, your wife send you not a worse.

PETRUCHIO
    I hope, better.

HORTENSIO
    Sirrah Biondello, go and entreat my wife
95   To come to me forthwith.
        [*Exit Biondello.*]

PETRUCHIO
                O, ho! entreat her!
    Nay, then she must needs come.

HORTENSIO
                I am afraid, sir,
    Do what you can, yours will not be entreated.
        Re-enter BIONDELLO.
100   Now, where's my wife?

BIONDELLO
    She says you have some goodly jest in hand.
    She will not come; she bids you come to her.

PETRUCHIO
    Worse and worse; she will not come! O vile,
    Intolerable, not to be endur'd!
105   Sirrah Grumio, go to your mistress;
    Say, I command her come to me.
        [*Exit Grumio.*]

LUCENTIO

85 I won't bear just half. I'll take the whole bet.
Enter BIONDELLO.
What's this? What happened?

BIONDELLO

Sir, my lady sends you a message
that she's busy and cannot come.

PETRUCHIO

What! She's busy and cannot come!
90 Is that a proper answer?

GREMIO

Yes, and a nice one, too.
You'd better pray, sir, that your wife doesn't send you a worse one.

PETRUCHIO

I hope for a better one.

HORTENSIO

Servant Biondello, go and beg my wife
95 to come to me at once.
Exit BIONDELLO.

PETRUCHIO

O ho! Beg her!
Well then, she has to come.

HORTENSIO

I'm afraid, sir,
that do whatever you like, your wife won't be begged.
Enter BIONDELLO.
100 Well, where's my wife?

BIONDELLO

She says you're playing some kind of trick.
She won't come. She asks you to come to her.

PETRUCHIO

Worse and worse! She won't come! O terrible,
intolerable, not to be stood!
105 Servant Grumio, go to your lady. Tell her that
I order her to come to me.
Exit GRUMIO.

HORTENSIO
I know her answer.

PETRUCHIO
What?

HORTENSIO
She will not.

PETRUCHIO
110   The fouler fortune mine, and there an end.
Re-enter KATHERINA.

BAPTISTA
Now, by my holidame, here comes Katherina!

KATHERINA
What is your will, sir, that you send for me?

PETRUCHIO
Where is your sister, and Hortensio's wife?

KATHERINA
They sit conferring by the parlour fire.

PETRUCHIO
115   Go, fetch them hither. If they deny to come,
Swinge me them soundly forth unto their husbands.
Away, I say, and bring them hither straight.
[*Exit Katherina.*]

LUCENTIO
Here is a wonder, if you talk of a wonder.

HORTENSIO
And so it is; I wonder what it bodes.

PETRUCHIO
120   Marry, peace it bodes, and love, and quiet life,
And awful rule, and right supremacy;
And, to be short, what not that's sweet and happy.

BAPTISTA
Now, fair befall thee, good Petruchio!
The wager thou hast won; and I will add

HORTENSIO
  I know what her answer will be.

PETRUCHIO
  What?

HORTENSIO
  She won't.

PETRUCHIO
110   My bad luck, then, and that will be an end to it.
          Enter KATHERINE.

BAPTISTA
  Now by a holy relic, here comes Katherine!

KATHERINE
  What did you want, sir, when you asked for me to come?

PETRUCHIO
  Where's your sister and Hortensio's wife?

KATHERINE
  They're sitting by the parlor fire and chatting.

PETRUCHIO
115   Go bring them here. If they refuse to come,
      drive them to their husbands with a sound beating.
      Go, I said, and bring them here at once.
              Exit KATHERINE.

LUCENTIO
  This is a wonder, if you speak of wonders.

HORTENSIO
  Yes, it is. I wonder what it means.

PETRUCHIO
120   Really, it means peace, and love, and a quiet life,
      a rule that will inspire respect and proper obedience.
      In short, everything that's sweet and happy.

BAPTISTA
  Well, good luck to you, good Petruchio!
  You've won the bet, and I'll add

125   Unto their losses twenty thousand crowns,
      Another dowry to another daughter,
      For she is chang'd, as she had never been.

PETRUCHIO
      Nay, I will win my wager better yet
      And show more sign of her obedience,
130   Her new-built virtue and obedience.
            Re-enter KATHERINA, *with* BIANCA *and* WIDOW.
      See where she comes and brings your froward wives
      As prisoners to her womanly persuasion.
      Katherina, that cap of yours becomes you not;
      Off with that bauble, throw it under-foot.
            [*Kate throws down her cap.*]

WIDOW
135   Lord, let me never have cause to sigh,
      Till I be brought to such a silly pass!

BIANCA
      Fie! what a foolish duty call you this?

LUCENTIO
      I would your duty were as foolish too.
      The wisdom of your duty, fair Bianca,
140   Hath cost me a hundred crowns since suppertime.

BIANCA
      The more fool you, for laying on my duty.

PETRUCHIO
      Katherina, I charge thee, tell these headstrong women
      What duty they do owe their lords and husbands.

WIDOW
      Come, come, you're mocking; we will have no telling.

PETRUCHIO
145   Come on, I say; and first begin with her.

WIDOW
      She shall not.

125   to their losses twenty thousand crowns—
      another dowry for another daughter
      because she has changed into someone totally different.

PETRUCHIO
      Wait, I'll win my bet even more convincingly
      and give you more proof of her obedience,
130   her new virtue and obedience.
            Enter KATE, BIANCA, *and* WIDOW.
      See, she's coming and bringing your stubborn wives
      as prisoners of her gifts of womanly persuasion.
      Katherine, that cap of yours doesn't become you—
      take that bauble off; trample it.

WIDOW
135   Lord! May I be spared all troubles
      until I do such a silly thing!

BIANCA
      How ridiculous! What kind of foolish obedience do you call that?

LUCENTIO
      I wish you were as foolish in your obedience, too.
      Your wise obedience, lovely Bianca,
140   has cost me a hundred crowns since supper.

BIANCA
      You're an even bigger fool for betting on my obedience.

PETRUCHIO
      Katherine, I order you, tell these headstrong women
      what obedience you owe your lords and husbands.

WIDOW
      Come, come, you're mocking us. We won't have a lecture.

PETRUCHIO
145   Come on, I said. Begin with her first.

WIDOW
      No she won't.

PETRUCHIO
I say she shall; and first begin with her.

KATHERINA
Fie, fie! unknit that threatening unkind brow,
And dart not scornful glances from those eyes,
150 To wound thy lord, thy king, thy governor.
It blots thy beauty as frosts do bite the meads,
Confounds thy fame as whirlwinds shake fair buds,
And in no sense is meet or amiable.
A woman mov'd is like a fountain troubled,
155 Muddy, ill-seeming, thick, bereft of beauty;
And while it is so, none so dry or thirsty
Will deign to sip or touch one drop of it.
Thy husband is thy lord, thy life, thy keeper,
Thy head, thy sovereign; one that cares for thee,
160 And for thy maintenance commits his body
To painful labour both by sea and land,
To watch the night in storms, the day in cold,
Whilst thou liest warm at home, secure and safe;
And craves no other tribute at thy hands
165 But love, fair looks, and true obedience—
Too little payment for so great a debt.
Such duty as the subject owes the prince
Even such a woman oweth to her husband;
And when she is froward, peevish, sullen, sour,
170 And not obedient to his honest will,
What is she but a foul contending rebel
And graceless traitor to her loving lord?
I am asham'd that women are so simple
To offer war where they should kneel for peace,
175 Or seek for rule, supremacy, and sway,
When they are bound to serve, love, and obey.
Why are our bodies soft and weak and smooth,
Unapt to toil and trouble in the world,
But that our soft conditions and our hearts
180 Should well agree with our external parts?
Come, come, you froward and unable worms!

PETRUCHIO
    I say she will. Begin with her first.

KATHERINE
    Shame, for shame! Stop scowling,
    and don't look with those scornful glances
150 at your lord, your king, your ruler.
    It mars your beauty as frosts bite the flowers,
    spoils your reputation as tornadoes shake lovely buds,
    and is in no way proper or lovable.
    An angry woman is like a churning fountain:
155 muddy, ugly, thick, stripped of beauty.
    And while it's like that, no one, no matter how parched and thirsty,
    will be willing to sip or touch one drop of it.
    Your husband is your lord, your life, your keeper,
    your ruler, your king. He's one who will care for you,
160 and to keep you in comfort, he dedicates himself
    to painful work, both by sea and land,
    keeping watch during stormy nights and during cold days
    while you're lying at home, safe and secure.
    And he doesn't ask any other favor from you
165 except love, kind looks, and true obedience—
    too small a payment for such a large debt.
    Such obedience as a subject owes to a prince,
    just such obedience does a woman owe her husband.
    And when she's stubborn, peevish, sullen, or sour
170 and does not obey his honorable will,
    what is she except a disgusting, seditious rebel
    and wicked traitor to her loving lord?
    I'm ashamed that women are so foolish
    as to fight when they should kneel to peace,
175 or seek leadership, dominance, and lordship
    when they have sworn to serve, love, and obey.
    Why are women's bodies so soft, weak, and smooth,
    unsuited to work and laboring in the world,
    unless our soft qualities and our tempers
180 should match our outer appearance?
    Come, come, you willful and lowly worms!

My mind hath been as big as one of yours,
My heart as great, my reason haply more,
To bandy word for word and frown for frown;
185 But now I see our lances are but straws,
Our strength as weak, our weakness past compare,
That seeming to be most which we indeed least are.
Then vail your stomachs, for it is no boot,
And place your hands below your husband's foot;
190 In token of which duty, if he please,
My hand is ready; may it do him ease.

PETRUCHIO
Why, there's a wench! Come on, and kiss me, Kate.

LUCENTIO
Well, go thy ways, old lad; for thou shalt ha't.

VINCENTIO
'Tis a good hearing when children are toward.

LUCENTIO
195 But a harsh hearing when women are froward.

PETRUCHIO
Come, Kate, we'll to bed.
We three are married, but you two are sped.
[*To Lucentio.*] 'Twas I won the wager, though you
hit the white;
And, being a winner, God give you good night!
[*Exeunt Petruchio and Katherina.*]

HORTENSIO
200 Now, go thy ways; thou hast tam'd a curst shrew.

LUCENTIO
'Tis a wonder, by your leave, she will be tam'd so.
[*Exeunt.*]

---

198 *white* Petruchio means the "bull's-eye of a target" and "Bianca" (which means "white" in Italian).

My mind was as once as puffed up as yours,
my spirit as great, my reason perhaps greater,
to trade word for word and frown for frown.
185 But now I see our lances are just straws,
our strength as weak, our weakness beyond comparison,
that we try hardest to be that which we're least able to do.
So swallow your pride, because it's useless,
and put your hands beneath your husband's foot.
190 To symbolize my obedience, if he chooses to accept it,
my hand is ready if he chooses to use it.

PETRUCHIO
Why, that's a woman! Come on and kiss me, Kate.

LUCENTIO
Well, go on, old lad. You've won the bet.

VINCENTIO
It's pleasant news to hear that children are obedient.

LUCENTIO
195 But bad news when women are willful.

PETRUCHIO
Come, Kate, let's go to bed.
We three are married, but you two are done for.
*(To Lucentio)*I'm the one who won the bet, though you
hit the white.
So, being a winner, God give you a good night!
Exit PETRUCHIO *and* KATE.

HORTENSIO
200 Well, go on. You've tamed a terrible shrew.

LUCENTIO
It's amazing, if you'll excuse me for saying so, that she has been so tamed.
They exit.

DISCUSSION QUESTIONS

Induction

1. **What purpose is served by the argument between Sly and the hostess at the beginning of the play?**

   The argument serves to set the tone of the play. Sly and the hostess engage in mock-serious battle, Sly turning each one of the hostess' threats into a pun. While tempers may flash, the bantering mood and Sly's blithe self-assurance make any real threat seem unlikely. The argument also introduces the theme of conflict between men and women. Sly's cavalier victory over the hostess may foreshadow Petruchio's own triumph over his noisy wife.

2. **What is the thematic purpose of the lord's plan to dupe Sly into believing he is a lord?**

   The lord's scheme foreshadows a number of themes in *The Taming of the Shrew*. First, the notion of an elaborate attempt to deceive others about identity is central to the lord's plan, as well to Petruchio's strategy for taming Kate. Lucentio, Tranio, Hortensio, and the pedant also play the game of disguise in the wooing of Bianca. Secondly, only the comic aspect of this change of identities is emphasized. The lord worries about his servants keeping a straight face—not what will happen when the jest comes to an end and Sly must have his true rude "awakening." Petruchio's cruel treatment of Kate and the pedant's threat to have Vincentio jailed are similarly treated as jokes. Thirdly, the object of disguising identities is the same for the lord and Petruchio: to alter the behavior of the deceived person. The lord contemplates his proposal to remake Sly and remarks, "Would not the beggar then forget himself?" Petruchio's tyrannical behavior is designed to make Kate forget her shrewish attitudes. Finally, both the lord's and Petruchio's deceptions are carried out under the false cloak of kindness. The lavish attentions to Sly are really attempts to mock him; Petruchio's exaggerated solicitude for Kate is merely a clever way to break her stubbornness.

3. **What parallels does the page's function as Sly's "wife" have to Katherine's relationship to Petruchio?**

The page appears to be a model of Elizabethan womanly virtue. "She" is lovely, modest, loyal, submissive, and solicitous.

Kate, apart from her beauty, seems the exact opposite of the page. But by the play's end, she too will cast aside her persona to fulfill the promise of the page's ideal woman.

4. **What purpose do the references to real local people and places have in Sly's speeches?**

The local color gives the character of Sly the ring of truth. References to familiar places also undoubtedly appealed to those in Shakespeare's audience looking for local color.

Shakespeare uses the factual details for ironic effect, too. One of the lord's servants protests that Sly has been babbling in his madness of phantom acquaintances: "twenty more such names and men as these/ Which never were nor no man ever saw." Once again, the conflict between the real and the apparent is raised.

5. **Does Sly truly believe that he is a lord?**

While Sly does not tip his hand, many critics argue that Sly does not swallow the lord's tale. He simply plays along with a fine opportunity. Sly, by his very name, seems too worldly-wise to be taken in by the lord's farce. Details like his request for small ale and his wish to address the page by a name rather than a title indicate that he refuses to put on the proper airs of a lord. He remains a simple man, seeking the enjoyments of his old life.

Act I

1. **What does Lucentio's opening speech reveal about his character?**

    Lucentio's sketch of his background and goals reveals his idealism and naivety. Lucentio places a high value on virtuous deeds—for him, virtue is the road to happiness. He has come to Padua full of the zest for knowledge, eager to fulfill his father's hopes for him.

    But behind Lucentio's lofty aims is uncertainty. He needs reassurance that his intentions are laudable. Tranio gives him that assurance but also points out that, in essence, all work and no play make Jack a dull boy. Tranio injects the element of reality and of good fun into his master's idealistic plans.

2. **How does Tranio's advice foreshadow future events?**

    Tranio advises Lucentio to seek the pleasures in life, particularly the delights of love. He even mentions Ovid—the poet Lucentio will later use to woo a lover. Finally, Tranio suggests that Lucentio simply "study what you most affect."

    The words are scarcely out of his mouth when Bianca appears, and Lucentio is immediately smitten. Lucentio's pursuit of Bianca will lead him to take Tranio's advice literally. He will study what he most affects by assuming the guise of a literature teacher. Under that mask, he will instruct Bianca in Ovid's love poetry to persuade her to love him.

3. **What does Kate's first appearance on the scene immediately reveal about her?**

    Kate shows herself to be as violent and hot-tempered as Bianca's discouraged suitors implied. A quick wit goes with her independent spirit, and she is more than a match for Hortensio and Gremio. She scornfully rejects the notion that she would ever stoop to marrying—if she would ever consider marrying—either one of them.

Kate appears resentful of her sister and angered by her father's affection for Bianca. These emotions may just be part of Kate's general peevishness. On the other hand, Kate also may be revealing her jealousy of Bianca's attractiveness to men. She may simply be protesting too much when she declares marriage does not interest her.

4. **What is the relationship between Tranio and Lucentio?**

Tranio and Lucentio's relationship goes beyond that of servant and master. Lucentio is an eager, naive young man who forms plans in a rush, then seeks reassurance that those plans are workable. He relies on Tranio, much as he would a good friend and confidant, to give assurances or suggestions.

Tranio serves as Lucentio's counselor, confessor, manager, and prompter, even though he may have doubts about the wisdom of Lucentio's aims. Lucentio's romantic, idealistic notions go against the grain of Tranio, the knowing and practical man. However, he obliges his master because he deeply cares for Lucentio.

Tranio and Lucentio are also linked by their role as co-conspirators. Together, they are responsible for cooking up the scheme to fool Baptista. The equal burden of guilt establishes an equality between the two.

However, Tranio's role as primary implementer of the deception puts him in control. His wry, manipulative use of the disguise also gives him an authority and appeal. The expert use of outrageous lies seems to make him the master of the situation. In contrast, Lucentio often seems the straight man and weaker partner in his relationship with Tranio. In an ironic sense, therefore, the exchange of identities is an accurate reflection of Tranio and Lucentio's real relationship.

5. **Why do Sly and company disapper from the play?**

Scholars have offered a number of explanations for the

221

disappearance of the subplot involving Sly and the lord. One supposition is that the portions of the play resolving the plot of the Induction were lost. In other words, a conclusion to Sly's story may have been acted on stage but was never printed. Another similar theory offers the explanation that most of the Sly speeches were ad-libbed by the players and, therefore, never written down.

Other critics believe Shakespeare deliberately dropped Sly from the play. Kate and Petruchio's tale was too engrossing to be diluted by more interruptions from the bored Sly, this school argues.

Some scholars offer a humbler, much more simple explanation for Sly's disappearance. They suggest Shakespeare simply forgot the characters of the Induction.

6. **How does Petruchio's stated purpose in coming to Padua differ from Lucentio's?**

Petruchio's arrival in Padua is a parody of Lucentio's. Lucentio comes to the city to steep himself in esoteric learning. He is full of naive enthusiasm for his plan, intending to make his father proud of him.

Petruchio, on the other hand, comes to Padua to try his fortune. His father is dead, and the only plan Petruchio has to honor the deceased is to make good use of the family money. Petruchio has no zest for scholarly learning. He intends to seek a wife. He bluntly tells Hortensio that he means to marry a wealthy woman.

Act II

1. **Why does Kate abuse Bianca?**

Kate's torture of her sister is a natural display of her shrewish nature. Once again, the loud, violent manner of the older sister is contrasted to the demure, reasoning behavior of the younger.

However, as Kate's protests to Baptista reveal, Kate is more concerned about being left an old maid than she may care to admit to her younger sister. Bianca's wealth in potential husbands galls Kate. In a typically passionate way, Kate shows her jealousy.

Kate is particularly irked by her sister's real or assumed indifference to the envious position of being wooed by several worthy catches. In fact, given the revelation of Bianca's calculating nature by the play's end, Bianca may be trying to insult Kate by offering to share wooers. Kate's anger would be fully justified in this case.

2. **How does Petruchio's first meeting with Baptista set the style for the rest of the courtship?**

Petruchio immediately demonstrates he is a quick-mover, self-assured, and a man of business. He makes a hasty bow to romantic conventions and then speedily moves on to the matter of Kate's dowry. Petruchio's praise for Kate's virtues also unfolds his scheme for taming his shrew. He pretends Kate is the ideal woman and refuses to acknowledge any demonstrations of her true nature, no matter how violent.

The other characters' reactions to Petruchio's blunt and self-assured actions are also established by this scene. Petruchio's taming methods will continue to shock and amuse his on-stage audience throughout the play.

3. **What kind of father does Baptista appear to be?**

Critics strongly disagree about Baptista's character. Some argue that Minola is actually responsible for Kate's shrewishness. According to this interpretation, Kate has become a brat not by overindulgence or natural temperament but through neglect. By unfairly favoring Bianca, Baptista makes Kate bitter and forces her to seek attention in the only way left to her—loud complaint. Supporters of this reading point to

Baptista's "selling" of both of his daughters for the best price.

However, Baptista seems to be depicted as more the harried parent than the cruel father. He scolds Kate and tries to reason with her. But ultimately he is reduced to a helpless protest after Kate's tongue-lashing: "Was ever gentleman thus grieved as I?"

Baptista also shows his concern by stipulating that he will not approve Kate's marriage unless Petruchio gains his daughter's love first. And when Kate appears to have been jilted, Baptista attempts to comfort her.

Finally, though Baptista does dwell on marriage settlements for both of his daughters, he is so impressed by Kate's reformation that he claps another twenty thousand crowns onto Kate's dowry. The generosity is hardly the action of a completely mercenary, arbitrary father.

4. **What purpose is served by Hortensio/Licio's account of his music lesson with Kate?**

First and foremost, Hortensio's tale is classic farce. His ludicrous appearance with the lute smashed over his head perfectly captures the slapstick element in farce. No harm has been done. Hortensio takes a blow that realistically would be extremely painful and comes back complaining only of injured pride. Consequently, Hortensio looks ridiculous, not pathetic. He remains the cardboard character typical of farce. He is there to give the audience a laugh, not to provide insightful reflection on reality.

The characterization of Kate also exemplifies typical farce. No one can honestly be surprised by her reaction. After the repeated attestations to her shrewish nature, her violence seems perfectly predictable and mechanical.

5. **Does Petruchio's soliloquy reveal a concealed character?**

No. Unlike many of Shakespeare's characters in his other dramas who use the soliloquy to declare deep motives and thoughts, Petruchio merely elaborates on his established persona. We already know this man— his cleverness and determination. His basic plan—the pretense that Kate is a paragon of virtue—has been revealed previously. Petruchio just sketches in a few more details and prepares the audience for an amusing fight between worthy opponents.

6. **Why are puns used so frequently in Kate and Petruchio's encounter?**

The puns contribute to the comic tone and fast-paced, bawdy fun sustained throughout the play. But the puns are also the weapons in Kate and Petruchio's battle for mastery. The witty exchange proves they are equals in intelligence, spirit, and determination.

The puns also dramatize the sifting for identity. The meanings of words shifts just like the personas the characters wear. Kate and Petruchio are just two of the players in the game to test another character without revealing their own true natures. The puns serve as barbs to penetrate each others' masks while turning aside attacks to their own disguises.

7. **Why is Petruchio's story about Kate's agreement to marry him so readily accepted?**

Petruchio's commanding manner and devastatingly quick decisions catch everyone off balance. He has also demonstrated that he can be a threatening man. His fits of temper, whether actual or bluff, may cow the other characters. And, of course, everyone (even Kate, to a certain extent, since she no longer needs to fear being left an old maid) profits by believing Petruchio.

8. **How does Tranio's decision to find a "father" reflect a theme of the play?**

Tranio, as the "supposed" Lucentio, seeks a "supposed" father. Another bluff is in the works; another disguise being planned. The Padua of this play is a world where a servant plays a master, masters play servants, clever women pretend to be modest maids, and a snappish man plays a considerate lover. Nothing is as it seems to be, and the normal order is inverted. Therefore, Tranio's declaration that "a child shall get a sire" comes as no surprise.

Act III

1. **What do the love scenes between Bianca and Lucentio and Bianca and Hortensio reveal about Kate's younger sister?**

Bianca's calculating play with her tutors shows the modest virgin of Act I in a new light. Lucentio's and Hortensio's declarations of love do not shock her. On the contrary, she enjoys the love games and admits that she has been merry with both of her teachers.

This sophisticated attitude is complemented by a spirit as strong as Kate's. When Lucentio and Hortensio quarrel over Bianca's attentions, she squarely steps in and asserts her rights to make the decision herself. But though her determination rivals Kate's, Bianca proves much more aware of proprieties and the need to mask her spirit.

2. **How does Kate and Petruchio's love scene contrast with Bianca's courtship?**

Kate and Petruchio openly confront and test each other. Their meeting seems more like combat than courting. Kate is angry, violent, and scornful of Petruchio's courtly compliments. She even tries to leave. Petruchio is mocking, judgmental, and pays humorous lip service to romantic notions. He quickly and willingly sets "all this chat aside" to state the bald fact that he means to marry Kate "will you, nill you."

In contrast, the courtly conventions deeply involve Bianca and her lovers. Bianca is wooed with charming persuasions and ardent requests—all in passionate earnestness and not in Petruchio's cynical vein. Bianca's lovers do not demand but beg their mistress' favor and they accept her decisions. Bianca, while displaying her sister's strong will, enjoys the love play. Though she has strong opinions about her suitors, she does not meet them in violent conflict. Instead, she dismisses them with regal aplomb.

3. **How does Petruchio's delay in appearing for the wedding affect Kate?**

Kate resents Petruchio's arrogant, mocking manner. His delay allows her to reproach her father and claim that he agreed to entrust his daughter to a "frantic fool." But the satisfaction of saying "I told you so" is tempered for Kate by her fear of being left an old maid. She frets "Now must the world point at poor Katherine/ And say, 'Lo! there is mad Petruchio's wife,/ If it would please him come and marry her.' " This is evidence that Kate's concern for the good opinion of others is beginning to outweigh her need for independence.

4. **What is the effect of Petruchio's shabby appearance?**

The immediate response to Petruchio's incredible costume is, of course, laughter. Biondello, serving as announcer, whets the audience's appetite with an exhaustive catalog of Petruchio's disreputable appearance. When anticipation is at a pitch, the punch line is delivered—Petruchio appears in person.

On the level of plot and character, Petruchio's poorman's dress serves another purpose. Appreciation of the joke leads to a heightened estimation for Petruchio. He proves himself master of the situation, again, and a true artist in his flair for the ridiculous. He shows, too, that he is willing to risk severe censure for his actions. Kate is already backing away from such demonstrations of independence. Petruchio's gaucheness is designed to increase her social awareness.

Petruchio's lesson also brings up the theme of appearances and disguises. Though Petruchio tries to shame and humble Kate, he also attempts to give her a lesson in discriminating between levels of appearance. Petruchio suggests that temperament and behavior are at least as equally important as looks. He declares: "To me she's married, not unto my clothes./ Could I repair what she will wear in me/ As I can change these poor accouterments,/ 'Twere well for Kate and better for myself."

That lesson was first delivered in the Induction. Sly remains a lowly tinker though decked in lord's clothes. So, too, Kate will remain a shrew, not fit to wear a lady's gown, as Petruchio later remarks, if she does not act like a lady.

5. **What purpose is served by Petruchio's rude behavior at the wedding?**

This scene parallels Petruchio's first shocking arrival earlier in the act. Once again, the scenerio milks the humorous aspect of the situation. The same purpose to Petruchio's crudity and the same thematic thread are repeated.

The scenes are similar in stucture, too. Both hinge on the impact of a messenger's graphic description. Biondello, the messenger announcing Petruchio's arrival, and Grumio, the herald who reports the wedding, are clownish characters. Both supply wonderfully detailed and comic pictures of events offstage. And both descriptions serve to build anticipation for the appearance of the characters involved.

6. **What is notable about Kate's reaction to Petruchio's announcement that they will leave before the wedding dinner?**

Though Kate ends up in a temper, asserting her rights, she begins her argument with Petruchio by trying to persuade him to stay. "Let me entreat you," she begs. She even tries the measure of his affection for her: "Now, if you love me, stay." Only when Petruchio publicly humiliates her does she fall back on her independent stance. Already, Kate is experimenting with the moderate, properly submissive role of an Elizabethan wife.

7. **What is ironic about Kate's statement "I see a woman may be made a fool/ If she had not a spirit to resist"?**

The irony of Kate's assertion is that Petruchio makes a fool of her when she does try to resist. He keeps to his game of ridiculous disguises and pretends the guests are hostile and dangerous. In reality, of course, only Kate seethes at his demand that they leave at once. Petruchio drags her off, playing to the end that he is serving Kate's own wishes. The guests are left to laugh and wonder in amazement about the "mad" couple.

Act IV

1. **What elements of farce are present in Grumio and Curtis' meeting?**

The running joke about the fire and the slapstick blow are examples of the obvious and superfluous comedy characteristic of farce. The mechanical development of character is also typical of farce. Curtis plays the dull-witted, bumpkinish straight man to Grumio's clever, rude comedian.

Grumio's story about the journey home with his master and mistress expands on the farcical tone. The graphic narrative of the three travelers stumbling about in the mud is another example of farcical physical comedy. Grumio's tales also rolls off with the usual, fast-paced tempo of farce.

2. **What evidence of change is apparent in Kate by Grumio's account and by her own behavior when she enters?**

As the servants conclude, Petruchio is proving more of

a shrew than his notorious wife. This estimation is partly based on Petruchio's shocking behavior, which makes Kate seem relatively mild. But Kate is actually changing, too. She wades through the mud to stop Petruchio from beating Grumio. In response to Petruchio's curses, she does not retort in kind. Instead, she pleads for Petruchio to show mercy. "How she prayed, that never prayed before," remarks Grumio.

When Kate and Petruchio—in fearsome bluster—appear on the scene, the servants' judgment is born out. Petruchio strikes a servant, and Kate begs for his patience—a virtue so alien to her own temper in past scenes. She also tries to calmly reason with her husband when he rejects the supper.

Perhaps the surest indication of Kate's budding reformation is the change in other characters' attitudes toward her. While the servants are probably amused by the show, they also pity Kate, the "poor soul."

3. **How does Petruchio compare his treatment of Kate to the taming of a falcon?**

Petruchio's metaphor compares two stubborn, aloof, and spirited creatures. He takes this similarity of nature as his key in taming Kate. He plots to refuse Kate food or sleep until she learns her lesson and submits to his will. Elizabethans tamed falcons in the same way. Food was withheld from a young falcon so that when the bird was flown outdoors, it would return to the trainer's hand when tempted with meat. Similarly, when a falcon was unruly and refused to be touched, the trainer would keep the bird awake until it became too tired to fight.

4. **How does Bianca and Lucentio's exchange in Scene 2 compare to their last meeting?**

The same playful mood prevails, but both lovers are much bolder now than in their previous encounter. Bianca's earlier distrust has vanished. Now she eagerly welcomes Lucentio's discussion of Ovid—and the affections she arouses in Lucentio. In fact, to the secret observers Tranio and Hortensio, Bianca's forwardness makes her look like the wooer. "See how beastly she doth court him," Tranio remarks in sham disgust.

Bianca's thawing can be attributed in part to her confidence in Lucentio's claim to be a wealthy merchant's son in disguise. Undoubtedly, too, Bianca's affection for Lucentio has grown. But certainly the fact that Bianca believes herself to be alone with Lucentio also leads her to drop her retiring mask and reveal her true lusty attitudes.

5. **Why is Hortensio's resolution to seek kindness in a woman and not beauty ironic?**

Hortensio rejects Bianca for the same reason he spurned Kate—Bianca, like her sister, may be beautiful and wealthy, but she is "proud" and "disdainful." (And a "haggard," just as Petruchio describes Kate in Scene 1.) Yet, after having dismissed both sisters, Hortensio seeks out the widow. In the final act, this lady proves the most shrewish of the three brides. Even though Hortensio attends Petruchio's taming school, he does not learn the master's lesson that there "is a way to kill a wife [or husband] with kindness."

Though Hortensio does not see past the widow's mask of kindness, he shows hints of astuteness in donning his own disguise. He seems to take to heart the resolution that affection in a bride outweighs everything else. But his quick shift of devotion and angry rejection of his former disguise as a lowly musician suggest Hortensio also seeks to recoup lost pride.

Hortensio's pointed reference to the widow's wealth shows he has one more, very ironic, interest in the new match. This hint of greedinesss brings Hortensio full circle. He becomes one of the "good fellows" he supposes exist who would marry a woman "with all faults, and money enough" (Act I, Scene 1).

6. **How does the recruitment of the pedant further the theme of deception?**

Tranio carries out his plan to find a man to play Vincentio by convincing the pedant to act the part. Tranio's plan works because he advances the scheme under the, by now, typical play of deceptive kindness. He tells the pedant that all travelers from Mantua are under sentence of death in Padua due to a quarrel between the dukes of the two cities. Tranio's "kind" offer to allow the pedant to assume Vincentio's role is gratefully accepted.

7. **What new awareness on Kate's part is revealed by her conversation with Grumio?**

Petruchio's starvation technique has begun to tell on Kate. She pleads with Grumio for any food he will bring her. Grumio devilishly assumes his master's part and teases her appetite—and temper—with tempting dishes. But he knows better than to cross Petruchio and finally promises to bring "mustard without the beef." Only when Kate realizes Grumio has been baiting her all along does her old temper reawaken.

Behind the comedy of the scene is Kate's awareness of her dependence on others for support. She feels in the same position as beggars who asked for charity at her father's door, and she shows appreciation for her father's policy of generosity. Kate begins to see that she "who never knew how to entreat,/ Nor never needed that I should entreat" must beg for her supper from the master of the house—Petruchio. Touching appeals to servants, like Grumio, will prove useless if the master does not approve.

8. **What does Kate's outburst at Petruchio over the cap and gown reveal?**

Kate's argument with Petruchio over the clothing is her last grand fit of temper. She clearly defines her values and, in the sea of deception and hypocrisy in the play, Kate's shrewishness suddenly seems a virtue. She asserts that she will honestly say what she feels: "My tongue will tell the anger of my heart,/ Or else my heart, concealing it, will break."

Moreover, Kate states again her old indifference to affection. "Love me or love me not," she tells Petruchio, she values her freedom of speech more than anything else.

Kate's professed indifference to love and her angry outbursts seem connected. Petruchio must bridle his wife's temper not only by cowing her, but by winning her heart, the guide of her temper.

9. **Is Petruchio's speech to Kate about the unimportance of clothing hypocritical?**

As before the wedding, Petruchio again states that appearance is unimportant since " 'tis the mind that makes the body rich." Though this may be a noble attitude, Petruchio may not be sincere. His previous fussiness about Kate's gown and cap might show how important every detail of dress was to him just a moment ago. On the other hand, these demonstrations may only have been Petruchio's way of setting up his argument that character is more fundamental than appearance.

The scene with the tailor plays like the homecoming dinner in Scene 1 and Grumio's baiting of Kate with savory dishes earlier in this scene. The temptation, fault findings, and Kate's inevitable disappointment is the pattern of those scenes and this one. Petruchio's commonplaces about the honor of shabby clothing may be as false and cliche as his concern about choleric meat.

Petruchio's philosophy on the honorableness of impoverished dress also may be ironic, given his motivation in marrying Kate. He plainly declared to Hortensio that he meant to marry a rich woman. The question remains, was he sincere, or was he also looking for a woman of equality and spirit?

The final piece of evidence that Petruchio is speaking

ironically is his advice, "If thou accounst it shame, lay it on me." His earlier retort to Kate may suggest his real attitude. Kate protests that "gentlewomen wear such caps as these." Petruchio assures her "When you are gentle you shall have one too—and not till then." Petruchio may be saying that Kate's poor behavior will earn her only poor clothing—the blame is hers.

On the other hand, he may be suggesting to her that superior spirits like Kate and himself must learn to wear certain masks—or "caps"—before the world. The actor playing Petruchio is given ample support for either interpretation.

10. **Why does Biondello remain behind after Tranio, Baptista, and the Pedant leave?**

Biondello knows his master Lucentio's hesitant nature. Just as Tranio earlier suggested, seconded, and organized Lucentio's plans, Biondello stays behind to prod Lucentio into action. In a previous scene, Lucentio had considered eloping with Bianca: " 'Twere good, methinks to steal our marriage." However, he needs Tranio's and Biondello's prompting to seize a likely opportunity. Biondello, in fact, tries to flatter his master's intelligence by merely dropping hints. Finally, however, he is forced to clearly explain the scheme.

Even with the plot clearly laid out, Lucentio still vacillates. "I may, and will, if she be so contented./ She will be pleased; then wherefore should I doubt?" At last he argues himself into a determined stand: "I'll roughly go about her."

11. **What do Petruchio's tests of Kate in Scene 4 prove?**

Petruchio's tests seem to prove Kate is finally tamed. She has grown so weary of arguing that, to please Petruchio, she denies even the fundamental fact of nature that the sun is shining. She gives up her right to voice her own opinions: "What you will have it named, even that it is;/ And so it shall be so for Katherine."

Kate's mood in accepting her obedient role is more clearly defined when Vincentio appears. She does not simply chime in with Petruchio's ridiculous statments. She heartily takes up her husband's amusing suggestion that Vincentio is a young girl. She even tries to top Petruchio's extravagance. The game of wits Kate and Petruchio played against one another in earlier scenes now becomes their joint conspiracy of humor against the world.

Act V

1. **What does Vincentio's reaction to Lucentio's and Tranio's deceptions reveal about his character?**

Vincentio's anger at being deceived is natural and makes for good comedy. But his temper also indicates he is not a man to be crossed by his servants. Even after Lucentio's explanation that Tranio and Biondello were merely following orders, Vincentio swears he will be "revenged for this villainy."

Another amusing aspect of Vincentio's character emerges in his quarrel with Tranio. When Vincentio first arrives in Padua, he merrily tries to bribe his way into Lucentio's house with a money gift for his son. But in the cross of deceptions, the conservative merchant's personality comes to the fore. He takes one look at Tranio and bursts into lamentations about the expense of the servant's clothing: "A silken doublet! a velvet hose! a scarlet cloak! and a/coptain hat! O, I am undone! I am undone! While I play the/good husband at home, my son and my servant spend all at the/university." As Gremio had gloatingly guessed earlier (Act II, Scene 1), Vincentio is "an old Italian fox" who wants to control the purse strings.

Yet, the scene also reveals Vincentio's love for his son. His hysterical conclusion that his son has been murdered and his relieved exclamation: "Lives my sweet son?" prove Vincentio is a loving father, if a masterful one.

235

2. How does Lucentio play on his assumed name?

Cambio means "exchange" in Italian. Lucentio, explaining his identity deception, remarks "Bianca's love/ Made me exchange my state with Tranio." Like many of the maskers in the play, Lucentio has fun with his disguise and drops a playful, witty clue as to his real identity and purpose.

3. Is Petruchio's request for a kiss in Scene 1 simply another test of Kate?

Petruchio is measuring Kate's obedience with his request, but there seems to be more to this test. After Kate agrees to kiss him, he remarks, "Is not this well?" His simple point is that agreement between married partners—the wife agreeing to a husband's request—is pleasurable and natural. In fact, as natural as kissing in public if one is happily married.

Petruchio also seems to be seeking an expression of his wife's love. He initially sought out Kate for her wealth. But he found her a worthy mate in spirit and wit. Lucentio plunged ahead into a match for love and only begins to discover his wife's true temper in the final scene. Petruchio knew and molded his wife's fiery spirit from the beginning. Now, as confirmed by the kiss, he and his wife seem to be finding love and harmony in an initially practical marriage. "Better once than never," Petruchio concludes, "for never too late."

4. What does Petruchio mean when he remarks "Padua affords nothing but what is kind"?

On the surface, Petruchio's remark is an apology to Baptista for his impatient exclamation, "Nothing but sit and sit, and eat and eat!" But coming from a bystander at Vincentio's recent fight with Tranio, et al., Petruchio's comment also should be considered as ironically intended. Most of the characters in the play, including Petruchio, have shown that the Padua brand of kindness can be a hollow virtue. Indeed, Hortensio immediately utters a wistful doubt about the truth of Baptista's statement.

Petruchio's bet with the other bridegrooms may hint of a final irony in his comment about kindness. Padua has indeed afforded a kindness little suspected—Petruchio's tamed, loving wife.

5. **How does Petruchio pursue an aim opposite to Lucentio's in the final scene?**

Lucentio intends the feast to be courteous and cheerful—in other words, kindness all around once again. He invites them to a banquet "to close our stomachs up"—literally close their stomachs and figuratively stop their fighting.

However, Petruchio finds such "good cheer" dull. He immediately seeks a way to liven up the feast. Petruchio's design is not really to make trouble but stir a lively exchange of wits. That his aim is good-natured is exemplified by his cupid-like urging of the widow to kiss Hortensio.

However, his close questioning of comments, punning, and nudging of guests to join the fray awakens a few tempers. Even Kate shows she has not lost her spirit or her tongue. And Petruchio, instead of trying to quiet her, actually urges her on. "To her, Kate!" he shouts like a man at a cockfight, and then wagers on her success.

This preliminary skirmish raises everyone's spirits—and competitive drive—for Petruchio's more conclusive and surprising bet on Kate. That bet brings the feast to a result just the opposite of Lucentio's goal. Instead of soothing tempers, Hortensio and Lucentio learn to their dismay how temperamental are their wives.

6. **How is suspense built up about the bet?**

The pointed remarks, exchange of barbs, and Petruchio's initial attempt to raise a bet on Kate all prepare the way for a more decisive conflict. The wealth of hunting similies throughout the scene adds to the suspense by suggesting that all the guests are searching for big game. Petruchio finds an appropriate challenge when his wife's obedience is questioned. Then, when the bet is agreed upon, he insists on raising the stakes. More money and more pride rest on the initially trivial wager.

Tension builds as Biondello is dispatched and the on- and off-stage audiences await his return. He delivers Bianca's refusal, first, and then the widow's. Both these reputedly kind women will not obey their husbands— the men jeer what then can Petruchio expect from his shrew? Even the off-stage audience, aware of Kate's submission to Petruchio in earlier scenes, may wonder. Kate's spat with the widow indicates her temper still flairs.

Finally, Grumio is sent to deliver the fateful message to Kate. The audience must wait several more moments before Kate obediently appears. Once again, Petruchio daringly raises the stakes by demanding more of his wife than Bianca or the widow would ever tolerate. Yet, Kate proves her devotion, and Petruchio wins his game.

7. **What is the essence of a wife's duty according to Kate?**

Kate lectures Bianca and the widow that all women owe their husbands beauty, obedience, and thoughtful attendance. She argues that women are innately weaker and softer than men—unfit for wordly labor. The mind should suit the body, then, she concludes. As the woman depends on her husband for her bodily needs, so, too, her mind should depend on his opinions.

Kate's speech may strike some modern readers as a one-sided statement. But a careful reader will note that Kate gives the husband obligations to fill. A good husband loves and cares for his wife. His duties keep him at unenviable tasks until unpleasant hours. Such is the wife's bargain, Kate states, that a wife quietly reaps the benefits of her husband's labor in return for respect.

DISCUSSION QUESTIONS

Motivation:

1. **Why does Petruchio want to marry Kate?**

   Kate is a wonderful catch by practical Elizabethan standards, apart from her shrewishness. Hortensio assures Petruchio that Kate is lovely, young, schooled, and of a good family. But seemingly the most important factor for Petruchio remains the temptation of Minola's gold. Petruchio plainly says that he has come to Padua for "wealth is burden of my wooing dance."

   Though greed may initially interest Petruchio in Kate, something more seems to motivate him. Petruchio is a gambler, a man who loves to test his wisdom, will, and daring against others. His catalog of experiences (Act I, Scene 2) proves he has lived an eventful life. Kate presents merely another challenge to this old adventurer. The odds seem against him. Everyone quickly protests that Kate is an unwinnable demon. But like the most dedicated gambler, Petruchio finds the challenge all the more fascinating.

   Petruchio's interest in the game continues to grow when he finds Kate a witty opponent. His determination to win increases, too. " . . . Never make denial;/ I must and will have Katherine to my wife," he declares.

   Finally, Petruchio's attraction to Kate as man to woman should not be slighted. Hortensio has told Petruchio that Kate is beautiful. Petruchio's ribald remarks when he meets Kate suggest he at least notes Kate's desirability.

2. **Why does Kate change from a shrew to an obedient wife?**

   Kate seems motivated to change for several reasons. She seems primarily motivated by fear when she takes her first step toward change by marrying Petruchio. The independent-minded woman dreads being mocked as an old maid.

239

The root of that fear—a value for the good opinion of others—continues to transform Kate once she is married. Petruchio's temper tantrums show her a rude mirror of her own behavior. She sees that the laughter and mockery roused by her husband's crude manners could just as well be directed against her own rude behavior.

Petruchio's taming method also simply teaches Kate the value of kindness and obedience. Almost unconsciously at first, and then with growing awareness, she begins to appreciate the gentle kindness she has belittled in the past. Petruchio, in the manner of a by-the-book behavioral psychologist, reinforces this realization by rewarding Kate when she responds with quiet obedience.

Kate's change may be partially due to love, too. In a cliche straight out of Hollywood, Kate may learn to love Petruchio when she sees he is a man who can stand up to her. Or she may be won by Petruchio's kisses and wild humor.

Other readers have suggested that Petruchio convinces neither Kate's heart nor her sense of propriety but her sense of self-preservation. Petruchio's exhausting starvation and sleepless night treatments simply wear down Kate's independence. She sees that only obedience and unquestioning respect for her husband will profit her.

Finally, some scholars believe Kate's conversion does not really occur at all. Kate merely assumes a submissive guise.

Strong arguments can be made for each of the explanations for Kate's change. The final interpretation of her character rests with the reader.

3. **Why does Lucentio fall in love with Bianca?**

Lucentio is an eager, impressionable young man. He is particularly receptive to the advice of his trusted councilor, Tranio. When Tranio advises Lucentio to seek the pleasures in life and remember the attractions of love, Lucentio takes the words to heart. Bianca arrives on the heels of their conversation, and the primed Lucentio falls in love with her instantly.

Bianca's apparent charms certainly account for much of Lucentio's attachment. Bianca seems to be a beautiful, modest, wise, and obedient woman. (Though by play's end, Lucentio will have reason to doubt all except her beauty.)

Finally, Lucentio is a romantic, a believer in courtly traditions. The courtship game attracts him. He seems fond of the playful courtly appeals to the lady on a pedestal. Like many an earnest youth of romantic literature, Lucentio's desire is at least partially fueled by his love of being in love.

4. **How does money motivate the characters and generate plot developments in the play?**

Money is a powerful motivator in *The Taming of the Shrew*. The characters come from merchant class households. Bargaining and sales are at the heart of their world.

Petruchio, for example, seeks his fortune in a wealthy bride. Along the way, he sweetens his marriage settlement with contributions from Bianca's suitors. He even bets on his wife's behavior.

Baptista, too, often displays the traits of the shrewd merchant. He insists Kate must be married before Bianca. Baptista undoubtedly loves Kate and does not want to make her feel unhappy and neglected. He also knows that matching an "old maid" to a wealthy husband is very difficult. Petruchio's opportune arrival seems too good to be true, and Baptista readily agrees to the fateful marriage. "I play a merchant's part," he confesses after settling the match, and he plays it smoothly.

Baptista's disposal of Bianca's hand also seems calculating. He accepts the suitor who has the most property to bid. His insistence that the supposed Lucentio produce his father to guarantee the valuable settlement generates another subplot. Tranio is forced to recruit the pedant to play Vincentio and promise the settlement.

Money influences other characters. Hortensio, after his disillusionment by Bianca, seems swayed by the widow's wealth as well as her seeming amiability. The pedant arrives on the scene to collect bills. Bianca remains wary of Lucentio until she feels certain he is really the proper youth he claims to be.

While money motivates characters at some levels, the generosity of these usually hospitable people should not be overlooked. To them, money is so precious in the making because it is so delightful in the spending.

Appearance and Reality:

1. **Is Kate's statement at the end of the play about a woman's duties sincere or ironic?**

The question of how Kate's lecture on wifely obedience should be read has been much debated. Some scholars interpet the speech as a straightforward declaration. After all, the philosophy expressed reflects a common attitude among Elizabethans about a woman's place.

There is an internal consistency to this reading, too. As the title alone suggests, Kate seems to genuinely reform. She reacts to the ugly picture of herself that Petruchio presents. Petruchio's deprivations teach her, too, that marriage means sacrifices and sharing. The selfish, demanding aspect of her nature is literally worn away.

However, other readers hold that there is room to doubt Kate's sincerity. Perhaps Petruchio has simply taught Kate the value of disguising her true opinion—quite different from the lesson that a husband's opinion must be respected and sincerely seconded. Like most of the characters in the play, Kate shows she knows the value of hypocritical behavior and dons a mask to cloak her real nature. Her speech to the rebellious brides may be her joke on Petruchio. Just as she tried to top his ridiculous lies about Vincentio, so she tries to beat him at the game of arguing a wife's "properly" obedient role.

Still other scholars suggest Kate's speech is a jest concocted between husband and wife. The joke gives the couple the last laugh on the derisory company and allows them to show up the less-than-perfect newlyweds. They also pocket a tidy wager (besides Baptista's sizeable dowry supplement).

More evidence can be assembled to support any of these theories. The question remains for the audience to answer: has Kate's heart been tamed or only her tongue?

2. **Does Lucentio's initial impression of Bianca match with her real character?**

At first glance, Lucentio sees in Bianca a maidenly, retiring Diana. She appears to passively accept her father's wishes and submissively retire to her studies. Her modesty and virginal demeanor would make one predict she would be a backward lover.

When Baptista is offstage, however, Bianca begins to shine with mischievous energy. Her love scenes with Hortensio and Lucentio show she is more of a lusty Venus than a chaste Diana. She proves to be fond of courtship and playful repartee.

Bianca also shows her independence. She refuses to be directed by her lovers—even the favored Lucentio. And though she does not boldly confront her father, the sly dalliance and eventual elopement with Lucentio show Bianca will choose her own lover. She weds without Baptista's permission, while her sister, renowned for shrewishness, is half-forced into a marriage.

The final scene fully reveals Bianca as the forceful, domineering woman she promised to be. Her witty, mildly risque retorts demonstrate her sense of freedom and ability to fend for herself. She even escapes Petruchio (when her supposedly more boisterous sister could not). Lucentio learns, to his chagrin, the extent of his wife's willfulness when Bianca refuses to answer his summons.

3. How does kindness serve as a false front in the play?

The lord's joke on Sly first introduces the theme of false kindness. The lord and his servants try to make Sly believe he really is a noble. They lay out the luxuries of a plush life with tempting cruelty. For, as with the seductive charms of "Lord" Sly's false wife, the delights will eventually be denied the tinker.

Petruchio's scheme to cure Kate of her shrewishness continues the theme of hypocritical kindness. He galls Kate by pretending to lovingly observe her best interests. He denies her meat on the grounds that it will inflame her temper. The bed is not fit for her to sleep on. The cap and gown are insults to her good taste and character. In reality, of course, Petruchio's kind protectionism is punishment. He privately gloats, "This is a way to kill a wife with kindness."

Bianca presents the feminine mask of false kindness. She appears respectful and obedient to her father and suitors. Beneath this guise, however, Bianca teases and defies men unmercifully. After putting down Lucentio and Hortensio, she begs them "take it not unkindly, pray/ That I have been thus pleasant with you both." Lucentio, to his regret, sees the full extent of this "pleasantness" by the end of the play. Similarly, Hortensio's "kind" widow proves to be a shrew.

Bianca's suitors know the politic value of apparent kindness. Their gifts to Baptista are actually bargaining chips in the game of marriage and dowries. Petruchio's presentation of Hortensio as the musician Licio is a particularly unkind gift. Hortensio sneaks past Baptista, like a Trojan horse, to woo Bianca against Baptista's will.

The servants even take up the mask of deceptive kindness. Tranio dupes the pedant into playing Vincentio by spinning a tale about immediate death sentences for all Mantuans in Padua. He mockingly concludes his offer of protection by remarking, "If this be court'sy, sir, accept of it." Of course, the display of generosity only goes to serve Tranio and Lucentio's end.

Grumio, too, plays the game. He offers the starved Kate one tempting dish after another—only to deny her anything in the end.

These examples may leave the reader with the picture of a play filled with manipulative, hypocritical characters. However, closer review turns up instances of genuine kindness: Baptista's pity for Kate on her wedding day; Kate's intervention to save the servants from Petruchio's beatings; Baptista's alms to the poor; Vincentio's loving offer of money to Lucentio; and numerous invitations to dine from different characters.

Yet, in the mix of motives, both characters and readers may still have proper doubts about the sincerity of kind actions. The exchange between Petrucho and Hortensio in the final scene perfectly captures this skeptical attitude:

PETRUCHIO
Padua affords nothing but what is kind.
HORTENSIO
For both our sakes I would that word were true.

4. **What elements of farce inevitably distort reality?**

Characters in farces are usually mechanical and one-dimensional. Complicating factors do not change their personalities. They speak to entertain, not to reveal inner characters or present deep philosophy.

In *The Taming of the Shrew*, only Kate, Petruchio, and Sly become more than cardboard personalities. The rest of the characters act predictably. They could even be labeled with convenient tags like Gremio, the Pantaloon.

Another element of farce that defies reality is familiar to any cartoon viewer: slapstick. Kate smashes a lute over Hortensio's head but does not hurt him. Grumio boxes Curtis on the ear, and Petruchio cuffs the priest. Both incidents are quickly forgotten—no harm done, no repercussions. No realistic plot or character development result from the insults and blows. The incidents are included simply to serve the broad comedy of farce.

In terms of comedy and characterization, farce sacrifices subtlety and complex development for the quick laugh.

Philosophical:

1. **How is romantic love portrayed in the play?**

    Most of the conventions of romantic love are present in Lucentio and Bianca's courtship. Lucentio blindly idolizes his lady love and makes romantic sacrifices to be near her. He pleads his love in urgent but gentle and respectful terms. Like Romeo and Juliet, the two elope, braving displeasure of their fathers. Love and beauty—not wealth or position—move Lucentio to court Bianca.

    The pretty pursuit of romantic love proves a frail basis for a marriage, in the end. Lucentio realizes he does not really know his wife when she asserts her independence in the final act. The picture of his ideal blinded him.

    Lucentio's treatment of Bianca during their courtship also sets up the young lover for disappointment. Lucentio worships his supreme mistress when he woos her. He is shocked to find Bianca refuses to relinquish the elevated position he thought he had temporarily granted her.

    Kate and Petruchio's match is concluded for much more practical reasons. Money, connections, and station are behind their marriage, not love. Only gradually does a measure of affection grow between the two after they establish a realistic (for the day and age) relationship. In contrast, Lucentio and Hortensio are left to contemplate the folly of marrrying for affection and allowing their wives to rule the house.

2. **What seems the ideal of marriage as presented in the play?**

    If Kate's speech in the final scene is taken at face value, then the best marriage would give the man dominance.

Ideally, the husband's opinion should rule the household. Business decisions and the protection of the family are his duties. The woman should support her husband by being thoughtful, submissive, and attractive.

Judging by Kate and Petruchio's match, Kate does not mention other virtues of a good marriage. A shared sense of humor and sharp wits keep their relationship strong. Their comparable wealth and positions make them social equals with similar tastes. Mutual courtesy (once Kate is tamed) also strengthens their marriage. Finally, a healthy sexual appreciation for one another enlivens Kate and Petruchio's relationship.

3. Is Petruchio's taming of Kate really kind?

On the surface level, Petruchio's taming methods are cruel though cloaked in external courtesy. But what about his end? Arguably, Petruchio does Kate a favor by taming her foul temper. Kate's acceptance of the role of model Elizabethan wife makes her a respected, desirable woman, rather than a mockery. The role and new image seem to cure Kate of her bitterness and envious resentment of Bianca.

The taming process appears to awaken Kate to the joys of love, too. As Petruchio concludes, Kate's transformation means "what not that's sweet and happy."

Modern readers may question if Petruchio's goal is really kind if he also strips Kate of her lively and honest opinions. Does he create a happy wife or a mindless minion? Evidence supporting the view of Kate as cured, not lobotomized, is found in her exchange with the widow. She parries with the widow using the fiery spirit and quick wit she possessed in the opening scene.

Even in her grand capitulation to male rule, Kate's distinctive character shines through. Her cogent reasoning, self-aware statements, and fire-and-brimstone style suggest her conviction is internal, not externally imposed. Unless Kate's long speech is to be taken ironically, the lady herself would certainly argue that her husband's taming scheme was a kindness.

4. **How do the characterizations in the play suggest Elizabethan notions of human psychology?**

Elizabethan playwrights often based their characters—particularly comic ones—on the "humors theory," the idea that four bodily substances, blood, phlegm, yellow bile, and black bile control human personality. Aberrations in human behavior were the result of an imbalance in these humors. Kate's choleric temperament comes from an excess of yellow bile; Petruchio seeks to correct this imbalance by imitating Kate's behavior. Grumio's mock concern with Kate's diet suggests a belief that food has a direct effect on the temperament.

Encore: Vocabulary Words

In each group below, the main word is found in *The Taming of the Shrew*. Mark the letter of the word in each group that comes closest in meaning to the main word.

Induction

1. rogues
    a. scamps
    b. fools
    c. judges

2. loathsome
    a. disgusting
    b. reluctant
    c. rough

3. antic
    a. clown
    b. joy
    c. scene

4. dispatched
    a. turned
    b. mended
    c. sent

5. homage
    a. honor
    b. curse
    c. freedom

6. raiment
    a. flood
    b. clothing
    c. treasure

7. bestrew
   a. push
   b. cover over
   c. lift up

8. beguiled
   a. deceived
   b. punished
   c. laughed

9. malady
   a. gentlewoman
   b. battle
   c. sickness

10. tarry
    a. paint
    b. pick
    c. linger

Act I

11. abjured
    a. left
    b. renounced
    c. spotted

12. importune
    a. scare
    b. estimate
    c. beg

13. chide
    a. peel
    b. season
    c. scold

14. pine
    a. yearn
    b. grow
    c. replace

15. thralled
    a. pleased
    b. enslaved
    c. injured

16. pate
    a. head
    b. gasp
    c. gallop

17. perused
    a. strolled
    b. played
    c. read

18. largess
    a. gift
    b. needle
    c. monument

19. chafed
    a. built
    b. worshipped
    c. irritated

20. quaff
    a. roar
    b. drink
    c. blow

Act II

21. dissemble
    a. break
    b. pretend
    c. hope

22. affability
    a. friendliness
    b. modesty
    c. misfortune

23. covenants
    a. contracts
    b. monastaries
    c. companions

24. peremptory
    a. unhappy
    b. persuasive
    c. dictatorial

25. askance
    a. modestly
    b. simply
    c. disapprovingly

26. commodity
    a. shop
    b. article
    c. suit

27. cavil
    a. quibble
    b. thrust
    c. protect

28. lave
    a. oil
    b. bake
    c. wash

29. kine
    a. china
    b. cattle
    c. villas

30. temperate
    a. angry
    b. decorated
    c. moderate

Act III

31. perogative
    a. privilege
    b. interest
    c. strength

32. rudiments
    a. basics
    b. insults
    c. languages

33. pithy
    a. smoky
    b. concise
    c. indirect

34. doff
    a. straighten
    b. remove
    c. burn

35. tedious
    a. suspenseful
    b. rude
    c. wearying

36. clamorous
    a. noisy
    b. blunt
    c. unfeeling

37. surly
    a. graceful
    b. sullen
    c. chilly

38. chattels
    a. property
    b. sweethearts
    c. blessings

39. appareled
    a. stunned
    b. enjoyed
    c. dressed

40. vex
    a. annoy
    b. jinx
    c. operate

Act IV

41. beseech
    a. surround
    b. implore
    c. answer

42. spruce
    a. scented
    b. tidy
    c. lonely

43. engenders
    a. produces
    b. separates
    c. bothers

44. continency
    a. travel
    b. belief
    c. moderation

45. unfeigned
    a. proper
    b. sincere
    c. suspicious

46. disdainful
    a. scornful
    b. weak
    c. inclined

47. credulous
    a. deadly
    b. restful
    c. trusting

48. lewd
    a. sewn
    b. indecent
    c. gigantic

49. marred
    a. spoiled
    b. educated
    c. quiet

50. habiliments
    a. dress
    b. horses
    c. invitations

Act V

51. notorious
    a. ridiculous
    b. infamous
    c. patient

52. dotard
    a. senile person
    b. pretender
    c. escaped criminal

53. giddy
    a. selfish
    b. dizzy
    c. handsome

54. galled
    a. puzzled
    b. feasted
    c. annoyed

251

55. bodes
    a. departs
    b. ends
    c. foreshadows

56. craves
    a. begs
    b. splices
    c. recovers

57. peevish
    a. lovely
    b. innocent
    c. irritable

58. frivolous
    a. obscene
    b. significant
    c. trivial

59. controversy
    a. invention
    b. argument
    c. valor

60. bandy
    a. exchange
    b. sip
    c. pronounce

Improvisation: Student Enrichment

Research:

1. Research the Elizabethan concept of wit.

2. Read *Kiss Me Kate,* an adaptation of *The Taming of the Shrew* by Sam and Bella Spewak. Compare the book to Shakespeare's play.

3. Compare Kate and Petruchio to another pair of Shakespearean lovers—Romeo and Juliet, Troilus and Cressida, Benedick and Beatrice, or Antony and Cleopatra.

4. Investigate the marriage customs and ceremonies of Shakespeare's day.

5. Compare and contrast John Fletcher's play *The Woman's Prize; or the Tamer Tamed* to *The Taming of the Shrew*.

6. Read George Bernard Shaw's review of the play and comment on his criticisms.

7. Research the use of comic "types" in *The Taming of the Shrew*, and how they relate to the commedia dell'arte and ancient Roman comedy.

Reaction:

1. Does *The Taming of the Shrew* seem more effective when read silently or performed? Explain the reasons for your choice.

2. Most scholars believe this play is one of Shakespeare's earlier works. Compare *The Taming of the Shrew* to comedies dated later in Shakespeare's career. Do you agree with the scholarly opinion? Why or why not?

3. Which character in the play appeals to you most? Why?

4. Do you think Baptista is a good and fair father? Why or why not?

Creation/Composition:

1. Prepare a rebuttal to Kate's conclusions about the woman's place.

2. Write another scene for the play viewing the three couples after they have been married for ten years.

3. Write a final act in which Sly reappears to comment on the play and see the conclusion of the lord's joke.

4. Petruchio's cousin Ferdinand is only mentioned once in the play and never appears (Act IV, Scene 1). Imagine you are Ferdinand. Give a sketch of yourself, Petruchio, and Kate.

5. Draw wedding portraits of each of the couples. Imagine how their clothing, stance, gestures, and expressions might vary.

Between the Lines: Essay Test

Literal Level

1. What part do the servants play in the drama?

2. How does Kate's image change during the play?

3. How do Petruchio's and Lucentio's methods of wooing differ?

4. Explain Kate's initial conflicting attitudes about marriage.

Interpretative Level

1. Compare and contrast Katherine and Bianca.

2. How does Petruchio get more than he bargained for when he marries Kate?

3. What are the elements of farce in the play?

4. Are there any inconsistencies in the play in terms of character, plot, or style of writing?

5. How does Shakespeare use the device of a play within a play?

Final Curtain: Objective Test

I. True—False

Mark each statement either T for True or F for False.

_____ 1. Sly immediately and easily accepts and falls into his part as a lord.

_____ 2. Baptista refuses all suitors to Bianca's hand until Katherine's marriage is set.

254

_____ 3. Petruchio says he came to Padua to marry the most spirited woman in the city.

_____ 4. Biondello pretends he is Lucentio.

_____ 5. All three of the weddings in the play take place in secret.

_____ 6. Hortensio and Gremio assume disguises to court Bianca.

_____ 7. Kate fears the fate of becoming an old maid.

_____ 8. The entire play takes place in Padua.

_____ 9. Bianca enjoys the game of courtship with her lovers.

_____10. Petruchio tames Kate like a falcon.

_____11. Petruchio depends on Grumio's good advice.

_____12. Kate believes Petruchio's excuses for depriving her of food, sleep, and clothing.

_____13. Hortensio marries a widow after he rejects Bianca.

_____14. Baptista rules Kate with an iron hand.

_____15. Petruchio's bet in the final scene proves he is the only husband who knows his wife.

II. Multiple Choice

Choose the answer that best completes each statement.

16. For his entertainment, Sly is offered a
    a. walk through the gardens.
    b. lavish feast.
    c. comic play.

17. Grumio is
    a. one of Bianca's suitors.
    b. Petruchio's servant.
    c. Lucentio's servant.

18. *The Taming of the Shrew* is a
    a. romance.
    b. fable.
    c. comedy.

19. Tranio disguises himself as
    a. a music teacher.
    b. Lucentio.
    c. Petruchio's servant.

20. The part of Sly's lady is played by
    a. the lord's page.
    b. the hostess.
    c. the widow.

21. Petruchio refuses to change his clothes for the wedding because
    a. he wants to shame Kate.
    b. he considers rich dress a sin.
    c. he owns no other clothes.

22. When Gremio is outbid for Bianca's hand, he decides to
    a. marry a widow.
    b. see if Vincentio agrees to the marriage terms.
    c. go to Petruchio's taming school.

23. Kate begs Grumio for
    a. some food.
    b. permission to stay at her wedding feast.
    c. a fire.

24. Hortensio says that a woman's most important virtue is
    a. beauty.
    b. kindness.
    c. nobility.

25. After Kate's horse slips in the mud, she tries to
    a. escape from Petruchio.
    b. scold her husband.
    c. stop Petruchio from beating Grumio.

26. Lucentio comes to Padua because the city has a reputation for
    a. great learning.
    b. beautiful women.
    c. lively entertainment.

27. Lucentio leaves many of his decisions up to
    a. Tranio.
    b. Biondello.
    c. Vincentio.

28. After deciding to marry, Hortensio seeks out Petruchio to
    a. arrange a marriage settlement.
    b. learn how to tame a wife.
    c. borrow money.

29. Petruchio says he will kill his wife with
    a. contempt.
    b. neglect.
    c. kindness.

30. On their way to Bianca's wedding feast, Kate and Petruchio meet
    a. Tranio.
    b. Vincentio.
    c. Hortensio.

31. Gremio and Hortensio join forces to
    a. buy music instruments for Bianca.
    b. chase Petruchio from Padua.
    c. find a husband for Kate.

32. The pedant agress to impersonate
    a. Lucentio.
    b. Baptista.
    c. Vincentio.

33. Petruchio bets Hortensio and Lucentio that Kate will
    a. prove the most obedient wife.
    b. happily agree to marry him.
    c. kiss in public.

34. Bianca and Lucentio marry
    a. after Lucentio signs a marriage agreement.
    b. in secret.
    c. with Vincentio's blessing.

35. Baptista rewards Kate's reverent behavior by
    a. doubling her dowry.
    b. comparing her to Bianca.
    c. kissing her in front of the guests.

III. Matching

A. Match the characters with their descriptions.

_____36. Baptista

_____37. Vincentio

_____38. Katherine

_____39. Gremio

_____40. Bianca

a. Lucentio's wealthy father

b. Bianca's crafty old suitor

c. secretly marries Lucentio

d. Minola's eldest daughter

e. Petruchio's father-in-law

B. Match the characters with their descriptions.

_____41. Grumio

_____42. Petruchio

_____43. Tranio

_____44. Hortensio

_____45. Lucentio

a. Vincentio's son

b. fortune-seeker from Verona

c. servant who suffers his master's wrath

d. Petruchio's Padua friend

e. servant who impersonates his master

C. Match the items with the proper description.

_____46. pantaloon

_____47. dowry

_____48. cap

_____49. comonty

_____50. dry meat

a. Baptista's bargaining chip

b. engenders choler

c. Sly's malapropism

d. "lewd" item prepared by haberdasher

e. ridiculous old man